REA's Test Prep Books Are ...

(a sample of the <u>hundreds of letters</u> REA receives each year)

" I felt [*REA's Testbuster® for the GRE CAT*] greatly improved my score, especially in the verbal and analytical sections, as quite a few of their techniques actually appeared on the GRE. This phenomenon was experienced by quite a few of my friends, too, and I must attest to the effectiveness of this book. "
Student, Bombay, India

" My students report your chapters of review as the most valuable single resource they used for review and preparation. "
Teacher, American Fork, UT

" Your book was such a better value and was so much more complete than anything your competition has produced — and I have them all! "
Teacher, Virginia Beach, VA

" Compared to the other books that my fellow students had, your book was the most useful in helping me get a great score. "
Student, North Hollywood, CA

" Your book was responsible for my success on the exam, which helped me get into the college of my choice... I will look for REA the next time I need help. "
Student, Chesterfield, MO

" Just a short note to say thanks for the great support your book gave me in helping me pass the test... I'm on my way to a B.S. degree because of you! "
Student, Orlando, FL

" The gem of the book is the tests. They were indicative of the actual exam. The explanations of the answers are practically another review session. "
Student, Fresno, CA

(more on next page)

" I just wanted to thank you for helping me get a great score
on the AP U.S. History... Thank you for making great test preps! "
Student, Los Angeles, CA

" Your *Fundamentals of Engineering Exam* book was the absolute best
preparation I could have had for the exam, and it is one of the major
reasons I did so well and passed the FE on my first try. "
Student, Sweetwater, TN

" I used your book to prepare for the test and found that the advice and the
sample tests were highly relevant... Without using any other material, I earned
very high scores and will be going to the graduate school of my choice. "
Student, New Orleans, LA

" What I found in your book was a wealth of information sufficient to shore up
my basic skills in math and verbal... The section on analytical ability was
excellent. The practice tests were challenging and the answer explanations
most helpful. It certainly is the Best Test Prep for the GRE! "
Student, Pullman, WA

" I really appreciate the help from your excellent book. Please keep
up with your great work."
Student, Albuquerque, NM

" I used your *CLEP Introductory Sociology* book and rank it 99% — thank you! "
Student, Jerusalem, Israel

" The painstakingly detailed answers in the sample tests are the most helpful
part of this book. That's one of the great things about REA books. "
Student, Valley Stream, NY

(more on back page)

TestBuster® for the GRE® GENERAL TEST

Pauline Alexander-Travis, Ph.D.
Assistant Professor of Reading
Southwestern Oklahoma State University
Weatherford, OK

David Bell, Ed.D.
Professor of Education
Arkansas Technical University, Russellville, AR

James W. Daley, M.A.
Educational Consultant
New York, NY

Anita Price Davis, Ed.D.
Professor Emerita of Education
Converse College, Spartanburg, SC

Michele DiBenedetto, M.A.
Educational Consultant
New Providence, NJ

Lucille M. Freeman, Ph.D.
Associate Professor of Educational Administration
University of Nebraska at Kearney

Alexander Kopelman, M.B.A.
Educational Consultant
New York, NY

Lutfi A. Lutfiyya, Ph.D.
Associate Professor of Mathematics
University of Nebraska at Kearney

James S. Malek, Ph.D.
Chairperson and Professor of English
DePaul University, Chicago, IL

Marcia Mungenast, B.A.
Educational Consultant
Private Test Preparation Instructor
Upper Montclair, NJ

Donald E. Orlosky, Ed.D.
Chairperson of Educational Leadership Department
University of South Florida, Tampa, FL

Mark Shapiro, M.A.
Adjunct Professor of Mathematics
University of Hartford
West Hartford, CT

Jerry R. Shipman, Ph.D.
Professor and Chairperson of Mathematics
Alabama A&M University, Normal, AL

Ricardo Simpson-Rivera, M.S.
Visiting Scientist
Oregon State University,
Corvallis, OR

Research & Education Association
Visit our website: www.rea.com
GRE Test Updates: www.rea.com/GRE

To Our Readers:

Educational Testing Service and the Graduate Record Examinations Board are gradually revising the GRE General Test. As these incremental changes are announced, you can count on REA to keep you up to speed at *www.rea.com/gre*.

Research & Education Association
61 Ethel Road West
Piscataway, New Jersey 08854
E-mail: info@rea.com

TestBuster® for the GRE® General Test with TestWare® on CD-ROM

Printed in the United States of America
Library of Congress Control Number 2009929630

ISBN-13: 978-0-7386-0327-8
ISBN-10: 0-7386-0327-9

About Research & Education Association

Founded in 1959, Research & Education Association is dedicated to publishing the finest and most effective educational materials—including software, study guides, and test preps—for students in middle school, high school, college, graduate school, and beyond.

REA's Test Preparation series includes books and software for all academic levels in almost all disciplines. Research & Education Association publishes test preps for students who have not yet completed high school, as well as high school students preparing to enter college. Students from countries around the world seeking to attend college in the United States will find the assistance they need in REA's publications. For college students seeking advanced degrees, REA publishes test preps for many major graduate school admission examinations in a wide variety of disciplines, including engineering, law, and medicine. Students at every level, in every field, with every ambition can find what they are looking for among REA's publications.

REA's practice tests are always based upon the most recently administered exams, and include every type of question that you can expect on the actual exams.

REA's publications and educational materials are highly regarded and continually receive an unprecedented amount of praise from professionals, instructors, librarians, parents, and students. Our authors are as diverse as the fields represented in the books we publish. They are well-known in their respective disciplines and serve on the faculties of prestigious high schools, colleges, and universities throughout the United States and Canada.

Today, REA's wide-ranging catalog is a leading resource for teachers, students, and professionals.

We invite you to visit us at www.rea.com to find out how "REA is making the world smarter."

Staff Acknowledgments

We would like to thank REA's **Larry B. Kling,** Vice President, Editorial, for supervising development; **John Paul Cording**, Vice President, Technology, for overseeing development of REA's exclusive GRE CBT TEST*ware*®; **Pam Weston**, Vice President, Publishing, for setting the quality standards for production integrity and managing the publication to completion; **Diane Goldschmidt,** Associate Editor, for coordinating revisions; **Ilona Bruzda,** Senior Graphic Designer, for the design, illustration, and graphic layout of our text and cover; and **Jeff LoBalbo** for post-production electronic processing.

We also gratefully acknowledge **James A. Corrick,** for ensuring the technical accuracy of the math sections; **Ellen Gong** for proofreading the manuscript; and **Wende Solano** and **Michael Cote** for typesetting the manuscript.

CONTENTS

CHAPTER 1

Introducing REA's Testbuster® for the GRE   3

Contents

CHAPTER 5

The GRE Vocabulary Enhancer   167

CHAPTER 6

Attacking Sentence Completion Questions   201

CHAPTER 7

Attacking Analogy Questions   231

CHAPTER 8

Attacking the Reading Comprehension Questions   251

CHAPTER 9

Attacking Antonym Questions   295

CHAPTER 10

Attacking the Problem Solving Questions   315

CHAPTER **11**

Attacking Quantitative Comparison Questions   **425**

Answer Sheets   **457**

About REA's TestWare®

Just by buying this book you are one step closer to busting the GRE General Computer-Based Test (CBT). Our exclusive TestWare® software will give you a further advantage on the test. The CBT software allows you to take three unique computer-based practice tests and automatically scores your progress. See more information on computer-based testing later in this book.

REA's TestWare® is designed to provide complete and accurate test preparation for the GRE. There are, however, a few important differences of which you should be aware:

• REA's TestWare® includes letters in the ovals next to the answer choices. On the actual GRE, the ovals are blank. We've included letters for your reference in the *Explanations* section.

• REA's TestWare® toolbar is slightly different from ETS's. Our toolbar is more colorful than ETS's, but the buttons function in basically the same way. In fact, throughout the exam, the differences between our toolbar and theirs are largely cosmetic. The important distinctions do not present themselves until you reach the *Explanations* mode in REA's TestWare®. Because there are no explanations on the actual GRE, the Explanations toolbar is unique to REA's TestWare®.

• REA's toolbar also has a *PAUSE* button, that will allow you to stop the clock. This can be convenient if you need to stop the test for a little while, but this option does not exist on the actual exam.

• REA's TestWare® offers a single essay topic for each question, and the entire essay section is timed as a single 75-minute unit. While this does offer greater flexibility for preparation purposes, you should keep an eye on the clock. On the actual exam, the two essay tasks will be timed separately at 30 and 45 minutes, respectively. Finally, while REA's TestWare® does not score your essay, you must enter some text in the essay window to receive an accurate score.

INSTALLING REA's TestWare®

SYSTEM REQUIREMENTS

Pentium 75 MHz (300 MHz recommended), or a higher or compatible processor; Microsoft Windows, 98, NT 4 (SP6), ME, 2000, or XP; 64 MB Available RAM; Internet Explorer 5.5 or higher, minimum 60 MB available hard-disk space; VGA or higher-resolution monitor, 800x600 resolution setting; Microsoft Mouse, Microsoft Intellimouse, or compatible pointing device.

INSTALLATION

1. Insert the GRE TestWare® CD-ROM into the CD-ROM drive.

2. If the installation doesn't begin automatically, from the Start Menu, choose the RUN command. When the RUN dialog box appears, type d:\setup (where *d* is the letter of your CD-ROM drive) at the prompt and click OK.

3. The installation process will begin. A dialog box proposing the directory "Program Files\REA\TESTware" will appear. If the name and location are suitable, click OK. If you wish to specify a different name or location, type it in and click OK.

4. Start the GRE TestWare® application by double-clicking on the icon.

REA's GRE TestWare® is **EASY** to **LEARN AND USE**. To achieve maximum benefits, we recommend that you take a few minutes to go through the on-screen tutorial on your computer.

TECHNICAL SUPPORT

REA's TestWare® is backed by customer and technical support. For questions about **installation or operation of your software**, contact us at:

Research & Education Association
Phone: (732) 819-8880 (9 a.m. to 5 p.m. ET, Monday–Friday)
Fax: (732) 819-8808
Website: http://www.rea.com
E-mail: info@rea.com

Note to Windows XP Users: In order for the TestWare® to function properly, please install and run the application under the same computer-administrator level user account. Installing the TestWare® as one user and running it as another could cause file access path conflicts.

Introducing REA's Testbuster® for the GRE General CBT

Busting the GRE General CBT

REA's Testbuster® for the GRE General CBT is the result of a massive effort to provide you with the best possible preparation for the GRE CBT (Graduate Record Examination–Computer-Based Test). The techniques, strategies, tricks, and tips you'll learn from this book have been tested and proven to work on the GRE General CBT. They are the same techniques and strategies used by the leading national coaching and review courses. REA's Testbusting techniques are proven to be effective and will help you score the best you possibly can on the GRE General CBT!

Bust it!

Bust it!

If you follow the strategies we teach you, you will do better on the GRE CBT than you ever thought possible. "But," you may ask yourself, "won't that mean I have to spend every spare moment I have studying the same stuff that I did in college?" No! The techniques we show you have nothing to do with what you learned in your undergraduate courses. We will teach you to beat the GRE. That means you will discover the methods to beat the people who write the GRE at their own game. We will teach you how to use the structure of the GRE to your advantage. Armed with this knowledge, you will go to the test center, sit at a computer, and take the GRE with the confidence that you will not be intimidated. In fact, the GRE should be intimidated by you because you will know its weaknesses!

What is the GRE?

Important Information!

The GRE, which stands for Graduate Record Examination, is considered an essential element for admission to a graduate school. Applicants for graduate schools submit their GRE test results together with undergraduate records, references, and work experience as part of the highly competitive admission process. Graduate schools use GRE scores to place prospective students on an equal footing. Your GRE score, along with the other information you must submit, aids graduate schools in predicting how well you will perform in their programs.

Who Makes the Test?

The GRE is developed and administered by ETS (Educational Testing Service). ETS is a very large "nonprofit" organization that not only develops and administers the GRE, but also does hundreds of other tests, such as the SAT and GMAT. You might have heard that ETS is a government agency or affiliated with Princeton University, neither of which is true. ETS is an organization that makes a lot of money developing and administering tests. The company uses a Princeton, New Jersey, mailing address (which is why some people assume that ETS is affiliated with Princeton University).

Important Information!

ETS is hired by another organization called the Graduate Record Examination Board, an organization affiliated with the Association of Graduate Schools and the Council of Graduate Schools, to write the GRE. Now that you know what ETS is—a company selling a product, no different than McDonald's or The Gap—we hope you won't be as intimidated by one of their best-selling items: the GRE.

What is a Computer-Based Test (CBT)?

Two of the three sections of the GRE are computer-adaptive. This means that you will use a computer to complete the GRE's Verbal and Quantitative Ability sections, and its software will determine which questions to ask based on your performance on the previous questions. In this way, the test will constantly adapt itself to

Important Information!

your level of ability. A correct response will be followed by a more difficult question, and an incorrect response will be followed by an easier question. Difficult questions increase your score in greater increments than moderate or easier questions.

*Important
Information!*

The Analytical Writing section is not computer-adaptive. The computer will randomly select your essay topics out of a pool of computer prompts. Then, you will type your essays. For the "Present Your Perspective on an Issue" task you can choose one out of two questions. The "Analyze an Argument" task won't give you a choice. All of the more than 100 topics that have been developed for each writing task are readily available beforehand because they are published by ETS.

On a traditional paper-and-pencil test,[†] every examinee sees the same or similar questions. Because of the adaptive nature of two parts of the CBT and the large pool of questions that are available, different test-takers are asked *different* questions. The test items have been designed to meet content and difficulty specifications that allow for an equitable comparison of scores.

Pros and Cons of Computer-Based Testing

*Important
Information!*

There are several advantages to computer-based testing. First, you will receive your unofficial scores for the multiple-choice sections of the test on the day you take your test. Second, the GRE CBT is offered much more frequently, and you may register just a few days in advance. Third, you may choose to take the test in the morning or afternoon—on a weekday or on a weekend. In addition, the testing

---

[†] Paper-based GRE General tests are offered in areas of the world where computer-based testing is not available.

venue is quieter and more orderly than traditional testing locations. In fact, you may be the only person in the room as you take the GRE CBT! Finally, there are fewer questions on the GRE CBT than there were on the traditional paper-and-pencil test.

Important Information!

Unfortunately, there are also some important disadvantages to the GRE CBT. People who are unfamiliar with computers may find the testing environment intimidating. While no computer skills are required, an unusual environment may have a psychological impact on your preparedness. In addition, you must answer the questions in the order in which they are presented. You cannot skip a question and return to it later—or return to an earlier question to change your answer. This is a significant disadvantage because it eliminates the important test-taking strategy of answering the easier questions first and returning to the more difficult questions if you have time. Also, don't be alarmed if the test seems very difficult to you. Because the GRE CBT software is continuously refining its estimate of your ability level, nearly all of the questions should seem difficult and challenging to you.

Beating the Multiple-Choice Questions of the GRE

The significance of a multiple-choice test is that the correct answer is always given, in contrast to "fill-in-the-blank questions" or essays where you have to come up with the answer yourself. Of course, finding the correct answer among the multiple choices is what the test is all about. Testbusting will teach you that sometimes it's easier to find the incorrect choices than the correct answer. By eliminating the incorrect choices you can home in on the correct answer. More about that later.

The Sections of the GRE

Important Information!

The GRE is divided into four sections: analytical writing, verbal ability, quantitative ability, and a trial section. You will be given three hours to complete the four sections. The first three sections are broken down as follows:

ANALYTICAL WRITING

Question Type	Number of Questions/Time
• Perspectives of an Issue	One 45-minute essay
• Analysis of an Argument	One 30-minute essay

Note: Although the bulk of the questions in the Quantitative and Verbal sections are multiple-choice, be prepared to encounter alternative question types as part of the effort by the test administrators to make incremental changes to the exam. Visit *www.rea.com/gre* for examples of the latest new question types.

QUANTITATIVE ABILITY

Question Type	Number of Questions/Time
• Quantitative Comparisons	
• Problem Solving— Discrete Quantitative	
• Problem Solving— Data Interpretation (charts)	28 multiple-choice/ 45 minutes

Important Information!

VERBAL ABILITY

Question Type	Number of Questions/Time
• Analogies	
• Sentence Completions	
• Antonyms	
• Reading Comprehension	30 multiple-choice/ 30 minutes

Important Information!

The allotted time given for each GRE General section is as follows:

> **Analytical Writing – 75 minutes**
>
> **Quantitative Ability – 45 minutes**
>
> **Verbal Ability – 30 minutes**
>
> **Trial Section – 30 minutes**

The Analytical Writing section will always be the first one on the test. The other three sections can appear in any order. The trial section is an "experimental" section that ETS uses to try out new questions. This will be another Verbal or Quantitative section. You are given 30 minutes to answer the questions in the trial section. **You will not be scored on the "experimental" section, nor will you be told which section it is. For example, if you get two verbal sections, one of them will be experimental, but you won't know which one. So do your best on all four sections.**

Also, you may be asked to complete an identified research section referred to by ETS as a "Pretest." This "Pretest" consists of additional experimental questions. The "Pretest" will appear at the end of the GRE. This part will have no effect on your GRE score; it is simply used by ETS as another way of developing and testing new questions for the GRE.

For practice purposes, we've omitted the "experimental" and "Pretest" sections in the practice test in this book and on the CD-ROM, and have presented only the counted and scored sections for the practice exam.

The Questions of the GRE

Let's take a quick glance at the types of questions you'll encounter on the GRE. Don't worry too much right now; this is just an overall summary. We'll go into further detail about each type of question you'll encounter on the GRE later in this book.

Analytical Writing Section

There are two types of essay questions on the GRE:

*Important
Information!*

- **Present Your Perspective on an Issue: (One 45-minute essay)**
  This essay requires you to analyze the stated issue and support your analysis with reasons and examples

- **Analyze an Argument: (One 30-minute essay)**
  This essay requires you to critique a given argument by analyzing its logical structure and soundness.

Quantitative Ability Section

There are three types of quantitative ability questions on the GRE:

- **Quantitative Comparison Questions: (13 – 15 questions)**
  These questions are designed to test your ability to determine the relationship between two quantities by asking you to select which quantity is larger than the other.

- **Problem Solving—Discrete Quantitative Questions: (8 – 10 questions)**
  These questions test your mathematical knowledge and skill through the basic multiple-choice format.

- **Problem Solving—Data Interpretation (Chart) Questions: (4 – 6 questions)**
  You will be required to read graphs and their data, and solve math problems based on those graphs.

Verbal Ability Section

In this section, you will encounter four question types:

- **Analogies: (6 – 8 questions)**
  These questions test your ability to identify the relationship between two words and choose a pair which shows a similar connection.

- **Sentence Completion: (5 – 7 questions)**
  A sentence will be given with either one or two words omitted. You will be required to choose the word or words that best fit the meaning of the sentence.

- **Antonyms: (8 – 10 questions)**
  These questions test your ability to identify the meaning of a word and choose the best OPPOSITE meaning from the words or phrases listed as answer choices.

- **Reading Comprehension:**
  (2 – 4 passages; 6 – 10 questions total)
  These questions are designed to test your critical reading skills, such as determining themes or arguments stated or implied in the passages.

Important Information!

How is the GRE Scored?

Important Information!

Scoring the Test

In traditional paper-and-pencil tests, every question is equal in value. The Verbal and Quantitative Ability sections of the GRE CBT are scored quite differently, since more difficult questions add more to your score than easier ones. As we've already pointed out, don't be alarmed if the test seems difficult to you. The GRE CBT software is continuously refining its estimate of your ability level, so nearly all of the questions should seem at least somewhat difficult to you.

When you complete a CBT exam using REA's TEST*ware*® software and return to the Main Menu, clicking on the VIEW SCORES button will generate a score report. REA's TEST*ware*® performs the raw score-to-scaled score conversion for you, and presents only scaled scores. In the Analytical Writing section, you will be asked to score your essays yourself, on a scale of 0 to 6, based on a given sample.

You will notice that the printed practice test in this book contains more questions than the actual GRE CBT. This is necessary to provide you with paper-and-pencil practice that is roughly comparable to the shorter computer-based test. Although the format is different, this test will give you an accurate idea of your strengths and weaknesses, just as with REA's TEST*ware*® practice tests. We'll explain how to score your printed practice test in the short introduction section that appears before the test.

The GRE provides three separate scores: a **Verbal Ability score** (Analogies, Sentence Completion, Antonyms, and Reading Comprehension); a separate **Quantitative Ability score** (Quantitative Comparison and Problem Solving); and a separate **Analytical Writing**

score (two analytical writing tasks). The Verbal and Quantitative Ability scores are reported on a scale of 200 to 800. The Analytical Writing section is scored on a scale of 0 (illegible, off-topic) to 6 (outstanding).

Scoring the Test

The Verbal and Quantitative Ability Sections are scored only by the computer. You will receive an unofficial score for these two sections right after taking the test at the test center. Each Analytical Writing essay is initially scored by one trained reader, then reviewed by e-rater, a computerized program developed by ETS. If the e-rater evaluation and the reader's score agree, the reader's score is used as the final score. If they disagree by a certain amount, a second reader will score your essay, and the final score is the average of the two readers' scores. Then, the scores for each essay are averaged together to give you your **Analytical Writing score** for the GRE CBT.

It is possible to receive half-point scores on the Analytical Writing Test: for example, if one reader gives a score of 4 and the other awards a score of 5, the grade would be 4.5.

Scoring the Test

Once your scores are scaled, they will be placed in a percentile group. The percentile assigned to your scaled score is the percentage of the last three years' test scores that were lower than the score you received.

Approximately two weeks after you take the GRE, you'll receive your official score report in the mail from ETS.

Your GRE scores are a very important factor when you apply to a graduate school. But we want to make it very clear that your GRE scores are not the only factor in getting into a graduate school. Graduate schools will also give strong consideration to your undergraduate performance, work experience, recommendations from former professors, or your essay response on your application. The best way to look at your GRE scores is to think of them as the first impression you give a school. And as you know, first impressions can be very important. But once a school gets to know you through the application process, the GRE will be one factor among many in deciding your admission.

Scoring the Test

How Should I Study for the GRE?

As a busy professional, you may be wondering how you will find time to work, have a social life, take care of family obligations, and still properly prepare for the GRE General Test. But don't worry, our GRE Pro Study Plan gives you a complete road map from now until test day. This flexible schedule allows you to work at your own pace and shows you how to prepare for the GRE as efficiently as possible. You'll get organized, stay on track, and make the most of your valuable study time.

If you are working a full-time job, you will need to set aside some time *every day* to study for the GRE. How and when you study is up to you, but consistency is the key to completing your GRE preparation. Make studying a priority and consider it a "second job" until you take the GRE exam.

Keep in mind that a high score on the GRE doesn't just help you get into a better grad school; it helps move your career forward. Therefore, a solid commitment to daily study is worth every minute of your time. The results will pay off in the long run!

Before you start a study session, be sure you have everything you need (pens, paper, your study materials, etc.) with you so you can work without interruption. Turn off the cell phone, television, radio, and eliminate other time-wasters and distractions. Remember, your primary goal right now is to get a high score on GRE—everything else can wait until after you've finished studying for the day.

Find a study routine that works for you and stick to it! Some people like to get up early and study for an hour or two before going to work. Others might choose to study while commuting, on their lunch hour, at the library, or at home after work. With our unique iPhone vocabulary App, you'll have access to instant test prep anywhere you go! Visit *www.rea.com/GRE* to learn more.

Whatever schedule you choose, make a commitment to study every day—even on weekends. Be sure to share your study schedule with family and friends and ask that you not be disturbed while studying. Daily focused concentration on the GRE test will help you retain more information, fully grasp the different concepts tested, and improve your overall GRE score.

The Pro Study Plan that we provide on the next page is designed to help you prepare for the GRE in a flexible time frame. The schedule presented is for an eight-week study course, but you can condense it to a four-week program by combining two weeks of studying into one. The more time you spend studying, the more prepared and relaxed you will feel on the day of the exam. If you choose to follow the eight-week schedule, plan to spend about an hour a day studying for the GRE.

Pro Study Plan

GRE CBT Pro Study Plan

Pro Study Plan

Week | Activity

- **Week 1**

  Get ready to bust the GRE General test! Start your study routine by taking the first GRE CBT practice exam using our REA TestWare® software to determine your strengths and weaknesses. Set aside at least 3 hours after work, on a weekend, or at another convenient time when you will not be disturbed. Take the test and try to do your best, even on sections where you may feel confused. Later in the week, study the detailed explanations for the questions you answered incorrectly. In the cases where you erred, find out why. Take notes and pay attention to sections where you missed a lot of questions. You will need to spend more time reviewing the related material.

- **Weeks 2 & 3**

  Make a firm commitment to study for at least an hour a day, every day for the next few weeks. It may seem hard to find time in your busy work/family schedule, but remember: the more you study, the better prepared you'll be for the GRE. **Week 2**: *Study the* **Vocabulary Enhancer** *and the review on* **Analogies**, *and answer the drill questions. Go back and review any items that you answered incorrectly.* **Week 3**: *Study the review on* **Sentence Completion** *and* **Antonym** *questions and answer the drill questions. Review any items that you answered incorrectly.*

Week | Activity

- **Weeks 4 & 5**

    Congratulations! You've reached the halfway point! Success is just around the corner, but keep going, there's more work to be done. **Week 4:** *Study the review on* **Reading Comprehension** *questions, and answer the drill questions. Be sure to review any items that you answered incorrectly.* **Week 5:** *Study the review on* **Quantitative Comparison** *questions, and answer the drill questions. Review any items that you answered incorrectly. If you feel you need extra GRE practice, why not review a chapter during your lunch hour or during your commute?*

- **Weeks 6 & 7**

    Keep working your way through the review chapters and practice drills. Your hard work is paying off! **Week 6:** *Study the review on* **Problem Solving** *and* **Chart** *questions, and answer the drill questions. Go back through the chapter and review any material that you answered incorrectly.* **Week 7:** *Study the* **Writing** *review, and answer the drill essays. Review any supplemental materials (such as a writing handbook) that will aid you in writing clearer, better-focused essays. You can also ask a coworker, spouse, or friend to give you feedback on your essay.*

- **Week 8**

    You've just about reached your goal! Now you're ready to take the second GRE exam on REA's Test-Ware®. Allow yourself at least 3 hours to take the practice test. Take your time, remember what you've learned, and answer every question to the best of your ability. After the test, thoroughly review all of the explanations for the questions you answered incorrectly. Restudy any areas in which you are still weak. After a day or two of additional study, take the third GRE practice exam in our software package. Continue to review all of the explanations for the questions you answered incorrectly. If you want further practice and reinforcement, you may wish to take the practice test printed in this book. Now is a great time to review vocabulary using our iPhone® vocabulary App.

Pro Study Plan

Congratulations! You've worked hard and you're ready for the GRE General Test!

A Look at the Computer Screen at the Test Center*

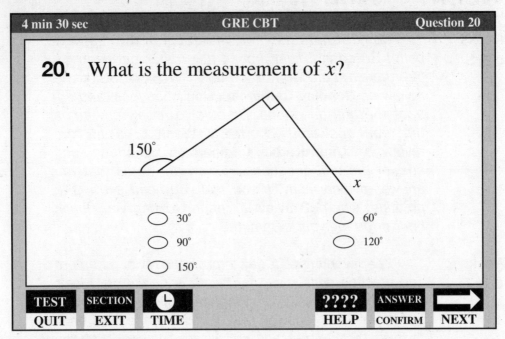

GETTING AROUND - You will use a mouse to navigate through the GRE CBT computer screen, and there are a few on-screen buttons you'll have to click on to get where you're going.

Test Quit - Click here to end the test.

Section Exit - Click this button to move on to the next section of the exam (if there is one) before time is up. Don't plan on using this button; if you finish before the clock runs out, you probably should have spent more time on the section.

Time - You can use this button to turn the on-screen clock on or off. When you start getting down to the wire (with about five minutes left in a section), the clock will start blinking and seconds will be added to the display.

Help - Here's another one you shouldn't use. The clock won't stop because you didn't memorize the directions. Learn how to take the test before you take the test.

Next - When you're sure about your answer choice, click here.

Confirm - After you've clicked "next," click here to move on to the next question.

*The software used for the essay sections contains standard word-processing features except for grammar or spell checks.

The Most Important Strategies for Beating the GRE

2

Don't Be Intimidated!

The single most important strategy you can use to beat the GRE is **NOT TO BE INTIMIDATED**. Test-taking anxiety, a very common factor when people sit down to take the GRE, can absolutely ruin your score. You've already learned that there are ways to beat the GRE by using its weaknesses against itself. You've already learned what ETS is and how it works. You've already learned what the GRE is and how it can help and hurt you. And you've already learned what types of questions to expect to see on the GRE. **You already know a lot about this test and you haven't really even begun to study for it!** So just remember, knowledge is power. **DON'T BE INTIMIDATED!**

Bust it!

The First Ten Questions on the GRE CBT

Earlier, we mentioned that when the GRE was changed to the computer-based testing format there were a lot of test-taking strategies taken away from you. Well, don't be too sad about that because the GRE CBT has given you one strategy that didn't exist on the paper-and-pencil format. In fact, this new strategy may be the easiest testbusting technique you'll learn in this book!

Important Strategy

To utilize this easy testbuster technique, you simply want to spend time and concentration on the first ten questions of the two multiple-choice sections of the GRE CBT. The reason for spending all of this time and effort on only ten questions is because the GRE CBT heavily relies on the first ten questions of each section to determine your score. These first ten questions have more to do with your final score than any of the remaining questions in the section.

This is true because the computer knows nothing about your knowledge or ability before you start a section. The computer doesn't have many questions with which to figure out how well you are doing, so it needs to make determinations of your ability as quickly as it can. In order to do this, the computer needs to use pretty big jumps in judgment in the first ten questions, and then use the remaining questions to "fine-tune" your score.

To illustrate: say the computer is asked to guess a number you've picked between 1 and 20. You can only tell the computer that the number you've picked is higher or lower than the one it guessed. Logically, the computer will pick 10 as its first number since the number you've picked will either be higher or lower than 10 and the computer can eliminate half the choices. If you tell the computer the number you've picked is lower than 10, it will next guess 5 because that will cut the possible choices by the most. If your number was lower than 5, the computer would pick 3 (once again cutting the possible choices the most). If your number is lower than 3, it has to be 1 or 2; if it is higher, the number must be 4. In this manner, the computer would use about four guesses to get to the right number. If it guessed randomly, it could take up to 20 guesses.

This example applies to the first ten questions of each section because the computer needs to determine your ability in the fewest number of guesses. Instead of using numbers to guess your score, the computer gives you questions that have an exact level of difficulty preassigned to them. By answering each question right or wrong, you are telling the computer whether your knowledge or ability is higher or lower than the level of difficulty preassigned to the questions.

Important Strategy

So, much like first guessing "10" in our example, the initial questions that the computer will give you in a section on the GRE CBT are designed to separate the best performers from the less stellar ones. Thus, mark well: The first several questions in either of the adaptive GRE sections will have a dramatic effect on your score; once the computer software pegs the level you're comfortable with, later questions will be presented with progressively finer adjustments in difficulty level and, as a consequence, those items will "count" for less and less in terms of your total score within that section.

Put another way, the more questions you answer, the less important they'll become. Why? Well, let's say you've answered 30 questions. If you answer the 31st question correctly, the computer will only increase your score by five or ten points (as opposed to increasing your score by perhaps hundreds of points in the first few questions).

Important Strategy

All of this means that, while you should try to answer every question on the GRE CBT correctly, you will gain the most points by spending more time double-checking the first ten questions of the two multiple-choice sections. The questions at the end of these sections warrant your lowest priority in terms of time and effort. Even if you spend so much time on the first ten questions that you run out of time and have to guess on the last ten questions, your score can only be improved!

Your Best Friend: The Process of Elimination

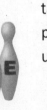

Eliminating Answer Choices

You probably already know how to use the process of elimination, but you may not realize it. More than likely, you've been taking multiple-choice tests for years. And you've been using the process of elimination to help yourself out while taking those tests. Let us show you:

Say you've been asked the following question on a history test (lucky for you there are no history questions on the GRE!).

Who was the 12th president of the United States of America?

(A)   Bill Clinton

(B)   Zachary Taylor

(C)   Gerald Ford

(D)   Thomas Jefferson

(E)   Franklin D. Roosevelt

Now, you may not know the order of presidents, but we bet you could still get the correct answer. Let's look at the answer choices. You know that Bill Clinton is definitely not it. You probably even know that he was the 42nd president. So you know this choice is incorrect.

~~(A)~~ **Bill Clinton**

Answer choice (B) may be tough for you, so we'll go on to the next choice.

Gerald Ford, answer choice (C), was president pretty recently and you probably know that. There have definitely been more than 12 presidents before Ford, so you can safely assume that answer choice (C) is incorrect.

~~(C)~~ **Gerald Ford**

You probably know that Thomas Jefferson was one of the United States' first few presidents. In fact, it is likely that you know that Jefferson was the 3rd president. You can easily label answer choice (D) as incorrect.

~~(D)~~ **Thomas Jefferson**

The final answer choice, Franklin D. Roosevelt, may give you some difficulty. You may know that he was president during World War II. You probably can say with confidence that Roosevelt couldn't have been the 12th president just by knowing he served during the 1930s and 40s, but a bit of math will tell you for sure. If World War II was fought in the 1940s, that means about 150 years had passed since the first president in 1790. Dividing 150 by 4 (the number of years in a presidential term) and you get a little over 37. There is no way that Roosevelt could have been the 12th president. This is an incorrect answer choice.

~~(E)~~ **Franklin D. Roosevelt**

Eliminating Answer Choices

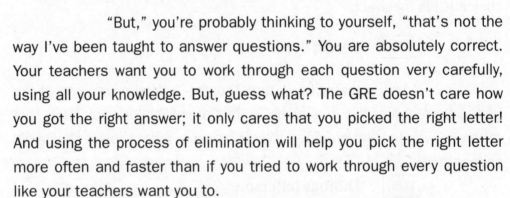

- [(A)] Bill Clinton
- [(B)] Zachary Taylor
- [(C)] Gerald Ford
- [(D)] Thomas Jefferson
- [(E)] Franklin D. Roosevelt

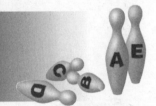

Eliminating Answer Choices

This question, at first glance, may have appeared a little more difficult than it was. By using process of elimination you were able to figure out that Zachary Taylor was our 12th president without knowing the exact order of presidents.

"But," you're probably thinking to yourself, "that's not the way I've been taught to answer questions." You are absolutely correct. Your teachers want you to work through each question very carefully, using all your knowledge. But, guess what? The GRE doesn't care how you got the right answer; it only cares that you picked the right letter! And using the process of elimination will help you pick the right letter more often and faster than if you tried to work through every question like your teachers want you to.

Now, we don't want to make you believe that every question on the GRE is going to be as easy to answer as the one we just showed you, because they aren't. But, by using the process of elimination, you can usually eliminate three of the five answer choices. This means you've taken a one-in-five, or 20%, chance of getting the correct answer, and turned it into a one-in-two, or 50%, chance of getting the correct answer! That sounds pretty good, doesn't it? You bet it does!

For reasons that will become clear later in this book, the ways you use the process of elimination will be different depending upon the question type you are attacking. Put simply, you will use the process of elimination in one manner for Quantitative Comparison questions and in a different manner for Sentence Completion questions. But don't worry about this now; we'll teach you what you need to know when you begin reviewing each particular question type.

Guessing on the GRE CBT—YES!

Because the Verbal and Quantitative sections of the GRE are computer-adaptive, you aren't allowed to skip the hard questions. Skipping the hard questions was an excellent strategy for beating the old paper-and-pencil GRE. In fact, it worked so well that ETS decided to stop the paper-and-pencil test so people couldn't skip questions!

But that doesn't mean you have to labor through every question that is given to you. If you can't get the answer quickly or have no idea how to begin to solve a question...GUESS! That's right, guess.

Since you can't skip questions on the GRE CBT, you'll have to guess if you want to get to the next question. You won't be able to answer all of the questions by working through them because the computer is constantly evaluating your performance and giving you questions that will challenge your skills. In order to avoid being stalled at the first question you can't work through, you'll need to take a guess.

Should I Guess?

Also, you'll need to guess if a question is taking too long for you to answer. Remember, the GRE is a timed test, and, as with any timed test, you'll need to keep an eye on the clock. If you are spending too much time on one question, guess and move on.

Now, we don't mean you should randomly guess (or blindly guess, as it's called by test-makers) on every question you can't answer. Before you do anything else, you should try to use the process of elimination. If you can eliminate any of the answer choices, you'll have a much better chance of guessing the correct answer. So, always use the process of elimination and then guess (this is called making an educated guess).

Should I Guess?

But using guessing as a technique to beat the GRE doesn't stop there. You see, the computer uses the number of questions you answered to calculate your overall score. So, it makes sense to answer every question that you can. If you are running out of time, start guessing, even if you don't have time to use the process of elimination. Even blindly guessing will help your GRE score in the long run. Don't just pick any letter, however. To use the laws of probability to your advantage, you must **PICK THE SAME LETTER** every time you blindly guess. Choose a letter, like C for example, and use it every time you need to blindly guess. This means, when you notice your time is beginning to run out, guess at the remaining questions, and be sure to use the same letter when you blindly guess.

Use Your Time Wisely

Watching the Clock!

As we've said, the GRE is a timed test. You'll be given one-and-three-quarters hours to work on the multiple-choice questions (this includes the unidentified trial section), and one-and-a-quarter hours for the Analytical Writing section. You'll need to work steadily, concentrating very hard on the questions. But you don't want to spend a lot of time on any particular question. If you find yourself stuck on one problem, try to make an educated guess and go on to the next question. If you find you are running out of time, answer as many remaining questions as possible, even if you have to blindly guess (and be sure to use the same letter every time you blindly guess).

Don't Look at the Directions!

The GRE is a standardized test. That means the directions and the types of questions will be the same from test to test, person to person. If you learn the directions and how to approach each type of question before your test day, you will save valuable time by NOT reading the directions before beginning to answer the questions. And as you've already learned, time is critical on the GRE. Also, knowing what to expect and how to handle all the question types before taking the GRE will enable you to avoid test anxiety and nervousness.

Important Information!

Use Your Scratch Paper

Our final tip for beating the GRE is to use the scratch paper. You'll be given scratch paper at the testing center to use on the quantitative section. It will be thrown out as soon as you finish, so scribble on it, mark it, make notes to yourself...do whatever you want!

One of the best ways to use your scratch paper is to work out math questions on it. Drawing diagrams and working out math problems can be very helpful when trying to solve complex analytical problems. No one will see that you had to use long division to figure out 100 divided by 5! Besides, it wouldn't matter if someone did see it. The only thing that matters is that you chose the right answer!

Important Strategy

Summary of the "Must Do" Testbusting Rules

On Target!

✔ **Don't Be Intimidated**

   Fear is your worst enemy. Studying this book will enable you to approach the GRE with confidence and poise.

✔ **Concentrate on the First Ten Questions of the Verbal and Quantitative Sections**

   The GRE administrators thought they were taking all the advantages away from you when they put the test on the computer. Well, they may have only made things easier! Since the first ten questions in each section determine so much of your score, if you are extremely careful and spend a lot of time on these first ten questions, you'll be able to dramatically increase your GRE score!

✔ **Use the Process of Elimination**

   One of the easiest and quickest ways to increase your score. Eliminating answer choices of the multiple-choice sections will lead you towards the right answer.

✔ **Guess When You Have To**

If you're stumped, blindly guess and move on without a second thought. Perhaps you're positive that one or two of the choices can't be correct; take solace in that, pick any of the remaining responses, and press on. The fact is, you've got a lot of ground to cover, so keep your eyes on the prize.

✔ **Use Your Time Wisely**

Working quickly is important. Don't spend too much time on one question. Remember, the more questions you answer, the better you'll do.

✔ **Don't Look at the Directions**

Why waste time reading what you already know? Learn the directions beforehand and ignore them during the test.

✔ **Use Your Scratch Paper**

They've given it to you, now use it! Make notes to yourself and draw diagrams. Work out math problems.

On Target!

GRE
Practice
Test

Now that you have some background information concerning the GRE, you are ready to take the practice test. This test is designed to help you identify where your strengths and weaknesses lie. This will help you make more effective use of your study time.

The practice test we've given you contains more questions than the actual GRE CBT. There are more questions in the Verbal and Quantitative sections because it is a paper-and-pencil version of the GRE. More questions are necessary in a paper-and-pencil version in order to provide a score that is roughly comparable to the shorter computer-based test. ETS has conducted numerous studies on this topic and has concluded that the scores received by taking the longer paper-and-pencil version do not vary from scores received through taking the CBT version. Although the format is slightly different, this test will give you an accurate idea of where your strengths and weaknesses lie, and it will provide guidance for further study.

GRE Practice Test

When you take the actual GRE, your essays will be scored by at least one official reader. Each essay is considered individually and graded according to scoring guidelines. There are no right or wrong answers. This makes grading your practice essays a little more difficult than scoring the other sections of the GRE. To score your practice essay responses, we suggest you give your essays to a professor or English major you may know (or someone else with a good grasp of grammar and composition writing). Supply him or her with the criteria for scoring the GRE essays. Ask him or her to grade your practice essay responses using these criteria so you can get a good idea of how GRE graders will score them.

GRE Practice Test

To take the practice test, situate yourself in a quiet room so that there will be no interruptions. Be sure to keep track of the time allotted for each section. After you complete the practice test, identify your strengths and weaknesses by scoring each section of the test. If you'd like to calculate your raw score for the practice test, count the number questions you answered correctly for the Verbal Ability and Quantitative Ability sections. This means, to determine your Verbal Ability raw score, only count the number of CORRECT ANSWERS in the Antonyms, Sentence Completion, Analogies, and Reading Comprehension sections. Do not count incorrect answers or answers that were left blank. This is your raw score for the Verbal section.

To determine your Quantitative Ability raw score, use the Quantitative Comparison and Problem Solving sections and follow the same steps as you did to determine your Verbal Ability raw score.

If you want to find your total raw score, add the number of correct answers you had for all sections of the practice test.

Here is an example of finding your Verbal Ability raw score:

IF YOU GET: 50 correct answers

AND YOU GET: 16 incorrect answers (these are not used to calculate your score)

YOU DID NOT ANSWER: 5 questions (these are not used to calculate your score)

YOUR RAW VERBAL ABILITY SCORE IS: 50

In the actual GRE test, this raw score is then taken and "corrected" by scaling it. ETS scales each year's GRE to make the scores comparable to previous years' scores. This is necessary because the same questions do not appear on the GRE every year (if they did, it would be much easier to study for the test!). Scaling helps "even out the playing field" from test to test. In other words, scaling makes up for the harder questions that may appear on one year's version of the GRE and the easy questions that appear on another year's version of the GRE. **A table of Scaled Scores and Percentile Rankings for the GRE CBT is provided.** It will give you a rough guide that you can use to judge how well you'll score on the GRE CBT.

GRE Practice Test

Once you've scored your practice test, study the reviews and answer the drill questions that follow. Then, after studying the reviews, take the practice test again and see how well you score.

There are other options for using this practice test. The first option is to take the practice test and study only the reviews in your weaker areas and then retake the test. A second option is to study all the reviews and answer all the drill questions first. Then take the practice test, and go back and review your weaker areas. You may already know where your weaknesses lie and want to read the review and answer the drill questions for that section, and then take the test.

Remember to employ all of the essential testbusting techniques introduced in previous chapters for beating the GRE. Begin using these techniques now so you can become comfortable with them before taking the actual GRE.

It is a good idea to photocopy the answer sheets for the practice test. By photocopying the answer sheets, you'll ensure that you have clean answer sheets no matter how many times you take the practice test.

SCALED SCORES AND PERCENTAGES FOR THE GRE CBT*

Raw Score	Verbal Score	% Below	Quantitative Score	% Below
72–76	800	99		
71	790	99		
70	780	99		
69	760	99		
68	750	98		
67	740	98		
66	720	96		
65	710	96		
64	700	95		
63	690	94		
62	680	93		
61	660	91		
60	650	89	800	98
59	640	88	800	98
58	630	86	790	98
57	620	85	780	97
56	610	84	770	95
55	600	82	750	92
54	590	80	740	90
53	580	78	730	89
52	570	75	720	87
51	560	73	700	83
50	550	71	690	81
49	540	68	680	79
48	530	65	670	77
47	520	63	650	72
46	510	60	640	71
45	500	57	630	68
44	490	55	620	65
43	480	52	600	61
42	470	49	590	59
41	460	45	580	56
40	450	43	560	52
39	440	40	550	49
38	430	37	540	46
37	420	34	530	44
36	420	34	510	39
35	410	31	500	37
34	400	28	490	34
33	390	26	480	32
32	380	24	460	27
31	370	22	450	26
30	360	18	440	23
29	360	18	430	21
28	350	17	410	18

(Table continues on next page)

(Table continues from previous page)

SCALED SCORES AND PERCENTAGES FOR THE GRE CBT*

Raw Score	Verbal Score	% Below	Quantitative Score	% Below
27	340	15	400	16
26	330	13	390	14
25	330	13	380	13
24	320	11	360	10
23	310	10	350	9
22	300	8	340	8
21	290	7	330	7
20	280	6	310	5
19	270	4	300	4
18	260	3	290	3
17	250	3	280	3
16	240	2	260	2
15	230	1	250	1
14	220	1	240	1
13	210	1	230	1
12	200	0	210	0
11	200	0	200	0
10	200	0	200	0
9	200	0	200	0
8	200	0	200	0
0-7	200	0	200	0

*Percent of examinees scoring below the scaled score is based on the performance of those who took the test in a recent multi-year period. It will give you a rough equivalency that you can use to judge how your scores on REA's practice tests compare to examinees' scores on the actual GRE CBT.

SCORE LEVEL DESCRIPTION FOR THE ANALYTICAL WRITING ASSIGNMENT

SCORE LEVELS 6 AND 5.5

The essays are well-focused and well-organized. They develop and support complex ideas with logical and highly persuasive examples. There is a superior understanding of sentence structure, grammar, and vocabulary with few, if any, errors.

SCORE LEVELS 5 AND 4.5

The essays provide a generally insightful analysis of complex ideas. They support main arguments with sound and well-chosen reasons. They are generally well-focused and display fluent use of language including effective sentence variety, appropriate vocabulary, and grammar.

SCORE LEVELS 4 AND 3.5

The writer provides a competent analysis of complex ideas with the support of relevant examples. The essays show a sufficient control of language. Sentence structure, grammar, and mechanics are satisfactory but there may be minor errors.

SCORE LEVELS 3 AND 2.5

The essays display some ability of critical thinking and writing. There is at least one of the following flaws: limited analysis, development, or organization; weak control of language; sentence structure and grammar. At times the essays lack clarity.

(Cont'd)

SCORE LEVELS 2 AND 1.5

At this level, the essays display serious deficiencies in analytical writing skills, resulting in incoherence. The content lacks analysis, there is little development, and there are severe errors in language, grammar, and sentence usage.

SCORE LEVELS 1 AND 0.5

There are fundamental deficiencies in the essays that result in incoherence. The content is confusing and irrelevant, there is little or no development, and severe errors make the essays incohesive.

SCORE LEVEL 0

The essays cannot be evaluated because they are merely attempts to copy the assignments, are in a foreign language, or are no text whatsoever.

GRE
Practice Test

Section 1 – Analytical Writing

Section 2 – Analytical Writing

Section 3 – Quantitative Ability

Section 4 – Verbal Ability

Section 5 – Quantitative Ability

Section 6 – Verbal Ability

To Our Readers

The questions in this REA practice test are also provided as part of our exclusive REA GRE CBT TEST*ware*® software. We strongly recommend that you take the adaptive test first to help you get a good feel for the actual CBT. Our software is designed to simulate your actual test-day experience. This printed practice test contains more questions than the CBT in order to provide a score that is roughly comparable to your score on the shorter computer-based test.

(Answer sheets appear in the back of the book.)

TIME: 45 Minutes
   1 Essay

DIRECTIONS: Present your perspective on the issue below by using relevant reasons and/or examples to support your views. Remember, there is no one "correct" response to the essay topic. Before starting, read the essay topic and its question(s).

Many non-smokers feel that secondhand smoke is hazardous to their health; recent medical research supports their allegations. Smokers feel that they have a right to enjoy this pastime, and that it would be a violation of their constitutional rights to deny them this privilege. The first group wants smoking made illegal, while the second group feels that they are being treated unfairly.

With whom do you agree, the smokers or the non-smokers? Using your own experience, reading, and observations, fully explain your reasoning.

STOP

Do not go on until you are instructed to do so. Use any remaining time to check your work on this portion of the test.

TIME: 30 Minutes
     1 Essay

DIRECTIONS: Critique the following argument by considering its logical soundness.

A new dog collar is now available with a new special feature—an underground electrical barrier that works with a receiver on your dog's collar. It beeps your dog when he nears the boundary and gives him a small electrical correction if he tries to cross it. It keeps your dog safe and out of trouble without having to resort to expensive fences, run ropes, or chains that could injure your pet.

Discuss how logical and/or convincing you find this argument. Be sure to analyze the reasoning and the use of any evidence in the argument. Include suggestions that would make the argument more acceptable and persuasive, and that would allow you to evaluate its conclusion more readily.

STOP
If time remains, you may go back and check your work.

TIME: 30 Minutes
     30 Questions

REFERENCE INFORMATION:

NUMBERS: All numbers are real numbers.

FIGURES: Position of points, angles, regions, etc. are assumed to be in the order shown and angle measures are assumed to be positive.

LINES: Assume that lines shown as straight are indeed straight.

DIRECTIONS: Each of the following given set of quantities is placed into either Column A or B. Compare the two quantities to decide whether

(A) the quantity in Column A is greater;
(B) the quantity in Column B is greater;
(C) the two quantities are equal;
(D) the relationship cannot be determined from the information given.

NOTE: Do not choose (E) since there are only four choices.

COMMON INFORMATION: Information which relates to one or both given quantities is centered in the two columns. A symbol which appears in both columns will indicate the same item in Column A and Column B.

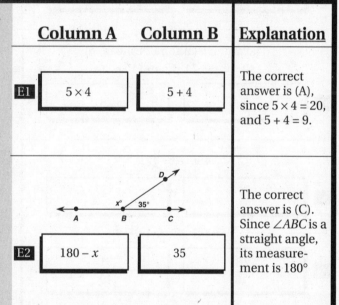

Column A	Column B	Explanation
E1 5×4	$5 + 4$	The correct answer is (A), since $5 \times 4 = 20$, and $5 + 4 = 9$.
E2 $180 - x$	35	The correct answer is (C). Since $\angle ABC$ is a straight angle, its measurement is $180°$

Column A	**Column B**

$x = 5, y = -3$

1. $(x + y)^2$ | $(x - y)^2$

2. $\dfrac{2}{3} + \dfrac{3}{2}$ | $\dfrac{5}{2}$

$x > 0, y > 0$

3. $x^2 + y^2$ | $(x + y)^2$

The average (arithmetic mean) of 40, 20, 30, 24, 27, and 15 is $\bar{x}$.

4. $\bar{x}$ | 26

$4w = 6x = 12y$

5. w | y

6. $\dfrac{13}{16}$ | $\dfrac{31}{40}$

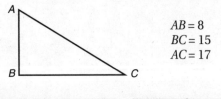

$AB = 8$
$BC = 15$
$AC = 17$

7. $\angle ABC$ | $90°$

Column A	**Column B**

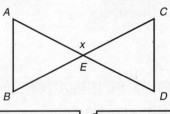

8. $2(\angle x)$ | $\angle A + \angle B + \angle C + \angle D$

$w : x = y : z$, x and z are not zero

9. $w + x$ | $y + z$

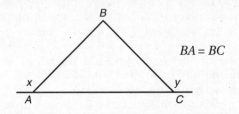

$BA = BC$

10. x | y

Square $EFGH$ is inscribed in circle $GO \perp OH$. Area of triangle $GOH = 12.5$

11. Area of shaded part of figure | 9π

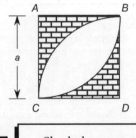

$ABCD$ is a square. The unshaded area represents the intersection of two quadrants.

12. Shaded area | Unshaded area

GO ON TO THE NEXT PAGE →

Column A	Column B

$$m > n > 1$$

13.

w^n	w^m

Jim buys a dozen oranges and ten apples for $2.20. Jane buys a half dozen oranges and four pears for $1.20. John buys a half dozen pears and three apples for $1.20.

14.

Cost of one apple and one pear	Cost of two pears

Column A	Column B

Given $2a = b$

15.

Area of a square, side = a	Area of an isosceles right triangle with leg = b

---

DIRECTIONS: For the following questions, select the best answer choice to the given question.

---

16. What part of three-fourths is one-tenth?

(A) $\dfrac{1}{8}$ (D) $\dfrac{3}{40}$

(B) $\dfrac{15}{2}$ (E) None of these

(C) $\dfrac{2}{15}$

17. Find the value of x in $2x + 12 = 3x + 9$.

(A) 1   (D) 4
(B) 2   (E) 5
(C) 3

18. Peter has five rulers of 30 cm each and three of 20 cm each. What is the average length of Peter's rulers?

(A) 25   (D) 26.25
(B) 27   (E) 27.25
(C) 23

19. Two pounds of pears and one pound of peaches cost $1.40. Three pounds of pears and two pounds of peaches cost $2.40. How much is the combined cost of one pound of pears and one pound of peaches?

(A) $2.00   (D) $.80
(B) $1.50   (E) $1.00
(C) $1.60

20. The sum of three consecutive odd integers is always divisible by (I) 2, (II) 3, (III) 5, or (IV) 6.

(A) I only   (D) I and III only
(B) II only   (E) IV only
(C) III only

Questions 21–25 refer to the charts on the following pages.

GO ON TO THE NEXT PAGE →

United States, Area and Population

Division	area*		population	
	sq mi	sq km	1970 census	1980 census
East North Central States	244,366	632,905	40,253,000	41,668,000
	248,283	643,050		
Illinois	55,877	144,721	11,114,000	11,418,000
	56,400	146,075		
Indiana	36,189	93,729	5,194,000	5,490,000
	36,291	93,993		
Michigan	56,818	147,158	8,875,000	9,258,000
	58,216	150,779		
Ohio	41,018	106,236	10,652,000	10,797,000
	41,222	106,764		
Wisconsin	54,464	141,061	4,418,000	4,705,000
	56,154	145,438		
East South Central States	179,427	464,714	12,804,000	14,663,000
	181,964	471,285		
Alabama	50,851	131,703	3,444,000	3,890,000
	52,609	133,667		
Kentucky	39,851	103,214	3,219,000	3,661,000
	40,395	104,623		
Mississippi	47,358	122,657	2,217,000	2,521,000
	47,716	123,584		
Tennessee	41,367	107,140	3,924,000	4,591,000
	42,244	109,411		
Middle Atlantic States	100,426	260,102†	37,199,000	36,788,000
	102,745	266,108†		
New Jersey	7,532	19,508	7,168,000	7,364,000
	7,836	20,295		
New York	47,869	123,980	18,237,000	17,557,000
	49,576	128,401		
Pennsylvania	45,025	116,614	11,794,000	11,867,000
	45,333	117,412		
Mountain States	856,633	2,218,669†	8,281,000	11,369,000
	863,887	2,237,457†		
Arizona	113,563	294,127	1,771,000	2,718,000
	113,909	295,023		
Colorado	103,794	268,825	2,207,000	2,889,000
	104,247	269,998		
Idaho	82,677	214,132	713,000	944,000
	83,557	216,412		
Montana	145,603	377,110	694,000	787,000
	147,138	381,086		
Nevada	109,889	284,611	489,000	799,000
	110,540	296,297		
New Mexico	121,445	314,541	1,016,000	1,300,000
	121,666	315,113		
Utah	82,381	213,366	1,059,000	1,461,000
	84,916	219,931		
Wyoming	97,281	251,957	332,000	471,000
	97,914	253,596		
New England States	62,992	163,149†	11,842,000	12,349,000
	66,608	172,514†		
Connecticut	4,870	12,613	3,032,000	3,108,000
	5,009	12,973		
Maine	30,933	80,116	992,000	1,125,000
	33,215	86,026		
Massachusetts	7,833	20,287	5,689,000	5,737,000
	8,257	21,386		
New Hampshire	9,003	23,395	738,000	921,000
	9,304	24,097		
Rhode Island	1,049	2,717	947,000	947,000
	1,214	3,144		
Vermont	9,274	24,020	444,000	511,000
	9,609	24,887		

Division	area*		population	
	sq mi	sq km	1970 census	1980 census
Pacific States	892,266	2,310,958	26,522,000	31,797,000
	916,728	2,374,315		
Alaska	566,432	1,467,052	300,000	400,000
	586,412	1,518,800		
California	156,537	405,429	19,953,000	23,669,000
	158,693	411,013		
Hawaii	6,425	16,641	769,000	965,000
	6,450	16,705		
Oregon	96,209	249,180	2,091,000	2,633,000
	96,981	251,180		
Washington	66,663	172,656	3,409,000	4,130,000
	68,192	176,616		
South Atlantic States	267,352	692,438†	30,671,000	36,942,000
	278,776	772,026		
Delaware	19,822	5,133	548,000	595,000
	2,057	5,328		
District of Columbia††	61	158	757,000	638,000
	67	174		
Florida	54,136	140,212	6,789,000	9,740,000
	58,560	151,670		
Georgia	58,197	150,730	4,590,000	5,464,000
	58,878	152,488		
Maryland	9,891	25,618	3,922,000	4,216,000
	10,577	27,394		
North Carolina	48,880	126,599	5,082,000	5,874,000
	52,586	136,197		
South Carolina	30,280	78,425	2,591,000	3,119,000
	31,055	80,432		
Virginia	39,841	103,188	4,648,000	5,346,000
	40,817	105,716		
West Virginia	24,084	62,377	1,744,000	1,950,000
	24,181	62,628		
West North Central States	508,192	1,316,211	16,320,000	17,183,000
	517,247	1,339,664		
Iowa	56,043	145,151	2,824,000	2,913,000
	56,290	145,790		
Kansas	82,056	212,524	2,247,000	2,363,000
	82,264	213,063		
Minnesota	78,289	205,358	3,805,000	4,077,000
	84,068	217,735		
Missouri	69,046	178,828	4,677,000	4,917,000
	69,686	180,486		
Nebraska	76,522	198,191	1,483,000	1,570,000
	77,227	200,017		
North Dakota	69,280	179,434	618,000	653,000
	70,665	183,022		
South Dakota	75,956	196,725	666,000	690,000
	77,047	199,551		
West South Central States	429,284	1,111,840†	19,320,000	23,743,000
	438,884	1,136,704		
Arkansas	52,175	135,133	1,923,000	2,286,000
	53,104	137,539		
Louisiana	45,155	116,951	3,641,000	4,204,000
	48,523	125,674		
Oklahoma	68,984	178,668	2,559,000	3,025,000
	69,919	181,089		
Texas	262,970	681,089	11,197,000	14,228,000
	267,338	692,402		
Total United States	3,540,938	9,170,987	203,212,000§	226,505,000§
	3,615,122	9,163,123†		

* Where two figures are given, the first is the land area, the second the total area.
† Converted area figures do not add up to total given because of rounding.
†† District of Columbia is a federal district.
§ Figures do not add up to total given because of rounding.
Source: U.S. government figures.

21. What is the land area in kilometers of the Pacific division?

(A) 892,266   (D) 2,374,315
(B) 916,728   (E) 26,522,000
(C) 2,310,958

24. What is the average increase of population from 1970–1980 per state in the New England region?

(A) 84,500   (D) 386,000
(B) 101,400   (E) 441,000
(C) 126,750

22. What are the divisions with the smallest and the largest land areas?

(A) New England – Pacific
(B) Mountain – New England
(C) Pacific – Pacific
(D) West North Central – New England
(E) Mountain – Middle Atlantic

25. If in the period 1980–1990 the rate of population increase is the same as in the 1970–1980 period, what will the population of East North Central be in 1990?

(A) 43,083,000   (D) 43,000,000
(B) 40,251,160   (E) 43,134,710
(C) 44,653,060

23. What percent of the land area represents the Pacific and East North Central divisions?

(A) 22.1   (D) 25.2
(B) 32.1   (E) 6.9
(C) 42.1

26. One number is 2 more than 3 times another. Their sum is 22. Find the numbers.

(A) 8, 14   (D) 4, 18
(B) 2, 20   (E) 10, 12
(C) 5, 17

27. The length of a rectangle is $6L$ and the width is $4W$. What is the perimeter?

(A) $12L + 8W$ (D) $20LW$
(B) $12L^2 + 8W^2$ (E) $24LW$
(C) $6L + 4W$

28. If the length of a rectangle is increased by 30% and the width is decreased by 20%, then the area is increased by

(A)   10%.   (D)   20%.
(B)   5%.   (E)   25%.
(C)   4%.

29. If n is the first of three consecutive odd numbers, which of the following represents the sum of the three numbers?

(A) $n + 2$ (D) $3n + 6$
(B) $n + 4$ (E) $6(3n)$
(C) $n + 6$

30. In the following figure, line l is parallel to line m. If the area of $\triangle ABC$ is 40 cm², what is the area of triangle $\triangle ABD$?

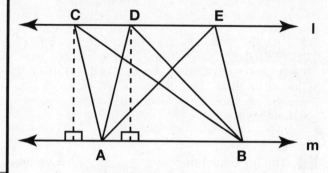

(A)   Less than 40 cm²
(B)   More than 40 cm²
(C)   The length of segment $\overline{AD}$ times 40 cm²
(D)   Exactly 40 cm²
(E)   Cannot be determined from the information given.

STOP

If time still remains, you may go back and check your work. When the time allotted is up, you may go on to the next section.

TIME: 30 Minutes
38 Questions

For each question in this section, select the best answer from among the given choices and fill in the corresponding oval on the answer sheet.

DIRECTIONS: Each of the given sentences has blank spaces which indicate words omitted. Choose the best combination of words which fit into the meaning and structure within the context of the sentence.

1. The frightened mother _____ her young daughter for darting in front of the car.

(A) implored   (D) admonished
(B) extorted   (E) abolished
(C) exhorted

2. The family left their country to _____ to Utopia and escape _____ because of their beliefs.

(A) emigrate...prosecution
(B) peregrinate...extortion
(C) immigrate...persecution
(D) wander...arraignment
(E) roam...censure

3. She responded so quickly with a _____ that it was evident the remark had been _____ until the proper time to use it.

(A) repartee...dormant
(B) wit...latent
(C) satire...hibernating
(D) humor...camouflaged
(E) sortie...disguised

4. After reading the letter, she _____ that the manager was attempting to _____ a contract with her.

(A) implied...abrogate
(B) inferred...negotiate
(C) imposed...nullify
(D) surmised...breech
(E) included...annihilate

5. The defense attorney was satisfied with the acquittal, but the prosecutor felt the judge's decision was _____ .

(A) ambiguous   (D) auspicious
(B) astute   (E) arbitrary
(C) arduous

6. Perhaps the most famous speech in all of Shakespeare's plays is Hamlet's _____ .

(A) colloquy   (D) quandary
(B) palindrome   (E) obloquy
(C) soliloquy

7. During the Middle Ages, many people were inspired to lead more religious lives by the _____ of St. Francis of Assisi.

(A) abnegation   (D) vacillation
(B) turpitude   (E) dichotomy
(C) calumny

DIRECTIONS: In the following questions, the given pair of words contains a specific relationship to each other. Select the best pair of choices which expresses the same relationship as the given.

8. MANDATORY:OPTIONAL::

(A) pious:indignant   (D) chaste:celibate
(B) competent:inept   (E) crass:boorish
(C) opaque:ornate

9. PUNISHMENT:FINE::

(A) hyacinth:flower   (B) orange:peel
(C) circulation:heart (D) puzzle:jigsaw
(E) sandals:shoes

GO ON TO THE NEXT PAGE

10. BANDAGE:WOUND::

   (A) collar:dog   (D) diaper:baby
   (B) stamp:envelope   (E) cast:fracture
   (C) gloves:hands

11. ESPOUSE:THEORY::

   (A) proponent:opponent
   (B) create:innovate
   (C) advocate:hypothesis
   (D) heretic:blasphemy
   (E) gourmand:gluttony

12. TRACTABLE:BIDDABLE::

   (A) torpid:lethargic   (D) colloquial:formal
   (B) viscous:liquid   (E) eccentric:aesthetic
   (C) truculent:contrite

13. DEIGN:CONDESCEND::

   (A) berate:commend
   (B) corroborate:repudiate
   (C) digress:stray
   (D) imbue:desiccate
   (E) vaunt:wither

14. FRAILTY:VICE::

   (A) felony:misdemeanor
   (B) aggravation:rage
   (C) trite:popular
   (D) secreted:veiled
   (E) cloister:monastery

15. ANALOGOUS:PARALLEL::

   (A) acidulous:saccharine
   (B) sinuous:tortuous
   (C) incongruous:homogeneous
   (D) pundit:tyro
   (E) mundane:celestial

16. FINE:AMERCEMENT::

   (A) loss:gain
   (B) forfeiture:reward
   (C) penalty:mulct
   (D) lottery:deposit
   (E) contraband:confiscate

DIRECTIONS: Each passage is followed by questions based on its content. After reading a passage, choose the best answer to each question. Answer all questions based on what is stated or implied in that passage.

Questions 17–24 are based on the following passage.

Line
(1)   Established firmly in popular culture is the notion that each of the two hemispheres of the brain has specialized functions. The left hemisphere, insist proponents of this theory,
(5) controls language and logic; the right hemisphere, espousers contend, is the more creative and intuitive half. Many proponents try to classify a person as "right-brained" or "leftbrained," suggesting that the two hemispheres do not work
(10) together in the same person and, thus, can be considered independent. Because of the supposed independent functions of the two hemispheres and because of their difference in specializations, an activity might engage one part of the brain while
(15) the other part is not used at all, they believe. "Right-brained" individuals are the creative, intuitive persons (artists, for instance) of society; "left-brained" persons are the verbal, language-oriented, logical individuals of civilization.
(20)   Opponents of the split-brain theory dispute the premise that the hemispheres operate independently simply because of specialized functions; they state that the very fact that the two hemispheres differ in purpose indicates that they
(25) must integrate activities and therefore result in processes which are different from and even greater than the processes of either hemisphere. These split-brain theory opponents base their arguments on the fact that when surgery is performed to
(30) disconnect the two sides, each can still function well (but not perfectly). They also argue that when a person writes an original story, the left hemisphere works to produce a logical work, but the right hemisphere helps with creativity. The third
(35) argument is based on the fact that if a patient has right hemisphere damage, major logical disorders are manifested; in fact, more logical disorders appear than if the left hemisphere suffers damage. The opponents to split-brain theory state that it is

GO ON TO THE NEXT PAGE →

(40) impossible to educate one side of the brain without educating the other. They state that there is no evidence that one can be purely right-brained or left-brained.

(45) Educators, then, who seek to modify the curriculum and methods to accommodate the split-brain theory must justify their demands. The burden of proof rests with these innovators who seek to restructure education as it currently exists.

17. To the assertion that the split-brain theory is accurate, the author would probably respond with which of the following?

(A) Unqualified disagreement
(B) Unquestioning approval
(C) Complete indifference
(D) Strong disparagement
(E) Implied uncertainty

18. Which of the following titles best describes the content of the passage?

(A) A Reassertion of the Validity of the Split-Brain Theory
(B) A Renunciation of the Split-Brain Theory
(C) Split Opinions on the Split-Brain Theory
(D) Modifying the Curriculum to Accommodate the Split-Brain Theory
(E) A New Theory: The Split-Brain Theory

19. The author uses the term "integrate activities" (line 25) to mean

(A) share synaptic connections.
(B) work together.
(C) coordinate functions.
(D) break down tasks into left- and right-brain segments.
(E) pass information from one hemisphere to the other.

20. According to the information given in the passage, which of the following statements are true?

I. The left hemisphere of the brain controls language and logic independently of the right hemisphere.
II. The two hemispheres of the brain control different functions.
III. Evidence exists that suggests that some logical functions are controlled by the right hemisphere.

(A) I only
(B) II only
(C) I and II only
(D) III only
(E) II and III only

21. The most compelling argument that the opponents of the split-brain theory present for their beliefs, according to the author, is which of the following?

(A) When surgery is performed to disconnect the two sides of the brain, both sides continue to operate well — but not perfectly.
(B) When a patient has right hemisphere damage, no logical disorders are manifested.
(C) Because of the independent functions of the two hemispheres, an activity might engage one hemisphere of the brain and not another.
(D) The hemispheres operate independently because of specialized functions.
(E) It is impossible to educate one side of the brain without educating the other.

22. According to the passage, the most significant distinction between proponents and opponents of the split-brain theory is which of the following?

(A) Their beliefs about teaching methods and the curriculum
(B) Proponents state that the two hemispheres differ in purpose and, therefore, must integrate activities.
(C) Opponents state that the hemispheres differ in function and, therefore, cannot integrate activities.
(D) Their beliefs about the functions of the hemispheres of the brain
(E) Their beliefs that the brain is divided into hemispheres

GO ON TO THE NEXT PAGE →

23. Which of the following statements is most compatible with the principles of the split-brain theory?

(A) The fact that the two hemispheres differ in purpose indicates that they must integrate activities.

(B) "Right-brained" individuals are the creative, intuitive persons of society; "left-brained" persons are the verbal, language-oriented, logical individuals of civilization.

(C) It is impossible to educate one side of the brain without educating the other.

(D) More logical disorders appear if the right hemisphere is damaged than if the left hemisphere is damaged.

(E) When surgery is performed to disconnect the two sides of the brain, each can function well.

24. To an assertion that education curriculum and methods should be altered to accommodate proponents of the split-brain theory, the author would most likely respond with which of the following?

(A) This is a definite need in our schools today.

(B) Educators have already made these important modifications.

(C) Justification for these alterations must be provided by proponents of the split-brain theory.

(D) It is impossible to educate one side of the brain without educating the other.

(E) Such alterations might be necessary since "right-brained" persons are the verbal, language-oriented, logical individuals.

Questions 25–27 refer to the following passage.

Line
(1)   Being born female and black were two handicaps Gwendolyn Brooks states that she faced from her birth, in 1917, in Kansas. Brooks was determined to succeed. Despite the lack of
(5) encouragement she received from her teachers and others, she was determined to write, and found the first publisher for one of her poems when she was 11.

    In 1945 she marketed and sold her first book;
(10) national recognition ensued. She applied for and received grants and fellowships from such organizations as the American Academy of Arts and Letters and the Guggenheim Foundation. Later she received the Pulitzer Prize for Poetry; she was the
(15) first black woman to receive such an honor.

    Brooks was an integrationist in the 1940s and an advocate of black consciousness in the 1960s. Her writing styles show that she is not bound by rules; her works are not devoid of the truth, even about
(20) sensitive subjects like the black experience, life in the ghetto, and city life.

    Brooks' reaction to fame is atypical. She continues to work—and work hard. She writes, travels, and helps many who are interested in
(25) writing. Especially important to her is increasing her knowledge of her black heritage and encouraging other people to do the same. She encourages dedication to the art to would-be writers.

25. Which of the following phrases best describes the passage?

(A) A discussion of the importance of Gwendolyn Brooks' writings

(B) An essay on the achievements of Gwendolyn Brooks

(C) An essay on Gwendolyn Brooks as a black female role model

(D) A biographical sketch on Gwendolyn Brooks

(E) A discussion of the handicaps faced by black women writers

26. The passage implies that Brooks received less credit than she deserved primarily because of which of the following?

(A) She tried to publish too early in her career.

(B) She was aided by funds received through grants.

(C) She was a frequent victim of both racial and gender discrimination.

(D) Her work was too complex to be of widespread interest to others.

(E) She had no interest in the accolades of her colleagues.

GO ON TO THE NEXT PAGE

27. According to the passage, Gwendolyn Brooks

    (A) marketed her first book when she was 11 years old.
    (B) achieved national recognition when she received the Pulitzer Prize.
    (C) advocated black consciousness in the 1940s.
    (D) received little encouragement from her teachers.
    (E) avoided "black" topics in her writing.

DIRECTIONS: Each of the following questions provides a given word in capitalized letters followed by five word choices. Choose the best word which is most <u>opposite</u> in meaning to the given word.

28. LUDICROUS:

    (A) mundane   (D) reasonable
    (B) semaphore   (E) fallacious
    (C) illogical

29. JEOPARDY:

    (A) danger   (D) conundrum
    (B) safety   (E) levity
    (C) perjury

30. AWRY:

    (A) earthy   (D) dubious
    (B) crooked   (E) straight
    (C) pied

31. INSIDIOUS:

    (A) precipitant   (D) conducive
    (B) incendiary   (E) imprudent
    (C) decadent

32. CAPRICIOUS:

    (A) impecunious   (D) copious
    (B) juxtaposition   (E) superfluous
    (C) scrupulous

33. COMPLACENT:

    (A) compliant   (D) contentious
    (B) decorous   (E) sumptuous
    (C) passive

34. DOCILE:

    (A) unruly   (D) uncouth
    (B) raucous   (E) strident
    (C) demure

35. POSTULATE:

    (A) mollify   (D) corroborate
    (B) conjecture   (E) refurbish
    (C) prognosticate

36. CONCORD:

    (A) succor   (D) vigilance
    (B) enmity   (E) nobility
    (C) grip

37. MALEFACTION:

    (A) affinity   (D) idiosyncratic
    (B) subsidy   (E) cognate
    (C) profligation

38. ZEPHYR:

    (A) tycoon   (D) taciturn
    (B) typhoon   (E) constellation
    (C) coracle

STOP
If time still remains, you may go back and check your work. When the time allotted is up, you may go on to the next section.

TIME: 30 Minutes
    30 Questions

REFERENCE INFORMATION:

NUMBERS: All numbers are real numbers.

FIGURES: Position of points, angles, regions, etc. are assumed to be in the order shown and angle measures are assumed to be positive.

LINES: Assume that lines shown as straight are indeed straight.

DIRECTIONS: Each of the following given set of quantities is placed into either Column A or B. Compare the two quantities to decide whether

(A) the quantity in Column A is greater;
(B) the quantity in Column B is greater;
(C) the two quantities are equal;
(D) the relationship cannot be determined from the information given.

NOTE: Do not choose (E) since there are only four choices.

COMMON INFORMATION: Information which relates to one or both given quantities is centered in the two columns. A symbol which appears in both columns will indicate the same item in Column A and Column B.

EXAMPLES:		
Column A	**Column B**	**Explanation**
E1 5×4	$5 + 4$	The correct answer is (A), since $5 \times 4 = 20$, and $5 + 4 = 9$.
E2 $180 - x$	35	The correct answer is (C). Since $\angle ABC$ is a straight angle, its measurement is 180°

Column A	Column B
1. Number of minutes in $2\frac{1}{2}$ hours	Number of hours in $6\frac{1}{4}$ days

$$w : x = y : z$$
$$x \neq 0, \quad z \neq 0$$

Column A	Column B
2. $wz - xy$	0

Column A	Column B
3. 35% of 7	0.7 of 35

$$\frac{1}{y} < 0$$

Column A	Column B
4. y	1

Column A	Column B
5. $\dfrac{2}{3} - \dfrac{1}{2}$	$\dfrac{4}{5} - \dfrac{2}{3}$

$$x + y = 6$$
$$3x - y = 4$$

Column A	Column B
6. $x - y$	0

Column A	Column B
7. $\left(1 - \sqrt{2}\right)\left(1 - \sqrt{2}\right)$	$\left(1 - \sqrt{2}\right)\left(1 + \sqrt{2}\right)$

Column A	Column B
8. Distance between $A(3, 4)$ and $B(-1, 1)$	Distance between $C(4, -2)$ and $D(-2, -2)$

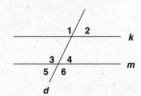

$k \| m$
$\angle 2 = 60°$

Column A	Column B
9. $\angle 5$	$60°$

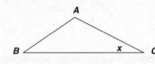

$\angle A = 100°$
$\angle B = 48°$

Column A	Column B
10. Side AB	Side BC

Column A	Column B
11. Product of the roots of $x^2 + 3x - 4$	Product of the roots of $x^2 + 4x + 4$

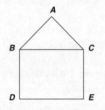

Area of triangle plus area of square = 125 and perimeter of square is 40

Column A	Column B
12. Twice the length of line segment BD	The shortest distance from point A to line segment DE

$$\frac{a+2}{a+1} = \frac{a-4}{a-3}$$

Column A	Column B
13. Value of a	1

GO ON TO THE NEXT PAGE

Column A	Column B		Column A	Column B

14.

The sum of all angles of a polygon whose sides are all equal

The sum of all angles of a square

15.

$$x < y < z$$

$|x^2 - y^2|$

$x^2 - z^2$

DIRECTIONS: For the following questions, select the best answer choice to the given question.

16. A runner takes nine seconds to run a distance of 132 feet. What is the runner's speed in miles per hour?

(A) 9 (D) 12
(B) 10 (E) 13
(C) 11

17. 35 is 7% of what quantity?

(A) 2.45 (D) 50
(B) 5 (E) 500
(C) 245

18. After taking four tests, Joan has an average grade of 79 points. What grade must she get on her fifth test to achieve an 83 point average?

(A) 83 (D) 95
(B) 86 (E) 99
(C) 87

19. If a triangle of base 6 units has the same area as a circle of radius 6 units, what is the altitude of the triangle?

(A) π (D) 12π
(B) 3π (E) 36π
(C) 6π

20. A given cube has a surface area of 96 square feet. What is the volume of the cube in cubic feet?

(A) 16 (D) 96
(B) 36 (E) 216
(C) 64

Questions 21–25 refer to the table below.

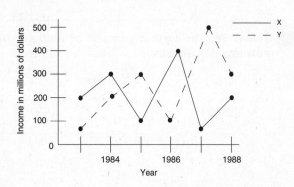

GO ON TO THE NEXT PAGE

21. What was the average income in millions of Company X during the years 1983 to 1986?

(A) 150   (D) 300
(B) 200   (E) 400
(C) 250

22. What was the largest difference in earnings (in millions) between the two companies in a given year?

(A) 100   (D) 400
(B) 200   (E) 500
(C) 300

23. What was the median income in millions of Company X from 1983 through 1988?

(A) 100
(B) 200
(C) 300
(D) 400
(E) Cannot be determined

24. What was the largest percent of increase in earnings of Company Y?

(A) 50%   (D) 300%
(B) 100%   (E) 400%
(C) 200%

25. What was the largest percent of decrease in earnings for either one of the companies?

(A) 50%   (D) 75%
(B) 100%   (E) 400%
(C) 200%

26. Solve the inequality $7 - 3x \le 19$.

(A) $x = 4$ (D) $x \le -4$
(B) $x = -4$ (E) $x \ge 4$
(C) $x \ge -4$

27. A truck contains 150 small packages, some weighing 1 kg each and some weighing 2 kg each. How many packages weighing 2 kg each are in the truck if the total weight of all the packages is 264 kg?

(A) 36   (D) 124
(B) 52   (E) 114
(C) 88

28. A wheel with a diameter of 3 feet makes a revolution every 2 minutes. How many feet will the wheel travel in 30 minutes?

(A) 3π (D) 30π
(B) 6π (E) 15π
(C) 45π

29. A waitress's income consists of her salary and tips. Her salary is $150 a week. During one week that included a holiday, her tips were $\frac{5}{4}$ of her salary. What fraction of her income for the week came from tips?

(A) $\dfrac{5}{8}$ (D) $\dfrac{1}{2}$

(B) $\dfrac{5}{4}$ (E) $\dfrac{5}{9}$

(C) $\dfrac{4}{9}$

30. Each of the integers h, m, and n is divisible by 3. Which of the following integers is <u>always</u> divisible by 9?

I. hm
II. $h + m$
III. $h + m + n$

(A) I only   (D) II and III only
(B) II only   (E) I, II, and III
(C) III only

STOP
If time still remains, you may go back and check your work. When the time allotted is up, you may go on to the next section.

**TIME: 30 Minutes
38 Questions**

For each question in this section, select the best answer from among the given choices and fill in the corresponding oval on the answer sheet.

DIRECTIONS: Each of the given sentences has blank spaces which indicate words omitted. Choose the best combination of words which fit into the meaning and structure within the context of the sentence.

1. The unmitigated truth is that the author of the essays was _____ in his writing; their publication _____ the teacher's chances for a promotion.

   (A) abusive...enhanced
   (B) laconic...obliterated
   (C) obtuse...obviated
   (D) profound...diminished
   (E) prolific...necessitated.

2. The sales associate tried to _____ trade by distributing business cards.

   (A) elicit   (D) elliptic
   (B) solicit   (E) conciliate
   (C) illicit

3. Many doctors now believe that a pregnant woman's _____ for odd foods supplements some lack in her regular diet.

   (A) quirk   (D) penchant
   (B) profusion   (E) stipend
   (C) pittance

4. The chairman complained that the committee was wasting too much time on _____ issues, instead of concentrating on the _____ one.

   (A) peripheral...essential
   (B) scurrilous...tedious
   (C) trenchant...superfluous
   (D) superficial...whimsical
   (E) munificent...desultory

5. The acquisition of exact knowledge is apt to be _____, but it is essential to every kind of excellence.

   (A) wearisome   (D) amorphous
   (B) equable   (E) eccentric
   (C) erratic

6. The biophysicist's lecture on molecular dynamics was too _____ for many of the students in the audience.

   (A) erudite   (D) inchoate
   (B) eclectic   (E) amorphous
   (C) abstruse

7. All her attempts to _____ the situation not only failed, but actually seemed to exacerbate the problem.

   (A) excoriate   (D) exculpate
   (B) disseminate (E) objurgate
   (C) ameliorate

DIRECTIONS: In the following questions, the given pair of words contains a specific relationship to each other. Select the best pair of choices which expresses the same relationship as the given.

8. GIGGLE:GUFFAW::

   (A) glove:gauntlet   (D) reprove:berate
   (B) fashion:vogue   (E) wheedle:whine
   (C) sob:weep

9. BENEFICIAL:BALEFUL::
   (A) amiable:anonymous
   (B) economical:thrifty
   (C) docile:compliant
   (D) benign:malice
   (E) favorable:ominous

GO ON TO THE NEXT PAGE

10. ILLUSION:MAGICIAN::

(A) trees:branches
(B) elements:chemistry
(C) disease:medicine
(D) recipe:cook
(E) aria:soprano

11. FUMBLE:FINESSE::

(A) frugal:fluent
(B) deceive:beguile
(C) facilitate:expedite
(D) impugn:extol
(E) abhor:appease

12. PUPA:MOTH::

(A) parapet:wall
(B) pommel:saddle
(C) stamen:flower
(D) tadpole:frog
(E) adolescent:adult

13. VACILLATE:DECISION::

(A) equivocate:commitment
(B) fluctuate:procrastinate
(C) conspire:collusion
(D) resolve:conclusion
(E) ameliorate:resolution

14. COALESCE:DISPERSE::

(A) umbrage:offense
(B) imprecate:consecrate
(C) incarcerate:remonstrate
(D) elucidate:prevaricate
(E) debilitate:mitigate

15. CONTUMACIOUS:MUTINEER::

(A) deleterious:renascence
(B) ephemeral:biennial
(C) obsequious:zealot
(D) pedagogic:neophyte
(E) irascible:connoisseur

16. FUSTIAN:BOMBASTIC::

(A) facetious:sardonic
(B) sanguine:saturnine
(C) loquacious:garrulous
(D) igneous:pecuniary
(E) nugatory:inordinate

DIRECTIONS: Each passage is followed by questions based on its content. After reading a passage, choose the best answer to each question. Answer all questions based on what is stated or implied in that passage.

Questions 17–22 refer to the following passage.

Line
(1)   Dr. Harrison Faigel of Brandex University has announced to standardized test-takers across the country the results of his experiment to improve the SAT scores of 30 high school students. Faigel
(5) was convinced that student nervousness had affected their scores; to reduce the anxiety of these students who had already been tested, he gave 22 of them a beta blocker before the re-administration of the test. Their scores improved an average of more
(10) than 100 points. The other eight (who did not receive the beta blockers) improved only an average of 11 points. Second-time test-takers nationwide improved only an average of 28 points.
    Beta blockers are prescription drugs which have
(15) been around for 25 years. These medications, which interfere with the effects of adrenalin, have been used for heart conditions and for minor stress such as stage fright—and now for test anxiety. These drugs seem to help test-takers who have low
(20) test scores because of test fright, not those who do not "know" the material. Since side effects from these beta blockers do exist, however, some physicians are not ready to prescribe routinely these medications to all test-takers.

17. The author of this article can be best described as which of the following?

(A) Pessimistic   (D) Resigned
(B) Unconcerned   (E) Optimistic
(C) Indifferent

18. The passage suggests which of the following?

(A) Many researchers will be dissatisfied with Faigel's study because he did not use a control group.

GO ON TO THE NEXT PAGE

(B) Second-time test-takers nationwide do fine without help; it is the first-time test-takers who experience anxiety and a lower score.

(C) Even without study, preparation, and knowledge of the test material, one can experience help by taking the beta blockers before taking a test.

(D) Adrenalin apparently increases minor stress which may result in lower test scores for already nervous students.

(E) Adrenalin has long been used for heart conditions and for minor stress such as stage fright—and now for test anxiety.

19. The passage implies that students' attitudes toward test scores can best be described as which of the following?

(A) Casual indifference
(B) Resignation
(C) Antagonism
(D) Pessimism
(E) Concern

20. The author mentions speculating on the average standardized test scores. Which of the following logically ensues?

(A) Retaking the SAT normally results in a significant increase on the scores because of the student's familiarity with the test format.

(B) The re-administration of tests will be decreased in the future since second-time test-takers routinely increase their average scores significantly.

(C) The beta blockers, if used routinely by nervous second-time test-takers, may result in an increase in the average standardized test scores for the nation.

(D) Only competitive students will attempt to utilize beta blockers; average test scores, therefore, will not be significantly affected.

(E) Competitive students will try to avail themselves of adrenalin; the average scores on standardized tests for the nation will be increased.

21. Which of the following best summarizes the author's main point?

(A) The study by Faigel indicates to the general public that help for general nervousness is at hand through the use of beta blockers.

(B) Adrenalin increased the performance of 22 second-time test-takers of the SAT.

(C) Beta blockers seem to improve the average scores of second-time test-takers of the SAT more than 100 points.

(D) Beta blockers should not be used since they may cause side effects.

(E) Nervousness does not seem to affect the test scores of students if they "know" the material in the first place.

22. Recognizing that nervousness may affect test scores and developing a plan to reduce the nervousness and to compare the test results is an example of Faigel using which of the following?

(A) Analysis   (D) Interpretation
(B) Synthesis   (E) Application
(C) Deduction

Questions 23–27 refer to the following passage.

Line
(1)   Amyotrophic lateral sclerosis (ALS) is a debilitating disorder which attacks the body's nervous system and renders muscles useless. The disease, which has no known cause or cure, is that
(5) which took the life of Lou Gehrig, a member of baseball's Hall of Fame. Even more perplexing is that three former San Francisco 49ers have also died from ALS, which is usually a rare disease. There exists no corroboration for speculations as to
(10) whether painkillers, steroids, or even the fertilizers used on playing fields triggered the disease. A solution to the enigma of ALS does not seem imminent.

GO ON TO THE NEXT PAGE

23. The author's attitude toward ALS is best described as which of the following?

(A) Amusement   (D) Approval
(B) Indignation   (E) Resignation
(C) Indifference

24. Which of the following statements is a correct example of deductive reasoning?

(A) At least four of the victims of the rare ALS have been athletes; the disease seems to affect active persons more often.
(B) Four sports figures have died from ALS.
(C) Since three football players and one baseball player have died from ALS, constant exposure to fertilizers on the playing fields may increase one's chances of developing ALS.
(D) Three football and one baseball player have died from ALS; the next victim will probably be a ball player also.
(E) All four of the most well-known victims of ALS have been males; the disease seems to affect only men.

25. Which of the following words would be the best substitute for the word "corroboration"?

(A) Support   (D) Analogy
(B) Evidence   (E) Confirmation
(C) Reason

26. The topic sentence is which of the following?

(A) A solution to the enigma of ALS does not seem imminent.
(B) The disease, which has no known cause or cure, is that which took the life of Lou Gehrig, a member of baseball's Hall of Fame.
(C) Even more perplexing is that three former San Francisco 49ers have also died from ALS, which is usually a rare disease.
(D) Amyotrophic lateral sclerosis (ALS) is a debilitating disorder which attacks the body's nervous system and renders muscles useless.
(E) There exists no corroboration for speculations as to whether painkillers, steroids, or even the fertilizers used on playing fields triggered the disease.

27. Which of the following questions does the passage answer?

(A) What are the causes of amyotrophic lateral sclerosis?
(B) Who was Lou Gehrig?
(C) What is the cure for amyotrophic lateral sclerosis?
(D) What is amyotrophic lateral sclerosis?
(E) What is the connection between ALS and professional athletes?

DIRECTIONS: Each of the following questions provides a given word in capitalized letters followed by five word choices. Choose the best word which is most <u>opposite</u> in meaning to the given word.

28. ODYSSEY:

(A) journey   (D) voyage
(B) errand   (E) cruise
(C) wandering

29. ADULTERATE:

(A) intermix   (D) miscegenate
(B) hybridize   (E) homogenize
(C) interface

30. RESPLENDENT:

(A) wan   (D) trite
(B) stolid   (E) palatial
(C) shoddy

31. ALTRUISTIC:

(A) dogmatic   (D) hedonistic
(B) abstemious   (E) apocalyptic
(C) fortuitous

32. VIRILE:

(A) effeminate   (D) choleric
(B) bestial   (E) lecherous
(C) equivocal

GO ON TO THE NEXT PAGE

33. BEMOAN:

   (A) laugh   (D) acclaim
   (B) exult   (E) eulogize
   (C) commiserate

34. MELANCHOLY:

   (A) sociability   (D) impulsiveness
   (B) serenity   (E) exhilaration
   (C) complacency

35. CLANDESTINE:

   (A) surreptitious   (D) candid
   (B) furtive   (E) lurid
   (C) egregious

36. PROPITIOUS:

   (A) conspicuous   (D) militant
   (B) auspicious   (E) aggregative
   (C) evanescent

37. MALAPROPOS:

   (A) congruous   (D) benign
   (B) specious   (E) propensity
   (C) ponderous

38. UNCOUTH:

   (A) melancholy   (D) boorish
   (B) ameliorating   (E) urbane
   (C) funereal

STOP
If time still remains, you may go back and
check your work. When the time allotted is up,
you may go on to the next section.

GRE PRACTICE TEST
ANSWER KEY

Section 3 – Quantitative Ability		Section 4 – Verbal Ability	
1. (B)	16. (C)	1. (D)	20. (E)
2. (B)	17. (C)	2. (C)	21. (A)
3. (B)	18. (D)	3. (A)	22. (D)
4. (C)	19. (E)	4. (B)	23. (B)
5. (D)	20. (B)	5. (E)	24. (C)
6. (A)	21. (C)	6. (C)	25. (D)
7. (C)	22. (A)	7. (A)	26. (C)
8. (C)	23. (B)	8. (B)	27. (D)
9. (D)	24. (A)	9. (D)	28. (D)
10. (C)	25. (E)	10. (E)	29. (B)
11. (A)	26. (C)	11. (C)	30. (E)
12. (B)	27. (A)	12. (A)	31. (D)
13. (D)	28. (C)	13. (C)	32. (C)
14. (B)	29. (D)	14. (B)	33. (D)
15. (B)	30. (D)	15. (B)	34. (A)
		16. (C)	35. (D)
		17. (E)	36. (B)
		18. (C)	37. (B)
		19. (C)	38. (B)

Section 5 – Quantitative Ability			
1. (C)	16. (B)		
2. (C)	17. (E)		
3. (B)	18. (E)		
4. (B)	19. (D)		
5. (A)	20. (C)		
6. (B)	21. (C)		
7. (A)	22. (D)		
8. (B)	23. (B)		
9. (C)	24. (E)		
10. (B)	25. (D)		
11. (B)	26. (C)		
12. (A)	27. (E)		
13. (C)	28. (C)		
14. (D)	29. (E)		
15. (D)	30. (A)		

Section 6 – Verbal Ability	
1. (C)	20. (C)
2. (B)	21. (C)
3. (D)	22. (B)
4. (A)	23. (E)
5. (A)	24. (C)
6. (C)	25. (E)
7. (C)	26. (D)
8. (D)	27. (D)
9. (E)	28. (B)
10. (E)	29. (E)
11. (D)	30. (C)
12. (D)	31. (D)
13. (A)	32. (A)
14. (B)	33. (B)
15. (B)	34. (E)
16. (C)	35. (D)
17. (E)	36. (D)
18. (D)	37. (A)
19. (E)	38. (E)

Detailed Explanations of Answers

Section 1 - Analytical Writing

PERSPECTIVES ON AN ISSUE ESSAY TOPIC

Sample Essay Response Scoring 6

Having known a heavy smoker, I can understand how difficult it is to break this habit. The chronic smoker continually asserts the enjoyment that he or she derives from smoking, but smokers often ignore the harmful effects that result for themselves and others around them. I realize that smoking is a powerful addiction, but why should others need to suffer the consequences of another's medical problem? I agree that smoking should be made illegal.

thoughtful opening

strong thesis

I have witnessed children wheeze after their parents smoked in the same room with them for several hours. I myself have often choked in a smoke-filled room, even though I was not the smoker. The odor of a cigarette smoker's clothes precedes him or her into every place that he or she goes. It becomes uncomfortable to visit a friend's home when it has the peculiar odor of old smoke; this makes it difficult for me to breathe freely.

the use of personal experience adds force to the argument

smooth transition

Until cigarettes are classified as the dangerous, addictive drug that they are, smokers will not seek the help they need. They must realize they are harming not only themselves, but the health of those with whom they come into daily contact (car pools, apartment houses, restaurants, etc.) We have come a long way from viewing smoking as romantic, but now it seems that only smokers are blind to the dangers of this habit. Smokers are "in denial." It is the responsibility of the nonsmokers to show this to them by making smoking illegal and offering smokers the health they deserve.

short & therefore strong sentence

well-executed transition between ideas

As for the help that smoking addicts need, we should concentrate on nicotine addiction in the same manner that we treat other drug addictions. There are always the personal, private clinics, but these are not affordable to everyone. City and state run clinics can service the rest of the smoking population. Perhaps government agencies could accept Medicare and Medicaid to offset the expense. Anti-smoking patches, psychotherapy, support groups, and even cigarette surrogates such as chewing gum could be offered free of charge.

good variation in sentence structure

If smoking were to be declared illegal because of its endangerment to everyone's health, then we could not abandon addicted people to their own devices. This would simply lead to an illegal, dangerous "smokers' market," similar to today's drug market. It is our responsibility to make certain that this does not happen; the addicted smoker forced into this position might be your mother, father, brother, sister, or even your child.

nice flow of arguments

nicely recapitulates the previous assertions; ability to be sympathetic w/ smokers adds force to argument

If I were a smoker, I think that I would feel desperate and lie to myself that I was not harming anyone. No amount of reading newspaper articles about the rise in lung cancer deaths would convince me this is unhealthy to myself and those around me. It would be like reading the Surgeon General's warning on the side of a cigarette box; I would know that something was there, but I would never fully understand its significance. It is a kind of unawareness that lets smokers practice their addiction near little children, invalids, and animals who have no say in the matter. I firmly agree that smoking should be made illegal, but we must provide for those former smokers who are suddenly left empty-handed and addicted.

strong concluding sentence

Analysis of Sample Essay Response Scoring 6

This paper earns a rating of 6 because it deals with the complexities of the issue: the health hazards of secondhand smoke, the smoker's unawareness of the damage that he or she is causing, the possible position of an addicted smoker if smoking were made illegal, and ways to rejuvenate the addicted smoker. The examples using children, animals, and family members persuasively appeal to the reader's emotions. The suggestion of smokers' clinics is well developed and insightful. The essay is clearly organized, separating the smokers' issues from those of the nonsmoker. The language, including diction and syntactic variety, is clear and controlled. The technical forms of sentence structure, grammar, spelling, and punctuation are satisfactory throughout the essay.

Section 2 – Analytical Writing

ANALYSIS OF AN ARGUMENT ESSAY TOPIC

Sample Essay Response Scoring 6

This argument is logical on the surface, because an electrical "correction" would stop a dog (or any species, for that matter) from continuing the same action which caused the "correction." Repeated doses of "correction" would eventually convince the dog to change direction. It is also feasible that an electrical barrier could be connected to a receiver on the dog's collar. *However, there is a flaw in the argument's overall logic.* Because "correction" means shock, one must wonder why a pet owner would subject his or her dog to continuous electrical shocks. How logical can it be to keep your dog "safe" by subjecting him to electrical shocks, which are not necessarily safe.

very effective transition

Sustained doses of electrical shock can jar the molecules in your body. Electric shock therapy is used in cases of mentally ill people in an attempt to reorganize their thinking. Who is to say that the same will not happen to dogs? I would like to see sufficient proof that the dog was not being harmed before I would even consider looking at such a product. I am convinced the product will perform as expected, but at what cost to the poor dog?

persuasive argument

effective appeal to emotion

I would also like to see several veterinarians' evaluations of this product. How much current is supplied in that electrical "correction"? How will this affect the dog? In what ways? Upon what research are the answers to these questions based? That raises another issue. If veterinarians take an oath to protect animals, how can they conduct this research at all? I cannot be convinced until I see the results of veterinarians' research that proves this product will not harm dogs. Yet they should not conduct research which may harm dogs. The problem is circular.

good transition between ideas

this shows the complexity of the subject

the initial essay's weakness becomes obvious through questions

I also feel the company that produces this product should be able to provide some verifiable research that explains how the product works. Some significant information that might be provided includes the following: 1) the specific electrical current for each "correction"; 2) how often a "correction" can be administered before it permanently damages the animal; 3) the person who decides on the guidelines for each of the numbers provided as well as his or her qualifications.

good
transition — (Furthermore,) I would like to read some testimonials from long-term users of this product; I would also like their telephone numbers, so that I might call them and personally verify that there was no ill effect on the dog.

What I find the most illogical and unconvincing aspect of this argument is the use of the word "safe" in conjunction with "electrical corrections." While the scientific reasoning makes sense, this segment of the argument is a paradox; it seems to invalidate the straightforward scientific explanation with a lot of shading, some of it apparently designed to mislead the reader.

cogent
summary
of earlier
raised
objections
- this is a
strong
conclusion

Analysis of Sample Essay Scoring 6

This essay earns a rating of 6: It clearly opposes the argument that this product should be used instead of chains, ropes, or fences to keep dogs within a certain boundary. A counter-argument is raised that makes the product appear unsafe. The essay's ideas are developed cogently, organized logically, and connected by smooth transitions. This can be seen in the paper's persuasive reliance on emotional and moral criteria that answer the coldly scientific argument for the use of this product. While there are minor flaws, the writer demonstrates superior control over language, including diction, syntactic variety, and the conventions of standard written English.

Section 3 – Quantitative Ability

1.   **(B)**   To compare $(x + y)^2$ with $(x - y)^2$, set $x = 5$ and $y = -3$ in each expression and calculate. We get

$$(x + y)^2 = [5 + (-3)]^2 = (5 - 3)^2 = 2^2 = 4 \text{ and}$$
$$(x - y)^2 = [5 - (-3)]^2 = (5 + 3)^2 = 8^2 = 64.$$

Since $64 > 4$ we can conclude that $(x - y)^2$ in Column B is larger than $(x + y)^2$ in Column A for $x = 5$ and $y = -3$.

If response (A) is chosen then perhaps an error was made in the computation after substituting the values for x and y, respectively. Or, it was assumed that $(x + y)$ is always greater than $(x - y)$ and thus

$$(x + y)^2 \text{ is greater than } (x - y)^2.$$

Response (C) implies that $(x + y)^2 = (x - y)^2$ for $x = 5$ and $y = -3$ which is not possible. Finally, response (D) as a choice is incorrect.

---

2.   **(B)**   Simplify Column A: $\dfrac{2}{3} + \dfrac{3}{2} = \dfrac{4}{6} + \dfrac{9}{6} = \dfrac{13}{6}$

Find a common denominator for the fraction in Column B: $\dfrac{5}{2} = \dfrac{15}{6}$

Therefore, Column B is larger than Column A.

---

3.   **(B)**   To compare the expression $x^2 + y^2$ in Column A with $(x + y)^2$, one should first assume that these expressions are equal. Then

$$x^2 + y^2 = (x + y)^2 \text{ implies } x^2 + y^2 = x^2 + 2xy + y^2. \qquad (1)$$

If x and y are both positive, their squares are also positive. So, a one-to-one comparison of the expression in Column B with the expression in Column A indicates that Column B is larger since it has an extra term, $2xy$, which is positive. Hence, response (B) is correct.

Response (C) is not possible. To see this add $-x^2$ and $-y^2$, respectively, on both sides of (1). So, one obtains

$$x^2 + y^2 - x^2 = x^2 + 2xy + y^2 - x^2$$
$$y^2 = 2xy + y^2$$
$$y^2 - y^2 = 2xy + y^2 - y^2$$
$$0 = 2xy$$

Note that $2xy = 0$ means that either $x = 0$, $y = 0$, or $x = y = 0$. So, the assertion of equality between the two statements leads to a contradiction since the original assumption is that both x and y are positive.

---

4. **(C)** The average (arithmetic mean), $\bar{x}$, of a set of numbers is defined as the sum of all the numbers in the set divided by the number of numbers, n. That is

$$\bar{x} = \frac{\text{sum of all numbers}}{n}$$

In this problem, calculating the average, $\bar{x}$, of the given numbers, we get

$$\bar{x} = \frac{40 + 20 + 30 + 24 + 27 + 15}{6}$$
$$= \frac{156}{6} = 26$$

So the two quantities in Columns A and B are equal.

5.　**(D)**　To determine the outcome consider the following:

If $4w = 6x = 12y$, then $^{4w}/_4 = {}^{12y}/_4$ or $w = 3y$. Thus, in general for positive numbers the value of w is always three times as large as the value of y. So response (A) would be correct. But, if one substitutes 0 for w, then w and y have the same value 0. So, the quantities are equal and response (C) is correct. Finally, if the values of w and y are both negative, then response (B) is correct. (For example, if $w = -12$, then $y = -4$ which is larger than w.) Thus, there is not enough information given to make a comparison.

6.　**(A)**　Perhaps the easiest way to approach the comparison of the two quantities is to first find the least common multiple for the denominators, 16 and 40, which is 80. Then, write equivalent fractions using the LCD. The results are

$$\frac{13}{16} \times \frac{5}{5} = \frac{65}{80} \text{ and } \frac{31}{40} \times \frac{2}{2} = \frac{62}{80}.$$

Since the numerator, 65, in the equivalent fraction in Column A is greater than the one in Column B, the fraction in Column A is greater.

7.　**(C)**　To understand this problem first assume that $\triangle ABC$ is a right triangle. With this assumption the Pythagorean Theorem applies as follows:

$$(AC)^2 = (AB)^2 + (BC)^2.$$

Since the length of the sides of the triangle are given $(AC = 17, AB = 8, BC = 15)$, substitute in the formula and observe whether the result is an equality.

$$(17)^2 = (8)^2 + (15)^2$$
$$289 = 64 + 225$$
$$289 = 289$$

Because the result is an equality, the assumption that the triangle is a right triangle is correct. So, the angle opposite the longest side ($\angle ABC$) must be a right angle. The quantities in the two columns are equal.

8. **(C)** To explain this answer one needs to first know that the exterior angle of a triangle equals the sum of the measure of both remote interior angles of the triangle. The exterior angle of $\triangle CDE$ is $\angle x$ and the remote interior angles are C and D. So, the sum of angles C and D equals $\angle x$. Similarly, the exterior angle of $\triangle ABE$ is angle x and the remote interior angles are A and B. So, the sum of angles A and B equals $\angle x$. Hence, by substitution, one gets that the quantities in the two columns are equal as follows:

$$\angle x + \angle x = (\angle A + \angle B) + (\angle C + \angle D) \text{ or}$$
$$2(\angle x) = \angle A + \angle B + \angle C + \angle D.$$

9. **(D)** Note that $w : x = {}^{w}\!/_{x}$, and $y : z = {}^{y}\!/_{z}$. Thus, ${}^{w}\!/_{x} = {}^{y}\!/_{z}$ is a proportion. Simplify the proportion by recalling that the product of the extremes equals the product of the means. The result is $wz = xy$. Since the values of w, x, y, and z are both positive and negative real numbers, there is not enough information that will allow comparison of the quantities $w + x$ and $y = z$.

10. **(C)** Since $\overline{BA}$ equals $\overline{BC}$, $\triangle ABC$ is isosceles. Thus, according to a well-known theorem, the angles BAC and BCA are equal. Since angles x and y are supplementary angles to BAC and BCA, respectively, it is clear that

$$\angle x + \angle BAC = 180° \text{ and } \angle y + \angle BCA = 180°.$$

But, since $\angle BAC = \angle BCA$ one can conclude that $\angle x = \angle y$. So, the quantities in the columns are equal.

---

11.   **(A)**   The quantity in Column A is determined by a series of steps. First, observe that radii *OG* and *OH* are equal legs of right triangle *GOH.* Since the area of the right triangle is 12.5, one can easily obtain the length of each leg of the triangle as follows:

$$\text{Area of } GOH = \left(\frac{1}{2}\right)(\text{leg})(\text{leg}) = \left(\frac{1}{2}\right)(\text{leg})^2 = 12.5$$

$$(\text{leg})^2 = 25 \Rightarrow \text{leg} = 5$$

Next, find the area of the square by using the Pythagorean Theorem to obtain the length of side *GH,* the hypotenuse of the right triangle, as follows:

$$(GH)^2 = (\text{leg})^2 + (\text{leg})^2 \Rightarrow (GH)^2 = 50$$

$$\text{or } GH = \sqrt{50} = 5\sqrt{2}$$

Then, the area of the square is $(GH)^2 = 50$.

Now, find the area of the circle as follows: Area $= \pi r^2 = (5)^2\pi = 25\pi$.

Finally, the area of the shaded part of the figure is approximately as follows:

Shaded area $= 25\pi - 50$
$\qquad\qquad = 25(3.14) - 50$
$\qquad\qquad = 78.5 - 50$
$\qquad\qquad = 28.5$

Comparing this value with the value in Column B, $9\pi = 9(3.14) = 28.26$, indicates that the quantity in Column A is larger.

12. **(B)** First, evaluate the shaded area with the following procedure: This half-shaded area can be expressed by

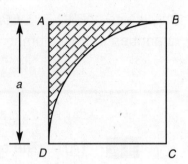

Half-shaded area

$$= \text{(Square area – Quadrant area)}$$

$$= a^2 - \frac{\pi a^2}{4} = a^2\left(1 - \frac{\pi}{4}\right)$$

because the quadrant represents one-fourth of the area of a circle with the radius a. Therefore, the shaded area in the problem will be

$$\text{Shaded area} = 2a^2\left(1 - \frac{\pi}{4}\right) = .43a^2.$$

The unshaded area can be expressed by

$$\text{Unshaded area} = \left(\text{Square area – Shaded area}\right)$$

$$= a^2 - 2a^2\left(a - \frac{\pi}{4}\right)$$

$$= a^2\left(\frac{\pi}{2} - 1\right) = .57a^2$$

Therefore, the unshaded area > the shaded area.

13. **(D)** Since nothing is given about the value of w, the value could be negative or positive. If the w is negative, the value of w^n and w^m can be negative or positive values. If w equals 0 or 1, Column A and B will be equal. If w is positive, then Column B will be greater than Column A.

14.   **(B)**   Set up three equations from the information given.

Let x = cost of one orange
Let y = cost of one apple
Let z = cost of one pear

First, solve for the cost of the pear.

$12x + 10y \qquad = 2.20$	(1)
$6x + \qquad 4z = 1.20$	(2)
$\qquad 3y + 6z = 1.20$	(3)

$12x + 10y \qquad = 2.20$	(1) Multiply equation (2) by 2; then sub-
$12x + \qquad 8z = 2.40$	tract equation (2) from equation (1)
$\qquad 10y - 8z = -.20$	(4)

$30y + 60z = 12$	Equation (3) multiplied by 10
$30y - 24z = -.6$	Subtract equation (4) multiplied by 3
$84z = 12.6$	
$z = .15$	Cost of one pear

$10y - 8(.15) = -.20$	Find the cost of one apple
$10y - 1.20 = -.20$	
$10y = 1.00$	
$y = .10$	Cost of one apple

Column A = .10 + .15 = .25
Column B = 2(.15) = .30

---

15.   **(B)**   The area of the square = a^2

The area of the right triangle in terms of $a = \dfrac{(2a)^2}{2} = \dfrac{4a^2}{2} = 2a^2$.

Therefore, Column B is greater than Column A.

16. **(C)**   First, observe that three-fourths is $\frac{3}{4}$ and one tenth is $\frac{1}{10}$. Let x be the unknown part which must be found. Then, one can write from the statement of the problem that the x part of three-fourths is given by

$$\frac{3}{4}x$$

The equation for the problem is given by $\frac{3}{4}x = \frac{1}{10}$. Multiplying both sides of the equation by the reciprocal of $\frac{3}{4}$ one obtains the following:

$$\left(\frac{4}{3}\right)\frac{3}{4}x = \left(\frac{4}{3}\right)\frac{1}{10} \text{ or } x = \frac{4}{30} \text{ or } x = \frac{2}{15}$$

which is choice (C).

Response (D) is obtained by incorrectly finding the product of $\frac{3}{4}$ and $\frac{1}{10}$ to be the unknown part. Response (B) is obtained by dividing $\frac{3}{4}$ by $\frac{1}{10}$.

---

17. **(C)**   Simplify
$$2x + 12 = 3x + 9.$$
$$12 - 9 = 3x - 2x$$
$$3 = x$$

---

18. **(D)**

$$\text{Average} = \frac{5 \times 30 + 3 \times 20}{8}$$

$$\text{Average} = \frac{150 + 60}{8} = \frac{210}{8} = 26.25$$

19. **(E)**   Let X = cost of one pound of pears

          Let Y = cost of one pound of peaches

$$2X + \;\; Y = 1.4 \qquad (1)$$
$$3X + 2Y = 2.4 \qquad (2)$$
$$\underline{\;\;\;\; X + Y = 1 \qquad \text{Subtract equation (1) from equation (2)}}$$

One pound of pears and one pound of peaches equals $1.00.

---

20. **(B)**   One can represent the three consecutive odd numbers as follows: $2x + 1$, $2x + 3$, and $2x + 5$, respectively. The sum of these numbers is

$$(2x + 1) + (2x + 3) + (2x + 5) = 6x + 9.$$

Clearly 2, 5, and 6 do not divide $6x + 9$ exactly (without a remainder). Hence, answer choices (A), (C), (D), and (E) are incorrect. So, answer choice (B) is correct, that is, the value 3 does divide the sum $6x + 9$ as follows:

$$\frac{(6x + 9)}{3} = \frac{3(2x + 3)}{3} = 2x + 3,$$

the quotient.

---

21. **(C)**   For area there are two columns, one in sq. mi. and the second in sq. km. In the latter appear two numbers for the Pacific division.

$$2,310,958$$
$$2,374,315$$

The first one is for land area and the second one for total area.

22. **(A)**   The largest division is the Pacific – (2,310,958 km^2 or 892,226 mi^2). The New England division has the smallest area – (163,149 km^2 or 69,992 mi^2).

---

23. **(B)**   Land area (U.S.) = 9,170,987 km^2
Pacific   = 2,310,958 km^2
East N. Central = 632,905 km^2

$$\text{percentage} = \frac{2,310,958 + 632,905}{9,170,987} \times 100\% = 32.1\%$$

---

24. **(A)**   To find the increase in population from 1970-1980 in the New England area, subtract the population of 1970 from the population of 1980.

$$1980 - 12,349,000$$
$$1970 - 11,842,000$$

Increase in the population of the New England area = 12,349,000 – 11,842,000 = 507,000.

To find the average increase in population of a state in the New England area, divide the increase in population from 1970-1980 by 6, the number of states in the region.

The average increase of a state in the New England area =

$$\frac{507,000}{6} = 84,500.$$

25. **(E)** First, calculate the rate in the period 1970-80 for the East North Central Division.

$$\frac{\text{Population 1980}}{\text{Population 1970}} = \frac{41,668,000}{40,253,000} = 1.0352.$$

The rate of increase is 3.52.

$$
\begin{aligned}
\text{Population 1990} &= \text{Population 1980} + (0.352 \times \text{Pop. 1980}) \\
&= 41,668,000 + (0.352 \times 41,668,000) \\
&= 43,134,710
\end{aligned}
$$

---

26. **(C)** Based on the information given in the first sentence of the problem one needs to first represent the unknown numbers. So let x be a number. Then, the other number is given by $3x + 2$, which is two more than 3 times the first number. So the two numbers are x and $3x + 2$.

Next, form an equation by adding the two numbers and setting the sum equal to 22 and then solve the equation for the two numbers.

$$
\begin{aligned}
x + 3x + 2 &= 22 \\
4x + 2 &= 22 \\
4x &= 20 \\
x &= 5, \text{ one of the numbers.}
\end{aligned}
$$

The other number is given by

$3x + 2 = 3(5) + 2 = 15 + 2 = 17$, the other number.

Hence, answer choice (C) is correct. The other answer choices fail to satisfy the equation $x + 3x + 2 = 22$.

---

27. **(A)** In order to find the perimeter of the rectangle, it is important first to understand the definition, that is, perimeter equals the sum of the dimension of the rectangle. Hence, for the given rectangle,

Perimeter = $6L + 4W + 6L + 4W$ (Add like terms)

$\qquad\qquad = 12L + 8W$

Answer choice (E), $24LW$, is incorrect because it represents the area of the rectangle, which is the product of the length and width. Answer choice (C), $6L + 4W$, is incorrect because it represents only one-half of the perimeter of the rectangle. Answer choice (D), $20LW$, is incorrect because this response is obtained by simply adding the coefficients of L and W which is an incorrect application of algebra. Finally, answer choice (B), $12L^2 + 8W^2$, is incorrect because it is obtained by using the definition of the perimeter of a rectangle incorrectly as follows: perimeter = $2L(6L) + 2W(4W)$.

---

28. **(C)**   Let x be the length of the rectangle. Then, a 30% increase in the length of the rectangle is given by $x + .3x$. Let y be the width of the rectangle. Then, a 20% decrease in the width of the rectangle is given by $y - .2y$. The original area is given by $A = xy$ and the new area is given by:

$$A = (x + .3x)\,(y - .2y)$$
$$= xy - .2xy + .3xy - 0.06xy$$
$$= xy + 0.04xy$$
$$= 1.04xy$$

So, the new area is 104% of the original area which is a 104% – 100% = 4% increase, which is answer choice (C). The other answer choices are found by either using the perimeter formula or incorrectly finding the increase and decrease in the length and width, respectively.

---

29. **(D)**   With n being the first odd number, it follows that $n + 2$ and $n + 4$ are the next two odd numbers. This eliminates answer choices (A) and (B) on the basis that each one of them represents only one of the two consecutive odd numbers that follow n. Since the sum of the three consecutive odd numbers is $n + (n + 2) + (n + 4) = 3n + 6$, it follows that neither of answer choices (C) and (E) is correct, which leaves answer choice (D) as correct.

30. **(D)**   The area of a triangle is equal to the product of the length of its base (any one of its sides) and the length of its altitude (the perpendicular segment drawn from the opposite vertex to the base of the triangle or to the line containing the base of the triangle).

For each of the triangles, the segment $\overline{AD}$ can be used as the base. The altitude of $\triangle ABC$ is the perpendicular distance from C to line m. The altitude of $\triangle ABD$ is the perpendicular distance from D to line m. Since C and D both lie on line l and lines l and m are parallel, then the altitudes of the triangles must be equal. Thus the area of $\triangle ABD$ is 40cm^2.

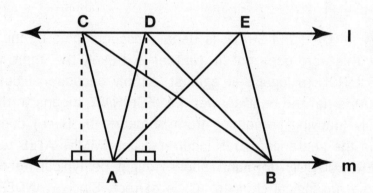

Section 4 – Verbal Ability

1.   **(D)**   IMPLORED (A) is a verb meaning begged; it does not fit well into the content of the sentence and is not the right answer. EXTORTED is to draw something (like money) from someone by force; (B) is not the correct answer. EXHORTED means to urge by words of good advice or to caution; since urging is not the issue here, (C) is incorrect. ADMONISHED seems to fit best since it means to warn, to reprove, to caution against specific faults. (D) is the correct answer. ABOLISHED (E) means to destroy or put an end to something; this word is too strong for the sentence.

2.   **(C)**   EMIGRATE is usually accompanied by the preposition *from;* this word does not fit. Neither is it likely that there would be a PROSECUTION (a legal suit against) simply because of beliefs, not actions. (A) is not the best answer. PEREGRINATE means to travel, but EXTORTION (drawing something from someone by force) does not fit logically in the sentence. (B) is incorrect. One IMMIGRATES to another place; PERSECUTION (torment, abuse) might be typical for one's beliefs. These are logical choices; (C) is correct. Since WANDER implies no set destination, this choice does not fit well. Coupled with the word ARRAIGNMENT (to bring before a court, to charge), (D) is clearly not a suitable choice. ROAM implies no set destination, this choice does not fit well. CENSURE indicates blame or criticism, but is not acceptable coupled with ROAM. Choice (E) is incorrect.

3.   **(A)**   A REPARTEE is a clever, witty retort; DORMANT suggests inactivity of that which is present. A person who bides her time before giving a statement would hold that retort or REPARTEE DORMANT. (A) is the best answer. WIT suggests the power to evoke laughter by remarks showing quick perception; it is not usually preceded by the article *a*. Only one statement is suggested by the sentence. LATENT stresses concealment. (B) is not the best answer. SATIRE is wit used for the purpose of exposing vice. HIBERNATING is the passing of winter in a lethargic state. These two words of choice (C) are not the best choices for the sentence. HUMOR is an ability to see the absurd and the comical in life's situations; it suggests a series of incidents rather than just one retort. CAMOUFLAGED implies that which is disguised. The sentence suggests not a disguising of the witty statement but rather a concealment of it until the proper moment. (D) is not the best answer. A SORTIE is a mission or an attack. It does not fit the sentence at all. DISGUISED could fit the sentence, but not when paired with SORTIE. (E) is not the best answer.

4. **(B)** IMPLIED is a transitive verb; it must have an object. There is no direct object here so IMPLIED does not fit well. ABROGATE is to annul, to abolish. Because IMPLIED does not fit well, (A) should not be selected. INFERRED is an intransitive verb in this sentence; it means to draw conclusions from data given. It fits well in this sentence. NEGOTIATE (procure) fits well in this sentence also. (B) is the correct answer. IMPOSED is to pass off or to obtrude. The word does not fit the meaning of the sentence well at all. NULLIFY (to make or render of no value) fits the sentence but not when coupled with IMPOSED. (C) is not the best choice. SURMISED is to imagine or to guess on slight charges. BREECH is to cover with breeches; a person who selected (D) probably confused BREECH with BREACH (to cancel). INCLUDED means contained; a person who chose (E) probably read the word as concluded, rather than INCLUDED. ANNIHILATE means to make void.

5. **(E)** The prosecutor was not satisfied with the judge's decision. That means that the correct adjective must be negative, to express this dissatisfaction. AMBIGUOUS (vague), ASTUTE (shrewd), ARDUOUS (laborious, difficult), and AUSPICIOUS (favorable) do not carry a negative connotation. Choices (A), (B), (C), and (D) are all inappropriate adjectives to complete the sentence. Only ARBITRARY (based on one's preference, not on reason) is the logical adjective to complete the sentence. (E) is the correct choice.

6. **(C)** The missing word must be some form of speech, so PALINDROME (B), a sentence that reads the same forward and backward, and QUANDARY (D), a state of doubt or perplexity, cannot be correct. COLLOQUY (A) is a dialogue, requiring two or more speakers; the sentence refers only to Hamlet, implying that there are no other speakers in the speech referred to. (A) is not the correct choice. SOLILOQUY (C) means a monologue that usually presents the character's inner reflections to the audience and is treated as if unheard by the other actors. Because the sentence refers to a speech and to only a single character, (C) is the correct answer. OBLOQUY (E) means to speak abusively or offensively. It is not an appropriate choice.

7. **(A)** People were inspired by the ABNEGATION, or self-denial, of St. Francis. (A) is the correct choice. TURPITUDE, which means depravity, is the opposite of the word sought. (B) is not an appropriate choice. CALUMNY (C) refers to false charges or misrepresentation; it is not the correct choice. VACILLATION (D) means indecision; it is not an appropriate word to complete the sentence. DICHOTOMY (E) means a division into two, often contradictory, groups.

8. **(B)** MANDATORY (required) and OPTIONAL are antonyms. COMPETENT and INEPT are also antonyms; the correct answer is (B). PIOUS:INDIGNANT (A) and OPAQUE:ORNATE (C) are unrelated pairs. CHASTE:CELIBATE (D) and CRASS:BOORISH (E) are synonymous pairs.

---

9. **(D)** A FINE is a form of PUNISHMENT, and JIGSAW is a form of PUZZLE; therefore, the correct answer is (D). Choices (A), HYACINTH: FLOWER, and (E), SANDALS:SHOES, reflect a specific:general relationship. ORANGE:PEEL reflects a whole:part relationship, so (B) is a wrong choice. HEART is the mechanism that provides CIRCULATION, so (C) is not the correct choice.

---

10. **(E)** The key pair and all of the choice pairs give a first term that is something that is put on the second term. However, a BANDAGE is put on a WOUND to promote healing. Only choice (E) reflects this aspect of the key pair. A CAST is put on a FRACTURE to promote healing.

---

11. **(C)** To ESPOUSE a THEORY is to support and promote it. To ADVOCATE a HYPOTHESIS is to support and promote it; the correct answer is (C). PROPONENT and OPPONENT are opposites; (A) is not the correct answer. CREATE and INNOVATE have synonymous meanings; (B) is not the correct choice. HERETIC:BLASPHEMY and GOURMAND: GLUTTONY both link a noun with an action associated with that noun. (D) and (E) are not correct answers.

12. **(A)** TRACTABLE and BIDDABLE are synonyms meaning obedient. TORPID and LETHARGIC are synonyms meaning lazy; (A) is the correct answer. VISCOUS:LIQUID and COLLOQUIAL:FORMAL have antonymous relationships; therefore, (B) and (D) are incorrect. TRUCULENT, meaning argumentative, and CONTRITE, or sorry, are unrelated; (C) is not the correct answer. ECCENTRIC (peculiar) and AESTHETIC (tasteful) are also unrelated, so (E) is not the correct answer.

13. **(C)** DEIGN:CONDESCEND have a synonymous relationship. BERATE (to belittle) and COMMEND (to praise) are antonyms, as are CORROBORATE (to support) and REPUDIATE (to deny). (A) and (B) are incorrect. DIGRESS and STRAY are synonyms; the correct answer is (C). IMBUE (permeate) and DESICCATE (dry out) are not related; (D) is not correct. VAUNT (boast) is unrelated to WITHER (shrivel); (E) is not the answer.

14. **(B)** A FRAILTY is an imperfection. The term VICE is used to denote a "serious" imperfection. The difference is in the degree, with a FRAILTY being milder. A FELONY is more serious than a MISDEMEANOR. The analogy, however, is inverted. (A) should not be selected. AGGRAVATION is irritation. PERNICIOUS is highly injurious. The degree, or intensity, of RAGE is greater than that of AGGRAVATION. Their relationship is that of FRAILTY:VICE, so (B) is the correct answer. TRITE means overworked, overused. POPULAR is common. The degree of the two is different, but the analogy is different from that of FRAILTY:VICE. (C) is not the correct answer. SECRETED is more carefully hidden than VEILED; again the order is inverted. (D) is incorrect. A CLOISTER implies seclusion from the world. A MONASTERY is a CLOISTER for monks. The relationship between CLOISTER and MONASTERY in choice (E) is not that which is sought.

15. **(B)** ANALOGOUS (similar) and PARALLEL (closely similar) are synonyms. ACIDULOUS (sour) and SACCHARINE (sickeningly sweet) are not synonyms so (A) is incorrect. SINUOUS and TORTUOUS both mean curving, winding. The two are synonymous and, thus, (B) is the right answer. INCONGRUOUS means dissimilar; it is an antonym to HOMOGENEOUS, which suggests similarity. (C) is wrong. A PUNDIT is an expert, while a TYRO is a novice. Since the two are antonyms, (D) is not, therefore, the correct answer. MUNDANE is common, everyday; CELESTIAL refers to heavenly. Because MUNDANE is opposite from CELESTIAL, (E) should not be selected.

---

16. **(C)** FINE and AMERCEMENT are synonymous for a penalty. LOSS and GAIN are opposites. FORFEITURE is a fine; REWARD is the opposite. (B) is incorrect since the pair does not have the same relationship as FINE:AMERCEMENT. PENALTY and MULCT are synonymous words. (C) is the correct answer. A LOTTERY is an affair of chance. DEPOSIT as a noun means that which is entrusted to the care of another, a pledge. The relationship between the pair is not the synonymous relationship sought. (D) is incorrect. CONTRABAND is illegal or prohibited commerce; it can also refer to goods or merchandise the importation or exportation of which is forbidden. CONFISCATE is a verb meaning to seize or appropriate; as an adjective it means appropriated or forfeited. The relationship is not that sought. (E) should not be selected.

---

17. **(E)** There is no evidence that the author disagrees so vehemently with the split-brain theory as to respond with UNQUALIFIED DISAGREEMENT. (A) is not the best answer. UNQUESTIONING APPROVAL is not the attitude of the author; rather she seems willing to listen to both sides, though she seems more inclined to disagree with the theory. (B) is not the best answer. The very fact that the author wrote the articles negates the idea that COMPLETE INDIFFERENCE is the best answer; (C) is not the best choice. Although the author seems to disagree with the split-brain theory, STRONG DISPARAGEMENT is not the best answer; (D) should not be chosen. IMPLIED UNCERTAINTY seems to be the best of the choices. (E) is the best answer.

18. **(C)** (A) is incorrect since the split-brain theory is not reasserted by the author in the article. Since the split-brain theory is not renunciated by the author, (B) is not the correct choice. (C) is the best answer since it implies what the article does—present both sides of the theory. Since modifying the curriculum is only one part of the article, (D) is incorrect. Since the split-brain theory is not new, (E) is inaccurate.

19. **(C)** The author is saying that, according to the opponents of the split-brain theory, both hemispheres work on tasks that proponents try to label "left-" or "right-brained," and that the cooperation between hemispheres yields a better result than if only one hemisphere had functioned. In this context, to "integrate activities" means to "coordinate functions" to produce the better result. This meaning includes working together (B), separating the task into functions for each hemisphere (D), and sharing needed information between hemispheres (E). There is no reference in the passage to synapses or synaptic connections, so (A) is an inappropriate choice.

20. **(E)** The passage states that "the premise that the two hemispheres operate independently" is currently being disputed. Opponents of the split-brain theory believe that the two hemispheres must coordinate their respective functions therefore statement I is false. Both proponents and opponents of the split-brain theory do, however, agree that different hemispheres perform specialized functions so statement II is true. Research has shown that "if a patient has right hemisphere damage, major logical disorders are manifested" therefore Statement III is also true. Choice (E), II and III only, is the correct response.

---

21. **(A)**   (A) is the correct answer. (B) is not the correct answer since damage to the right (as well as the left) side of the brain may result in logical disorders. (C) is not the right answer since it has not been proven to the satisfaction of everyone that one hemisphere may be engaged to the exclusion of the other. The article suggests that the two sides work cooperatively. (D) is, therefore, incorrect. The writer suggests that education involves both (not just one) side of the brain. (E) is incorrect.

---

22. **(D)**   Proponents and opponents do disagree about methods and curriculum but that is not a fundamental difference; (A) is incorrect. (B) is false; proponents do agree that the purposes of the hemispheres do differ but that the integration of activities is not urged, or even thought possible, by many. Opponents do not always state that the two hemispheres differ significantly in function nor do they always believe that integration of the activities is impossible; (C) is incorrect. The beliefs about the functions of the two hemispheres of the brain are the fundamental differences between proponents and opponents of the split-brain theory; (D) is the correct answer. Both groups agree that the brain is divided into hemispheres; this is not the DISTINCTION between the two groups. (E) is not the correct answer.

23. **(B)** (A) is a statement that OPPONENTS, not PROPO-NENTS, of the split-brain theory might espouse; (A) is incorrect. (B) is the correct answer. (C) is incorrect; this is a belief of the OPPONENTS of the split-brain theory. (D) is not the correct choice; this finding is one OPPONENTS of the split-brain theory often make known. Statement (E) is one OPPONENTS of the theory use.

---

24. **(C)** The author would disagree with (A). (B) is certainly incorrect; the modifications have neither already been made nor are they on the agenda of most educators. (C) is the correct answer. (D) is incorrect; the author's open-minded point of view is not illustrated by this statement. The reader should immediately see (E) as erroneous since it reverses the hemisphere associated by proponents of the theory with language and logic.

---

25. **(D)** The passage does include a discussion of the importance of Brooks' writing (A), mentioning the awards she's won and her use of black topics; a list of her achievements (B); a discussion of her importance as a role model (C), referring to her helping young writers and encouraging blacks to learn about their heritage; and does discuss the handicaps of being black and female (E). All of these phrases, however, are too specific to describe the passage well, because the passage encompasses all of these themes. The best phrase to describe the passage is (D), a biographical sketch on Gwendolyn Brooks.

---

26. **(C)** Brooks was a published writer by eleven; (A) is incorrect. Grants did not lessen, but heighten, her prestige. (B) is incorrect. Brooks was, however, a frequent victim of both racial and gender discrimination. (C) is the correct answer. After her first book was sold, she received nationwide recognition; (D) is wrong. Brooks takes an interest in others; (E) is incorrect.

27. **(D)** All of the statements are false except (D). It was Brooks' first poem that was published when she was eleven; her first book was not marketed until 1945. Choice (A) is false. Brooks received national recognition after her first book was published, before she won the Pulitzer Prize; choice (B) is false. Brooks was an integrationist in the 1940s and advocated black consciousness in the 1960s; choice (C) is false. Brooks did write about the black experience; so choice (E) is false. Brooks did receive little encouragement from her teachers (D), and succeeded despite this.

28. **(D)** LUDICROUS means illogical, senseless or absurd. MUNDANE means earthly; it does not relate to LUDICROUS. (A) is not the correct answer. A SEMAPHORE is an apparatus for signaling. (B) does not relate to LUDICROUS. ILLOGICAL is a synonym for LUDI-CROUS; (C) is not the best choice. REASONABLE is the opposite of LUDICROUS; (D) is the correct answer. FALLACIOUS (E) means logically unsound; it is closely related to the key word and not the right choice.

29. **(B)** DANGER (A) is synonymous to JEOPARDY. SAFETY is the opposite of JEOPARDY, so the correct answer is (B). PERJURY means false swearing. CONUNDRUM is a puzzle. LEVITY means frivolity. (C), (D), and (E) are incorrect choices.

30. **(E)**   AWRY means askew or bent. EARTHY means unrefined or natural; (A) is not the right answer. CROOKED is a synonym for AWRY; (B) is not correct. PIED means spotted; (C) is incorrect. DUBIOUS means doubtful; (D) is not correct. STRAIGHT (E) is the opposite of AWRY, and the right answer.

31. **(D)**   INSIDIOUS means wily, sly. PRECIPITANT (A) means rushing ahead. It is not an antonym for INSIDIOUS. INCENDIARY means tending to excite or inflame. (B) should not be selected as the antonym. DECADENT is deteriorating, declining. It is not the opposite of INSIDIOUS; (C) is not the correct answer. CONDUCIVE means helpful. (D) is the opposite of INSIDIOUS. IMPRUDENT means lacking in caution, indiscreet. (E) is not the opposite of INSIDIOUS.

32. **(C)**   CAPRICIOUS means fanciful, inconstant, apt to change suddenly. IMPECUNIOUS means poor, habitually without money. (A) does not bear an antonymous relationship to CAPRICIOUS. JUXTAPOSITION means place side by side as for the purpose of comparing. (B) is not the correct answer. SCRUPULOUS (C) means to be careful, exact; the dictionary gives it a meaning of faithful, steadfast — the opposite of CAPRICIOUS. COPIOUS means plentiful, abundant. (D) is not the opposite of CAPRICIOUS. SUPERFLUOUS means excessive, more than enough. (E) is not the antonym sought.

33. **(D)**   CONTENTIOUS, meaning quarrelsome, is the opposite of COMPLACENT, which means contented or smug. The correct choice is (D). COMPLIANT (A) means obedient. DECOROUS (B) means having good taste. PASSIVE (C) is submissive. SUMPTUOUS (E) means luxurious.

34. **(A)** The antonym of DOCILE (manageable) is UNRULY (disobedient), so the correct choice is (A). RAUCOUS (B) and STRIDENT (E) are synonyms for harsh. DEMURE (C) means coy, and UNCOUTH (D) is crude.

35. **(D)** To POSTULATE is to merely guess or to hypothesize. MOLLIFY is to appease, to calm. (A) is not the antonym of POSTULATE. CONJECTURE is to guess based on insufficient evidence. (B) is synonymous and not an antonym. PROGNOSTICATE (C) is to guess. It is synonymous with POSTULATE. CORROBORATE is to establish, to confirm. It is the opposite of guessing; (D) is the correct answer. REFURBISH is to brighten or to freshen up. (E) is not directly related to the key word and is not the answer sought.

36. **(B)** CONCORD is a state of agreement, harmony. SUCCOR is aid, help. (A) is not an antonym for CONCORD and should not be chosen. ENMITY is ill will or hatred; it is the opposite of CONCORD. (B) is the correct answer. A GRIP is one who moves scenery on a movie set. (C) bears no relation to CONCORD and should not be selected as the correct choice. VIGILANCE means alertly watchful. It is not directly related to CONCORD. (D) is an inappropriate choice. NOBILITY means state or quality of being admirable. (E) is not the opposite of the key word and should not be selected.

37. **(B)** A MALEFACTION is an evil deed, an offense. AFFINITY means an attraction, a likeness. (A) is not the opposite for MALEFACTION. A SUBSIDY is a gift, a form of aid; a SUBSIDY would be the opposite of MALEFACTION (an evil deed). (B) is the correct answer. PROFLIGATION means the act of wasting. It is not the opposite of

MALEFACTION. (C) should not be chosen as the correct answer. IDIO-SYNCRATIC (D) means peculiar, eccentric. (D) is not an antonym for MALEFACTION. COGNATE means of a similar nature. Since the term is not directly related to MALEFACTION, (E) should not be chosen.

---

38. **(B)** A ZEPHYR is a gentle wind. A TYCOON is a wealthy, powerful individual. (A) is incorrect. A TYPHOON is a violent cyclonic storm, just the opposite of a ZEPHYR; (B) is the correct choice. A CORACLE (C) is a small boat and not the answer sought. TACITURN is an adjective meaning quiet, soft-spoken. (D) is not the correct choice. A CONSTELLATION is a pattern of stars. (E) is not the antonym sought.

1. **(C)**

Column A
Column B

$2\frac{1}{2}$ hours $= \dfrac{60 \text{ minutes}}{1 \text{ hour}} \times \dfrac{5}{2}$ hours $= 150$

$6\frac{1}{4}$ days $= \dfrac{24 \text{ hours}}{1 \text{ day}} \times \dfrac{25}{4}$ days $= 150$

---

2. **(C)** Note that $w : x = {}^{w}\!/_{x}$ and $y : z = {}^{y}\!/_{z}$. Thus, ${}^{w}\!/_{x} = {}^{y}\!/_{z}$. Adding the opposite of ${}^{y}\!/_{z}$ to both sides of the equation, we get

$$\frac{w}{x} + \left(-\frac{y}{z}\right) = \frac{y}{z} + \left(-\frac{y}{z}\right)$$

$$\frac{w}{x} - \frac{y}{z} = 0$$

Multiplying through by xz, the LCD, we have

$$(xz)\left(\frac{w}{x}\right) - (xz)\left(\frac{y}{z}\right) = (xz)(0)$$

$$wz - xy = 0$$

Hence, the quantities in both columns are equal.

---

3. **(B)**

Column A   35% of 7 = .35 × 7 = 2.45
Column B   0.7 of 35 = .7 × 35 = 24.5

Therefore, Column B is greater than Column A.

4.   **(B)**   The only way for $\frac{1}{y}$ to be negative is for y to be negative since the numerator is a positive 1. For example, if $y = 2$, then $\frac{1}{2}$ is not less than 0. So, y is always < 0. Therefore, 1 in Column B is the larger quantity.

---

5.   **(A)**

Column A $\dfrac{2}{3} - \dfrac{1}{2} = \dfrac{4}{6} - \dfrac{3}{6} = \dfrac{1}{6}$

Column B $\dfrac{4}{5} - \dfrac{2}{3} = \dfrac{12}{15} - \dfrac{10}{15} = \dfrac{2}{15}$

Find a common denominator and compare the fractions.

Column A $= \dfrac{5}{30}$ Column B $= \dfrac{4}{30}$.

Therefore, Column A is greater than Column B.

---

6.   **(B)**   The given equations form a system which can be easily solved by the elimination method. By elimination one simply adds the two equations together in order to easily eliminate the y variable and solve for the x variable as follows:

$$\begin{array}{l} x + y = 6 \\ \underline{3x - y = 4} \\ \quad 4x = 10 \end{array} \qquad \text{(sum of the equations)}$$

$$\dfrac{4x}{4} = \dfrac{10}{4} \text{ or } x = \dfrac{10}{4} = \dfrac{5}{2}$$

The next step is to substitute the value of x in $x + y = 6$ and solve for the variable y. The result is

$$\frac{5}{2} + y = 6$$

$$\frac{5}{2} + y + \left(-\frac{5}{2}\right) = 6 + \left(-\frac{5}{2}\right)$$

$$y + 0 = \frac{12}{2} + \left(-\frac{5}{2}\right)$$

$$y = \frac{7}{2}$$

Finally, note that $x - y = {}^5\!/_2 - {}^7\!/_2 = -1$. Hence, the quantity in Column B is greater than the quantity in Column A.

---

7. **(A)** In Column A expand the indicated product by using the foil method or some other method. Thus, the product of

$$(1 - \sqrt{2})(1 - \sqrt{2}) = 1 - \sqrt{2} - \sqrt{2} + (\sqrt{2})(\sqrt{2})$$
$$= 1 - 2\sqrt{2} + \sqrt{4}$$
$$= 1 - 2\sqrt{2} + 2$$
$$= 3 - 2\sqrt{2}$$

which is positive.

Similarly, in Column B one expands the indicated product to get

$$(1 - \sqrt{2})(1 + \sqrt{2}) = 1 - \sqrt{2} + \sqrt{2} - (\sqrt{2})(\sqrt{2})$$
$$= 1 - \sqrt{4}$$
$$= 1 - 2$$
$$= -1$$

Thus, the quantity in Column A is larger.

8. **(B)** To determine the comparison one needs to know the formula for finding the distance between two points in the plane. The distance between $A(3, 4)$ and $B(-1, 1)$ is found by using the following formula where the subscript 1 refers to coordinates in point A and subscript 2 refers to coordinates in point B.

$$\sqrt{(x_2 - x_1)^2 + (y_2 - y_1)^2} = \sqrt{(-1 - 3)^2 + (1 - 4)^2}$$
$$= \sqrt{16 + 9}$$
$$= \sqrt{25} = 5$$

The distance between $C(4, -2)$ and $D(-2, -2)$ is found using the same formula as follows where the subscript 1 refers to coordinates in point C and subscript 2 refers to coordinates in point D.

$$\sqrt{(-2 - 4)^2 + [-2 - (-2)]^2} = \sqrt{(-6)^2 + (0)^2}$$
$$= \sqrt{36} = 6$$

Hence, the distance from C to D is greater than the distance from A to B.

---

9. **(C)** By definition $\angle 4$ and $\angle 5$ are vertical angles and by a theorem vertical angles are equal. Since line segments k and m are parallel, by a theorem the corresponding angles are equal. What are the corresponding angles? They are $\angle 1$, $\angle 3$, and $\angle 5$ on the left side of the diagonal d and $\angle 2$, $\angle 4$, and $\angle 6$ on the right side of the diagonal. It is given that $\angle 2 = 60°$. Since $\angle 4 = \angle 2$, then $\angle 4$ equals 60°. Finally, since $\angle 4$ and $\angle 5$ are equal vertical angles, then $\angle 5$ equals 60°. So the quantities in both columns are equal.

---

10. **(B)** Recall that $\triangle ABC$, as well as any triangle, contains 180°. Thus, the measure of $\angle x$ must be the smallest since $\angle A$ is 100° and $\angle B$ is 48°. That is,

$$100 + 48 + x = 180°$$
$$148 + x = 180$$
$$148 + x - 148 = 180 - 148$$
$$x = 32°$$

Now since $\angle A$ (100°) is the largest in $\triangle ABC$, then it is a well-known theorem that the side (BC) which is opposite this angle is the largest side. Thus, it follows that side BC in Column B is greater than side AB in Column A.

---

11.   (B)   Factor each equation.

Column A

$$x^2 + 3x - 4 = (x - 1)(x + 4)$$
$$x = 1, -4$$
$$\text{Product} = -4$$

Column B

$$x^2 + 4x + 4 = (x + 2)^2$$
$$x = -2, -2$$
$$\text{Product} = 4$$

Therefore, Column B is greater than Column A.

---

12.   **(A)**   Observe that each side of the square must be 10 since its perimeter is 40. So the information in Column A yields the value 2(10) = 20 units, twice the length of line segment BD.

In Column B the length of the shortest distance from point A to line segment DE is given by the length of a side of the square plus the height of the triangle. The distance from DE to the base of the triangle is 10 units.

The length of the base of the triangle is also 10 units. In order to find the height of the triangle, the area must be known first. The area of the combined figures is given to be 125 square units. But, the

$$\text{area of the square} = e^2 = (10)^2 = 100 \text{ square units.}$$

Thus, the area of the triangle is 25 square units since the total area of the figures is 125 square units.

The formula for the area of the triangle is $A = (\frac{1}{2})bh$. Thus, the height of the triangle is given by

$$h = \frac{2A}{b} = \frac{2(25)}{10} = \frac{50}{10} = 5 \text{ units.}$$

So, the value of the quantity in Column B is $10 + 5 = 15$ units. Hence, the quantity in Column A is larger.

---

13. **(C)**

$$\frac{a+2}{a+1} = \frac{a-4}{a-3}$$
$$(a+2)(a-3) = (a-4)(a+1)$$
$$a^2 - a - 6 = a^2 - 3a - 4$$
$$a^2 - a - a^2 + 3a = -4 + 6$$
$$2a = 2$$
$$a = 1$$

Therefore, the two quantities are equal.

---

14. **(D)** Observe that in order to attempt to compare the two statements there is a need to analyze each. The statement in Column B indicates that a representation of the sum of the angles of a square must be made. Since each of the four angles of a square is a right angle, then one can write the sum of the angles as follows:

$$4(90°) = 360°.$$

On the other hand, the statement in Column A indicates that a representation of the sum of all the angles of a polygon whose sides are equal must be made. The sum of all the angles of any polygon with equal sides will increase with the increasing number of sides of the polygon. Thus, it is not possible to compare the results from the two columns.

---

15. **(D)** Try some values into the equations.

If $x = 0$, $y = 1$, and $z = 2$, then Column A = 1 and Column B = –4.
If $x = -2$, $y = -1$, and $z = 0$, then Column A = 3 and Column B = 4.

Therefore, more information is needed to solve the equation.

---

16. **(B)** First one must determine the equivalent of 132 ft./ 9 sec. in terms of miles/hour in order to solve the problem. Recall that 1 hour = 60 min. = 3,600 sec. and 1 mile = 5,280 ft. Thus, one can set up the following proportion:

$$\frac{132 \text{ ft}}{9 \text{ sec}} = \frac{x \text{ ft}}{1 \text{ hr}} = \frac{x \text{ ft}}{3,600 \text{ sec}}$$

and solve for x. The result is

$$\frac{9x \text{ ft}}{\text{sec}} = \frac{132(3,600) \text{ ft}}{\text{sec}}$$
$$x = \frac{475,200}{9} = 52,800 \text{ ft or 10 miles.}$$

Hence, the speed is 10 miles per hour.

17. **(E)**

$$\text{Let } x = \text{number}$$
$$.07x = 35$$
$$\frac{.07x}{.07} = \frac{35}{.07}$$
$$x = 500$$

Therefore, the correct choice is (E).

18. **(E)** Let x = the score of Joan's last test

$$83 = \frac{4(79) + x}{5}$$
$$83(5) = 316 + x$$
$$415 - 316 = x$$
$$99 = x$$

19. **(D)** To find the altitude of the triangle one must recall that the area of a triangle is given by

$$A = \left(\frac{1}{2}\right)bh,$$

where b denotes the base and h denotes the altitude. Also, one must recall that the area of a circle is given by

$$A = \pi r^2,$$

where r denotes the radius of the circle.

Since $b = 6$ units then $(\frac{1}{2})(6)h = 3h = A$, the area of the triangle. In addition, since $r = 6$ units, then $A = \pi r^2 = \pi(6)^2 = 36\pi$, the area of the circle. But the area is the same for both figures. Thus,

$$3h = 36\pi$$
$$h = 12\pi$$

is the altitude of the triangle.

---

20. **(C)** One needs to first recall that a cube has six equal sized faces. Thus, the area of each face is found by dividing 6 into 96 to obtain 16 square feet. Since each face contains 16 square feet, then one can conclude that each edge of a face is 4 feet long. So, the volume of the cube, given by the formula,

$$V = (\text{length of edge})^3 \text{ is found to be}$$
$$V = (4 \text{ feet})^3 = 64 \text{ cubic feet.}$$

---

21. **(C)** The average income for Company X is obtained by finding the sum of the income over the years 1983 and 1986 and dividing by 4.

$$\frac{(200 + 300 + 100 + 400)}{4} = 250$$

---

22. **(D)** By observation one needs only to find the largest spread between corresponding plotted points on the two lines representing the companies. Thus, the largest difference occurred in 1987 where the difference was 400 million (500 – 100).

23. **(B)** The median is the middle annual earnings for X Company arranged in ascending order. Over the indicated years, the annual earnings in millions are 200, 300, 100, 400, 100, 200, respectively. Arranging these values in ascending order and taking the average of the two in the middle gives the value of 200 million for the median.

24. **(E)** From the graph notice that the largest increase in earnings of Y Company occurred between 1986 and 1987. The amount of the increase was 400 million. Recall that in order to find the percent of increase use the following formula:

$$\text{Percent increase} = \frac{\text{Amount of increase}}{\text{Original amount}} \times 100$$

$$= \frac{400}{100} \times 100 = 400\%$$

The other answer choices are incorrect as a result of either misapplying the formula or not observing the largest increase in earnings of Y Company.

25. **(D)** Of the two companies, Company X had the largest decrease in earnings which occurred between 1986 and 1987. The amount of the decrease was 300 million. Recall that in order to find the percent of decrease one uses the following formula:

$$\text{Percent decrease} = \frac{\text{Amount of decrease}}{\text{Original amount}} \times 100$$

$$= \frac{300}{400} \times 100 = 75\%$$

The other answer choices are incorrect as a result of misapplying the formula for the percent of decrease or not observing the largest decrease for X Company on the graph.

26. **(C)** Simplify

$$7 - 3x \leq 19$$
$$-3x \leq 19 - 7 \qquad \text{Add } -7 \text{ to both sides.}$$
$$x \geq 12 \div (-3) \qquad \text{Divide both sides by } (-3)$$
$$x \geq -4 \qquad \text{The sense of the inequality}$$

Add –7 to both sides.
Divide both sides by (–3)
The sense of the inequality changes when multiplied or divided by a negative number.

---

27. **(E)** One way to attack this problem is to solve it algebraically.

Let x represent the number of packages weighing 2 kg each. Then $(150 - x)$ represents the number of packages weighing 1 kg each.

Therefore,

$$2x + 1(150 - x) = 264$$
$$2x + 150 - x = 264$$
$$x = 264 - 150$$
$$x = 114$$

Thus, there are 114 packages weighing 2 kg each on the truck.

Another way to solve this problem is to test each of the answer choices. Note that if, for example, the number of packages weighing 2 kg each is 36 (answer choice (A)), then the number of packages weighing 1 kg each will be $(150 - 36) = 114$. Testing the answer choices yields:

(A)　　$(36)(2) + (150 - 36)(1) = 72 + 114 = 186$　(wrong)
(B)　　$(52)(2) + (150 - 52)(1) = 104 + 98 = 202$　(wrong)
(C)　　$(88)(2) + (150 - 88)(1) = 176 + 62 = 238$　(wrong)
(D)　$(124)(2) + (150 - 124)(1) = 248 + 26 = 274$　(wrong)
(E)　$(114)(2) + (150 - 114)(1) = 228 + 36 = 264$　(correct)

28.   (C)   The wheel will travel in 1 revolution (2 minutes) $C = \pi d = \pi(3) = 3\pi$ feet. In 30 minutes it will travel $^{30}\!/_2 = 15$ revolutions. Thus, the wheel will travel $15(3\pi) = 45\pi$ feet in 30 minutes.

---

29.   (E)   Note that tips for the week were $\left(\dfrac{5}{4}\right)(150)$. Thus, the total income was as follows:

$$(1)\,(150) + \left(\frac{5}{4}\right)(150) = \left(\frac{4}{4}\right)(150) + \left(\frac{5}{4}\right)(150)$$

$$= \left(\frac{9}{4}\right)(150)$$

Therefore, tips made up $\dfrac{\left(\dfrac{5}{4}\right)(150)}{\left(\dfrac{9}{4}\right)(150)} = \dfrac{\dfrac{5}{4}}{\dfrac{9}{4}} = \dfrac{5}{9}$ of her income.

Notice that one could figure out the total income in order to arrive at the solution; however, this would be a waste of time.

---

30.   (A)   Since h, m, and n are divisible by 3, first represent each as follows: $h = 3i$, $m = 3j$, and $n = 3k$, where i, j, and k are integers. Now consider the hm as follows:

$$hm = 3i(3j) = 9ij.$$

But clearly, $^{hm}\!/_9 = {}^{9ij}\!/_9 = ij$. So, hm is divisible by 9.

Using the same technique or by a simple example, it is clear that II and III are not possible. Hence, the other answer choices are not possible.

Section 6 –
Verbal Ability

1. **(C)** (A) is incorrect; ABUSIVE means treating badly or harshly. The term does not fit the sentence very well; ABUSIVE writing probably would not ENHANCE one's chance for a promotion. (B) is not an appropriate choice. Since LACONIC means brief and to the point, this type of writing does not seem grounds to OBLITERATE (wipe out) a teacher's chances for promotion. (C) is the correct answer. OBTUSE means blunt, stupid, not sharp. (For instance, an obtuse angle is not sharp, like an acute angle; it is larger than a right angle.) Such writing might OBVIATE (eliminate) one's chances of a promotion. (D) is incorrect; since PROFOUND means not superficial, and clearly marked by intellectual depth, it does not stand to reason that such writing would DIMINISH (or make less) one's chances for a promotion. The best answer is not (E). The publication of PROLIFIC (many) writings alone does not make necessary (NECESSITATE) the promotion of a teacher.

2. **(B)** (A) is not the best choice. ELICIT means to draw out in a skillful way something that is being hidden or held back. Giving business cards is not unique. The best answer is (B). SOLICIT means to ask earnestly, to try to get. Since ILLICIT (C) means illegal, it is an incorrect choice. ELLIPTIC (D) means shaped like an ellipse (with ovals at both ends). CONCILIATE (E) is to win over, to soothe. The word is an inappropriate choice.

3. **(D)** A QUIRK is a peculiar behavior trait; a pregnant woman's desire for odd foods is a temporary condition, not a behavior trait; (A) is incorrect. Choice (B), PROFUSION (abundance), is inappropriate. A PITTANCE is a small amount of money; (C) is not the correct choice. A STIPEND is a monetary payment; therefore, (E) is also incorrect. (D) is the appropriate choice; a PENCHANT is a desire or craving.

4. **(A)** Of the choices, (A) makes the most sense. A chairman would be likely to complain that time was being wasted on PERIPHERAL (auxiliary or side) issues, instead of on the ESSENTIAL (central or main) one. SCURRILOUS means coarse or indecent language; TEDIOUS means boring. (B) is not an appropriate choice. TRENCHANT, meaning distinct or clear-cut, and SUPERFLUOUS, meaning unnecessary, would be appropriate choices if their order was reversed, but as it is, (C) is incorrect. SUPERFICIAL, or surface, is an appropriate adjective for the first blank, but WHIMSICAL (fanciful) is not appropriate for the second; (D) is not the correct answer. MUNIFICENT (lavish) and DESULTORY (without order) are not logical adjectives for this sentence. Choice (E) is incorrect.

5. **(A)** AMORPHOUS, ECCENTRIC, and ERRATIC are all synonyms meaning inconsistent, sporadic. EQUABLE suggests a uniform methodical occurrence. WEARISOME is the correct choice, indicated by the key words "exact," "and," "but," and "essential."

6. **(C)** ABSTRUSE (C), meaning difficult to comprehend, is the most appropriate choice. A lecture on molecular dynamics would be inherently ERUDITE, or learned; (A) is not the correct choice. The lecture focused on a single topic, so it was not ECLECTIC (varied, diverse). (B) is not the correct answer. INCHOATE (unformed) and AMORPHOUS (having no determined form) are unrelated to the sentence topic, so (D) and (E) are incorrect answers.

7. **(C)** The clues to this sentence are "not only failed" and "exacerbate." These words imply that the correct choice must be the antonym of EXACERBATE (to worsen). EXCORIATE (to abrade), DISSEMINATE (to spread), EXCULPATE (to clear from fault), and OBJURGATE (to chide vehemently) are all inappropriate choices. AMELIORATE (to improve, to make better) is the necessary antonym; the correct answer is (C).

---

8. **(D)** The relationship between GIGGLE and GUFFAW is one of degree. GLOVE:GAUNTLET, FASHION:VOGUE, and SOB:WEEP all exhibit synonymous relationships. Therefore, (A), (B), and (C) are incorrect. (E) WHEEDLE (to entice by flattery) and WHINE (to use a plaintive tone of voice) might both be considered methods of manipulation, but they are not different degrees of the same thing. REPROVE (to kindly correct a fault) and BERATE (to scold vigorously) are different degrees of remonstrating. The correct answer is (D).

---

9. **(E)** AMIABLE (friendly) and ANONYMOUS (unknown) are unrelated, as are BENIGN (gentle, mild) and MALICE (desire to cause pain); (A) and (D) are incorrect answers. ECONOMICAL:THRIFTY and DOCILE:COMPLIANT are synonymous relationships. FAVORABLE and OMINOUS are antonyms, as are BENEFICIAL (conferring benefits) and BALEFUL (evil or harmful). The correct answer is (E).

---

10. **(E)** A MAGICIAN performs an ILLUSION; a SOPRANO performs an ARIA; therefore, (E) is the correct choice. BRANCHES do not perform TREES; CHEMISTRY does not perform ELEMENTS; MEDICINE treats DISEASE; and a COOK follows a RECIPE. (A), (B), (C), and (D) are incorrect.

11. **(D)** FUMBLE (to handle something clumsily) and FINESSE (to handle skillfully) are antonyms. FRUGAL (thrifty) and FLUENT (facile in speech) are unrelated. ABHOR (to loathe) and APPEASE (to pacify) are also unrelated. (A) and (E) are not correct choices. DECEIVE and BEGUILE are synonyms, as are FACILITATE and EXPEDITE, meaning to accelerate the process. (B) and (C) do not share the relationship sought. Only IMPUGN (to attack another's character) and EXTOL (to praise highly) share the antonymous relationship; therefore, the correct choice is (D).

12. **(D)** A PUPA is an immature form of a MOTH, which has to undergo a period of metamorphosis (striking physical change) to become an adult moth. A TADPOLE is an immature form of FROG that also must change significantly to become an adult frog. (D) is the correct choice. PARAPET:WALL are synonyms, so (A) is incorrect. POMMEL:SADDLE and STAMEN:FLOWER exhibit a part:whole relationship; (B) and (C) are incorrect. Choice (E) is inappropriate. An ADOLESCENT is the immature form of many animals, but no striking physical changes occur before it becomes an ADULT.

13. **(A)** VACILLATE is a verb meaning to waver. DECISION is a noun meaning the act of committing or deciding. A verb and noun which are opposite in meaning are needed from the choices given. EQUIVOCATE is a verb meaning to hedge. COMMITMENT is a noun meaning the act of declaring. The analogy in (A) is the same as for VACILLATE:DECISION. FLUCTUATE is a verb meaning to be changing continually. PROCRASTINATE is a verb meaning to postpone. (B) is not the appropriate answer. CONSPIRE is a verb meaning to act or plan together secretly; COLLUSION is a noun meaning the act of secretly planning together. The relationship of choice (C) is not the same as that between VACILLATE:DECISION. RESOLVE is a verb meaning to come to a decision; CONCLUSION is a noun meaning the close of an argument, debate, or reasoning. (D) is not the correct answer. AMELIO-RATE means to lessen, to make mild; RESOLUTION is a noun meaning the act of deciding or determining something. The analogy between AMELIORATE:RESOLUTION (E) and between VACILLATE:DECISION is not the same.

14. **(B)** COALESCE (to come together) and DISPERSE (to spread out) are antonyms. The only other antonym is (B): IMPRECATE (to curse) and CONSECRATE (to bless). UMBRAGE:OFFENSE (A) are synonyms. INCARCERATE (to jail) and REMONSTRATE (to reprove); ELUCIDATE (to make clear) and PREVARICATE (to lie); and DEBILITATE (to weaken) and MITIGATE (to mollify) are all unrelated terms. (C), (D), and (E) are incorrect.

15. **(B)** CONTUMACIOUS means stubbornly disobedient; a MUTINEER is one who resists lawful authority. Being contumacious is an innate quality of a mutineer. Only (B) reflects the same relationship. A BIENNIAL is a flowering plant that only lives for two years; EPHEMERAL means short-lived. Being EPHEMERAL is an innate quality of a BIENNIAL. Choices (A), (C), (D), and (E) do not reflect this relationship. RENASCENCE (rebirth or rising again) is not inherently DELETERIOUS (harmful). A ZEALOT (fanatic) is anything but OBSEQUIOUS (subservient). A NEOPHYTE (beginner) is not likely to be PEDAGOGIC (befitting a teacher). CONNOISSEUR means expert, IRASCIBLE means irritable; connoisseurs are no more likely to be irascible than anyone else.

16. **(C)** FUSTIAN and BOMBASTIC are synonyms meaning pretentious speech or writing. LOQUACIOUS and GARRULOUS are synonyms meaning talkative; therefore, (C) is the correct answer. (A) and

(D) are unrelated terms. FACETIOUS means joking and SARDONIC means bitterly ironic. IGNEOUS means having the nature of fire, and PECUNIARY means relating to money. (B) and (E) are antonymous terms. SANGUINE means optimistic and SATURNINE means gloomy. NUGATORY is insignificant and INORDINATE is excessive.

17.   **(E)**   The author of this article is not pessimistic (A) in tone; rather the author seems encouraged by the results of Faigel's study. The author does not have an unconcerned attitude toward the study by Faigel. The very fact that the article was written shows some concern on the part of the author. (B) is not an appropriate answer to the question. Indifferent (C) is not the tone of the writing. The writer is careful to point out the difference in scores between second-time test-takers who had been administered the beta blockers and second-time test-takers who had not been administered the drugs. The author of this article is not resigned. The author states that the drugs "seem to help test-takers"; on the other hand, the writer cautions that side effects do exist. (D) is not correct. The author of the article can best be described as optimistic (E). Again, the writer states that beta blockers "seem to help test-takers who have low scores because of test fright."

18.   **(D)**   A control group of eight students was used in Faigel's study. (A) is false. Second-time test-takers increase only 28 points nationally. (B) is not the best answer. The article states that the beta blockers cannot help those who do not "know" the material. (C) should not be selected. Adrenalin does increase minor stress and may result in lower test scores; (D) is the best answer. Beta blockers, not adrenalin, have long been used for heart conditions and for minor stress; therefore, (E) is false and not the best answer.

19. **(E)** Casual indifference (A) does not seem to aptly describe students who become nervous when taking the SAT. Resignation (B) is not the best descriptive adjective for students who continue to take the SAT to try to improve their test scores. Antagonism is not the attitude suggested by the article. No mention is made of students' possessing an antagonistic attitude or of their trying to eradicate standardized testing; (C) is not the best answer. Pessimism (D) is not the attitude mentioned in the article or suggested by students who continue to retake a standardized test to improve their grades. Concern best describes the attitudes of students who take (and retake) the SAT to try to increase their score and even experience nervousness during the test-taking. Concern (E) seems to be the answer implied (though not stated) by the article.

---

20. **(C)** Second-time test-takers nationwide improve only an average of 28 points—not a significant increase. Statisticians would attribute this insignificant increase to the fact that the test is a *reliable* test; students seem to achieve the same test scores each time it is administered unless they do something different in-between test administrations. (A), therefore, is false and an incorrect answer. The author of the passage makes no speculation on limiting the number of administrations of the SAT. (B) is false and should not be chosen. If beta blockers are used, the article suggests that scores of nervous second-time test-takers may be raised. This, in turn, will raise the national average. (C) is correct and the best choice. Raising test scores of even one group of students will affect the national average. (D), therefore, is false and should not be chosen as the correct answer. Adrenalin has not been shown to increase test scores. (E) should be avoided as the correct answer. It is beta blockers that seem to reduce nervousness and increase test scores.

21. (C) The study by Faigel focuses on SAT test-takers. Faigel does not attempt to make any predictions on how the beta blockers might affect the general public should they take them for nervousness; to the contrary, Faigel cautions that beta blockers do have certain side effects. (A) is not the best answer. It was not adrenalin but beta blockers which increased the performance of second-time test-takers of the SAT. (B) is an incorrect answer and should not be selected. Since beta blockers do seem to improve the average scores of second-time test-takers (particularly nervous second-time takers) of the SAT, (C) is a true, appropriate answer. Faigel recognizes that beta blockers do have side effects, but he in no way implies that they should never be used. (D), therefore, is an incorrect answer and should not be chosen. Nervousness *does* seem to affect the test scores of students who "know" the material. Faigel's study suggests by administering beta blockers to help control this nervousness, students can raise their test scores. (E) is not the best answer to this question.

22. (B) Analysis involves separating or breaking down into parts. Faigel's work primarily involved developing a plan (synthesizing), rather than a separating (analysis). (A) is not the best answer. Synthesis involves putting together, combining to form a whole. Developing a plan to reduce the nervousness and developing a plan to compare the test results is certainly a synthesizing. (B) is correct and should be chosen. Deduction (C) involves reasoning from the general to the particular. Deduction does not apply to developing a plan to reduce nervousness and to compare test results. Interpretation is used when one gives an explanation; developing a plan does not necessarily involve interpretation. (D) is not the correct answer. Application means the act of using a particular case or for a particular purpose; Faigel synthesized, rather than applied, when he developed his research plan. (E) is inappropriate.

23. **(E)** Amusement is certainly not the author's tone in this passage. (A) should not be chosen. Indignation (B) is not the author's tone. The author has no source upon which to vent indignation in this passage. The very fact that the author bothered to write the passage negates the idea that the author shows indifference. (C) should not be selected as the best answer. Approval is not the best choice for the author's attitude. There is little that a well-meaning author could approve in this passage. (D) is not an appropriate choice. Resignation (E) is the best choice for the author's attitude. The author is not resigned to never having a cure for ALS; the author admits that there may be a waiting period for this cure, however.

24. **(C)** Deductive reasoning moves from the general to the particular. Choice (A) leads from the particular (victims of ALS who are athletes) to the general (active persons are more often affected by ALS); therefore, (A) is not the correct answer. Alternative (B) is not a deduction; it is simply a restatement of a fact presented in the passage. Choices (D) and (E) offer faulty reasoning. The fact that the four victims discussed in the passage were all athletes and were all male does not give enough evidence to predict that the next victim will be an athlete (D) or a male (E). One cannot predict that the next victim will follow a pattern based on so small a subset of the total number of ALS victims. Only choice (C) is an example of deductive reasoning. It moves from the general (victims who were athletes) to the specific (exposure to possibly harmful fertilizers might be one of the causes of ALS).

25. **(E)** Confirmation is synonymous with corroboration; both mean supported by evidence. Support (A) and evidence (B) alone do not carry the same connotation. Evidence can be interpreted in different ways, and support is not always based on evidence. Analogy (D), meaning similarity or correlation, is an inappropriate choice. Using reason (C) in this sentence would imply that all speculations about possible causes of ALS are pointless, thus changing the meaning of the sentence considerably.

26. **(D)**   The non-imminent solution to ALS is a disturbing fact presented in the passage, but it does not give the topic of the paragraph. (A) should not be selected. Statement (B) gives an important supporting detail from the passage but does not give the topic of the paragraph to the reader. Statement (C) adds additional facts, but it does not present the main subject. (D) informs the reader of the topic of the paragraph. It is the correct choice. Statement (E) is taken from the passage and gives supporting details about the puzzle of ALS; it does not, however, give the topic of the sentence.

27. **(D)**   The passage states that the causes (A) and cure (C) for amyotrophic lateral sclerosis are not known; therefore, the passage cannot answer these questions. Furthermore, the passage only mentions who Lou Gehrig was (B), and it makes it clear there is no known connection between ALS and professional athletes (E). The purpose of the passage is to inform readers about amyotrophic lateral sclerosis (D).

28. **(B)**   An ODYSSEY is a long series of wanderings. Since a JOURNEY (A) is a very long trip, it is synonymous with ODYSSEY and an incorrect answer. An ERRAND (B) is a short trip, the opposite of ODYSSEY, and the correct answer. A WANDERING (C), like an ODYSSEY, is a moving about aimlessly; it is not the opposite of ODYSSEY. A VOYAGE is a long journey by water, much like an ODYSSEY; (D) is not the correct answer. A CRUISE is sailing about from place to place; (E) is very similar to ODYSSEY and should not be selected as the right answer.

29. **(E)** The correct answer is (E). The opposite of ADULTERATE (corrupt, make impure) is HOMOGENIZE (purify). INTERMIX (A) is to mix together. HYBRIDIZE (B) is to interbreed. To INTERFACE (C) is to connect. MISCEGENATE (D) is to mix races.

30. **(C)** The antonym for RESPLENDENT (splendid, dazzling) is SHODDY (C) (inferior, badly made). WAN (A) is pale; STOLID (B) means dull; TRITE (D) refers to commonplace; and PALATIAL (E) is large and ornate.

31. **(D)** ALTRUISTIC means unselfishly putting the needs of others before one's own. DOGMATIC (A) means opinionated; it is not the correct answer. ABSTEMIOUS (B) is not the opposite being sought; it refers to using sparingly. FORTUITOUS (C) means a lucky accident. HEDONISTIC (D), meaning seeking pleasure for oneself, is the antonym of ALTRUISTIC. The last choice, APOCALYPTIC (E), refers to revelation or discovery.

32. **(A)** The antonym of VIRILE (masculine, manly) is EFFEMINATE (A), which means having feminine qualities. BESTIAL (B) refers to having the qualities of a beast. EQUIVOCAL (C) means doubtful. CHOLERIC (D) is easily angered. LECHEROUS (E) means sexually voracious.

33. **(B)** To BEMOAN is to express grief, to lament. The correct antonym is (B) EXULT, which means to express joy, to rejoice greatly. (A) LAUGH implies joy but it refers to the audible sound not emotional state. To COMMISERATE (C) is to express sorrow for which is in a synonymous relationship to bemoan. (D) ACCLAIM means to announce or welcome with loud approval and (E) EULOGIZE is to praise highly. Neither (D) nor (E) reflect the same relationship of BEMOAN and EXULT in the expression of emotional states.

34. **(E)** The noun MELANCHOLY is derived from the Greek words for "black" *(melas)* and "bile" *(chole),* and it means sadness and depression of spirits. Its opposite is (E) EXHILARATION, which means stimulated, lively, gay, and comes from the Latin prefix *ex* (interns) and *hilaris* (glad). (Our word "hilarity" also comes from this Latin root.) Alternatives (A), (B), (C), and (D) are wrong because they fail to include the idea of lively and gay. (A) SOCIABILITY means liking the company of others; (B) SERENITY means undisturbed or calm; (C) COMPLACENCY means self-satisfied or smug; and (D) IMPULSIVENESS is acting upon impulse.

35. **(D)** CANDID (D), meaning open and honest, is the opposite of CLANDESTINE, which means hidden or private. The correct answer is (D). SURREPTITIOUS (A) and FURTIVE (B) are synonymous with clandestine. EGREGIOUS (C) means flagrant, and LURID (E) means gloomy.

36. **(D)** PROPITIOUS means favorably disposed, graciously inclined. CONSPICUOUS (A) means obvious to the eye or mind. The two are not antonyms. AUSPICIOUS is a synonym for PROPITIOUS; both mean favorable, fortunate. (B) is, therefore, not the correct answer. EVANESCENT (C) means dissipating like vapor, vanishing. It is a word that is not related to PROPITIOUS and should not be selected.

MILITANT means warlike, fighting. MILITANT is the opposite of PROPITIOUS, or favorably inclined. (D) is the correct answer. AGGREGATIVE means taken together, collective, tending to aggregate. (E) is not a suitable choice as an antonym of PROPITIOUS.

---

37. **(A)** MALAPROPOS means not appropriate. (The prefix *mal-* means not.) CONGRUOUS means fit, right, suitable; congruous (congruent) angles, for instance, are of the same size and shape. MALAPROPOS and CONGRUOUS are antonyms; (A) is the correct answer. SPECIOUS stresses a clear suggestion of fraud. It does not bear the opposite relationship to MALAPROPOS sought; (B) should not be selected. PONDEROUS (C) means heavy, dull, and bulky. It is certainly not the antonym sought. Since BENIGN means mild, kind, and gentle, it is not an antonym for a word meaning not appropriate. (D) should not be selected. PROPENSITY (E) means a natural inclination or bent. It does not suggest an opposite relationship to MALAPROPOS.

---

38. **(E)** UNCOUTH means uncultured, crude, boorish, or clumsy. MELANCHOLY is gloomy, depressed. Since an UNCOUTH person can be MELANCHOLY, (A) is not an antonym or opposite. AMELIORATING means making milder. It does not have an opposite relationship to UNCOUTH; (B) is not the correct answer. FUNEREAL is an adjective meaning dismal or mournful; it is not the opposite of UNCOUTH. (C) should not be selected as the correct answer. BOORISH is synonymous with UNCOUTH. (D) is not the correct choice. URBANE (E) means polite or civil; it is opposite from UNCOUTH and is the correct answer.

4

Attacking the Analytical Writing Section

An Introduction to the Analytical Writing Section

In the Analytical Writing section, you are given the opportunity to write two essays. One essay task asks you to present your perspective(s) on an issue. The other essay question wants you to evaluate the reasoning of someone else's argument. These essays are used to demonstrate your writing skills to the graduate schools to which you apply. The writing tasks will assess skills that are an essential part of the work done by graduate students in most fields: critical thinking and analytical writing.

Important Information!

The Analytical Writing section is administered by a computer, but is the only section that is NOT computer-adaptive. The computer will generate your essay questions from a large pool of topics.

Important Information!

You should be familiar with basic word-processing functions like delete, insert, and cut and paste. There won't be a spell or grammar check. Typing skills are also essential to succeed in this section. Practice typing on a computer or even a typewriter. Don't worry about typing as fast as you can; concentrate on accuracy. Accurate typing will make up for time wasted correcting mistakes you made while trying to go as fast as you can.

In many ways, composing an essay on a computer is much easier than using paper and pencil. With practice, you'll be able to type much faster than you can write. Also, using the basic word-processing functions will enable you to edit and rewrite your essay without unsightly erasures and insertions. But you must be comfortable with the computer and typing before you enter the testing center, or your ability to express your thoughts and ideas clearly and fluently will be impaired. And, after all, the Analytical Writing task is not testing your typing skills, but your ability to coherently express your thoughts!

Important Information!

Your essays will be scored at a later time and sent to you as part of your official score report. Your essay scores will not be part of the unofficial scores you receive the day you take the GRE. While the computer is checking your answers to multiple-choice questions, your essays will be scored by an official grader. Your official score report will include a separate score for each section of the test.

The two essays you are going to write differ in nature. The first essay, "Present Your Perspective on an Issue," asks you to analyze a certain issue and give your opinion. You must take a position on a topic and support that position with logical reasons, examples, and observations.

The second essay, "Analyze an Argument," asks you to explore an argument already made by another writer. After reading this other writer's argument, you must then write an essay supporting or condemning the argument. You must examine each idea presented in the argument, judge the merit of its conclusion, and make suggestions that would improve the argument.

Each of the essays has its own time limit. The "Present Your Perspective on an Issue" essay has a 45-minute time limit and the "Analyze an Argument" has a 30-minute time limit. Both essays will be scored on a 0–6 scale by two graders each. The scale has half-point increments. If the score the reader assigns your essay differs substantially from the computerized e-rater's score, a second reader will grade it. The scores for both essays will then be averaged to give you one single writing score, which will also be on the 0–6 scale. We'll go into the particulars of how the GRE scores your essays later in this chapter.

Important Information!

About the Directions

Perspective on an Issue Directions

The directions for the "Present Your Perspective on an Issue" task present you with an issue and then ask you to explain your views on that issue. Because there is no correct answer, you should not waste your time attempting to "figure out" what the graders want to read.

The graders are trained to keep their personal viewpoints out of their grading. Furthermore, given that there might be two people grading the test, these people are likely to have different personalities and grading styles. You have absolutely no way of knowing the temperament of the person who will grade your exam.

Additionally, the topics given are usually so uninspiring that most graders—especially after having read 10 to 15 essays on a particular topic—are not likely to be overly passionate about a topic.

For all of the reasons mentioned, we recommend that you write that which you honestly believe to be the truth. If you try to write what you think someone else wants to hear, you run the risk of creating an unconvincing argument.

Analyze an Argument Directions

The directions to the "Analyze an Argument" task are significantly different from those of the "Present Your Perspective on an Issue" essay. **The key difference between the two types of essays is that the argument essay asks that you critique the argument, while the issue essay asks for your opinions on the issue.**

Only do what you are being asked to do. **Do not** explain why the argument presented is true or false; rather, evaluate whether the conclusions and assumptions are validly drawn from the statements. **Do not** explain why you agree or disagree with the argument; rather, analyze the reasoning that underlies the argument. **Do not** express your personal views on the subject, as in the Issue task; rather, scrutinize the logical soundness of the given argument.

The purpose of this essay question is to give you a chance to demonstrate that you have the perceptive reading, analysis, critical thinking, and evaluation skills necessary for graduate work.

"Analyze an Argument" is essentially a critical thinking exercise. As a result, the analytical skills displayed in your essay carry more weight than the form and style of your writing.

The Analytical Writing Scoring Guide

The essays you will write are graded according to a scoring guide, which can be found on the GRE website. There is one scoring guide for the "Present Your Perspective on an Issue" essay, and there is a different scoring guide for the "Analyze an Argument" essay.

Scoring the Test

A look at the scoring guide can help you formulate a strategy for the essays. We begin with the "Present Your Perspective on an Issue" scoring guide. The guide is divided according to grade, with the grades ranging from 0–6. The guide then tells us what qualities will be possessed by each of the grades.

If you look at the official requirements for a score 6 essay, you will note that there are five. The first requirement is that your position is insightful. The second point deals with the content of your essay: your ideas, reasons, and examples. The third point concerns your organization of those ideas, reasons, and examples. The fourth and fifth points concern the manner in which you go about expressing those ideas (your control of the language, your diction, and your understanding of the rules of standard written English).

If you now look at the requirements for a score 5 essay, you will notice that the criteria have not changed much. The first requirement is that your position is well-considered. The second point still concerns your ideas, the third concerns your organization, and the fourth and fifth concern your writing ability. The difference between an essay with a score of 5 and an essay with a score of 6 is that the score 6 essay has better structure and content than the score 5 essay.

The score 6 essay has "insightful" reasons, while those of the score 5 essay are deemed only "well-considered." The score 6 essay is "well-focused, well-organized," while the score 5 is "generally well organized." If you look at the characteristics of the score 4, 3, and 2 essays, you would note that the pattern continues, in a somewhat downward spiral.

Scoring the Test

The essays are being judged according to three criteria:

1) **the content of your essay,**

2) **the organization of your essay, and**

3) **the expression of the content in your essay.**

These criteria are also found, with certain changes, on the scoring guide for the "Analyze an Argument" essay. The most important change seems to be that analysis is the focus of the argument essay whereas persuasion is the focus of the issue essay.

The first criterion unique to the argument essay wants you to analyze the structure of the given argument. To meet this criterion you must pay very close attention to how THEIR argument was put together. The third criterion concerns how well you support your main ideas. This is also called a content-based criterion.

Additionally—and this is very interesting—there is no difference between the writing skill demonstrated on the score 5 essay and the writing skill demonstrated on the score 6 essay. If you read the scoring guide, the last two criteria for the score 6 essay are exactly the same, word for word, as the last two criteria for the score 5 essay.

Scoring the Test

From this equability, we can conclude that the difference between the score 5 and the score 6 essay rests completely with the content and organizational portions of the grading. This emphasis on content fits in extremely well with the change of the directions we noted earlier in our discussion. **Content is definitely more critical for the argument essay than for the issue essay.**

About the Writing Assignment

Important Information!

It may be helpful if you break down the writing requirement into three discrete tasks. First, you must read the issue or argument and generate a few ideas that will form the basis for your essay. Second, you MUST OUTLINE your essay. Finally, you must write your essay.

Perspective on an Issue Essay

Important Information!

Generating a few ideas in the issue essay is a relatively easy task. All that is generally required is that you read the question, think about the issue presented, and ask yourself how you genuinely feel about the issue. Once you know how you genuinely feel about the issue, ask yourself why you feel as you do. Jot down a number of reasons as they come into your head. Now all that remains to do is to pick three or four of these reasons and structure your essay around them.

EXAMPLE

Sample Issue Essay Topic:

> Many new businesses are finding it difficult to survive in modern times without an enormous amount of financial backing. Many people recall "the good old days," when a person with a smart head, an ambitious heart, and a pocketful of change could start a potentially prosperous business. Today, however, larger companies continually swallow up smaller companies, or offer the type of competition against which no small business could ever hope to survive. However, larger corporations provide the country with a certain economic stability that would be lost if the nation were overrun solely with tiny businesses struggling to keep themselves alive.

> Which type of business described above, the small business or the large corporation, do you feel is more beneficial to both consumers and the business community at large? Explain your position, using relevant reasons and/or examples drawn from your own experiences, observations, or readings.

Bust it!

A possible answer is that if large-scale businesses are swallowing up small companies, it is because large companies can better serve consumers and the business community. Large-scale companies are, therefore, more beneficial to the individual and business consumer. A few examples are needed.

Point Number One: Large corporations create convenience.

When we want to buy a CD or a tape, where do we want to go? Do we want a mom-and-pop store where we would have two or three thousand CDs or tapes from which to choose? Or would we go to a place like Tower Records that might have just about every CD or tape we could imagine? Most shoppers would probably prefer the larger store with the broader selection. This is an instance where a large corporation creates a great deal of convenience for the consumer.

Point Number Two: Large corporations mean lower prices.

Given the choice, we would all rather pay less for a particular item. Huge stores, more akin to warehouses than actual stores, are cropping up all over the United States. Because of the enormous quantities these stores buy and sell, they are able to offer very low prices to the consumer.

Bust it!

Point Number Three: Large corporations create uniformity.

Many times shoppers are looking for uniformity, and large corporations can deliver uniformity. Suppose you are in a strange town and you want something to eat. In front of you are two stores: the local McDonald's and the local diner. Which you choose is up to you, but the local diner presents the bigger gamble. You order something from the local diner and you have no idea what you will be served. You order a cheeseburger, fries, and a Coke from a McDonald's and, whether you place your order in New York City or Memphis, Tennessee, you will be receiving exactly the same meal. At times, uniformity is what the consumer desires. Large-scale businesses offer a uniformity that a small business cannot hope to achieve.

Point Number Four: Provide examples to support the three points given.

These three advantages also apply to the business community as well as to individual consumers. A business that is trying to upgrade its computer system would probably prefer to work with a store that has more options. A business would rather buy its copying paper from a warehouse where the business could get the lowest price. And a business may well prefer to have its traveling employees stay with a national hotel chain where the service to the employees would be uniform.

Bust it!

At this point, you should essentially be able to see the structure of the essay. We have four paragraphs. One of them deals with the advantages large businesses have in the area of selection. A second concerns the issue of price. A third concerns the issue of uniformity. And the fourth paragraph gives examples of how these three issues can benefit the business community as well as the individual consumer.

These four paragraphs will make up the body of the essay. All we need to do now is add an introductory and concluding paragraph and the essay is complete. What we did here is essentially what you must do. A few clearly developed ideas with an introduction and a conclusion is all the graders expect from you.

Before going into the actual examples, it was stated that large-scale companies are more beneficial to the individual and business consumer. This statement may not, however, entirely reflect one's true feelings on the issue.

Although large-scale corporations are advantageous in certain circumstances, there are certain businesses where a smaller company will be preferable. The area of fine dining comes immediately to mind.

The creation of different, at times exotic, dishes is not susceptible to the same cooking methods as is a cheeseburger. Cooking at a certain level becomes an art. The chef has an idea and wants to experiment with it and develop it. The ambiance of the restaurant might be affected by the city in which it is located, and the ambiance might have to change as the city changes. When individuality comes into play, the small business has an advantage over the large corporation.

Bust it!

We see, therefore, a difference between small dining establishments and large-scale companies. It appears then, perhaps neither the large business nor the small business is the most beneficial. The nature of the business will dictate what size business can best serve that particular market. In the record store, all you want is the record. It matters not where you buy a particular record. The quality of the record does not depend upon the place of purchase. Thus, the only issue is price.

Yet, it is impossible to explain this in the essay outlined. This is due to the fact that one's true feelings are too complicated to be developed in a 30-minute essay. This example may illustrate a problem some of you have. Your honest thinking may be too multi-sided or too complex to be reduced to the 30-minute formula.

Bust it!

If you have this problem, you must simplify your thinking. Deal with only one side of an issue and write about that side clearly and forcefully. While this method will not present all of your ideas on a subject, this method will prove to be much more effective within the context of the time limit.

Analyzing an Argument Essay

Although the scope of the argument essay is somewhat more limited than the scope of the issue essay, generating ideas for the argument essay should not be a difficult task. Indeed, the directions for the argument essay point you in the direction the test-makers expect you to take.

In the directions, you are told to "Discuss how well reasoned you find this argument." This would require you to:

a) **examine the reasoning and**

b) **examine the use of evidence.**

As examples of how you might perform these tasks, you might discuss:

a) **questionable assumptions,**

b) **alternate explanations that weaken the conclusion,**

c) **counterexamples that weaken the conclusion,**

d) **evidence that would refute the argument,**

e) **evidence that would strengthen the argument,**

f) **what changes to the argument would improve it, and**

g) **what changes would help you evaluate the argument.**

Important Information!

The interesting thing about these items is that if we rearrange them slightly, they provide an outline for the essay. As you can well imagine, you will end up writing an introductory paragraph, a body of the essay, and a conclusory paragraph. Why don't you take these prompts, and fit them into your basic outline?

Voila!

Basic Outline for Analyze an Argument Essay

Introductory Paragraph

Our conclusions about:

a) **the reasoning and**

b) **the use of evidence.**

The Body of the Essay

We will discuss:

a) **questionable assumptions,**

b) **alternate explanations that weaken the conclusion,**

c) **counterexamples that weaken the conclusion, and**

d) **evidence that would refute the argument.**

Important Information!

The Conclusory Paragraph

We will discuss:

a) evidence that would strengthen the argument,

b) changes that would improve the argument, and

c) changes that would help you evaluate the argument.

Important Information!

Developing an Argument

We will now demonstrate how we can use this outline to evaluate an argument. To do so, we will need an argument:

Newspaper recycling is a wasteful exercise that should be abandoned. Recollected paper is so abundant that less than ten percent is ever put to a second use, and few dealers can survive the over-supplied market. America's recycling campaign has not prevented newspapers from filling our nation's garbage dumps—it has only made them more neatly stacked, at a cost which most towns must pass on to their citizens.

Important Strategy

Before we can apply our outline to their argument, we must first understand the nature and logic of their argument.

The argument is somewhat simple. The first sentence provides the conclusion and a suggestion for a policy change. The second sentence is the primary reason for the conclusion. The third sentence is a result of the second sentence.

Look!

Important Strategy

Now we can start to apply our outline to their argument. It is best if we start from the middle of our outline. What questionable assumptions does the argument contain? Two come immediately to mind.

The first assumption the author makes is that the amount of newspaper recycling that occurs is not a significant quantity. How do we know this to be an assumption of the author?

The author has implicitly admitted there to be some recycling by NOT saying there has been no recycling. And the author has been saying we should simply forget about this level of recycling. Thus, the author must believe the level of recycling is not worth preserving.

This assumption, however, is subject to attack. The author is talking about nationwide recycling. Can you imagine the number of newspapers that are sold in this country every day? Multiplying that number by 365, we realize that a staggering number of newspapers is sold in this country every year. Even if only 10 percent of recycled newspapers is eventually reused, this could still represent an enormous savings of forest.

The second assumption the author makes is that the 10 percent figure will not be significantly increased in the future. If, for example, within the next three years technology will allow 75 percent of recycled newspaper to be reused, then the author's argument that the entire system be abandoned has been severely weakened.

The directions next suggest that we consider alternate explanations that weaken the conclusion. Perhaps the reason that only 10 percent of recycled newspaper is being reused is that the paper is not getting to the recycling plants in a reusable condition. Perhaps consumers are allowing it to get wet before it is picked up. Or maybe the people picking it up are tossing it into the back of a dirty garbage truck and making the newspapers no longer recyclable.

Next, we are told to consider counterexamples that weaken the conclusion. Perhaps there are countries that have recycling programs that use 80 percent of their recycled paper.

Look!

Important Strategy

We are also told to consider evidence that would refute the argument. Here we would note that the argument does not cite any authority for its figure at all. Perhaps the 10 percent figure is inaccurate. How do we know? How can we judge? A situation such as this, where there is no authority for the only statistic used, must be considered ripe for an attack by additional evidence.

At this point, you can probably see that what we have written so far can, with a few minor adjustments, become the body of our paper. We are now in a position to write the introductory paragraph. Recall that in the outline of our introductory paragraph we would state our conclusions about:

a) the reasoning and

b) the use of evidence.

An acceptable introductory paragraph might be as follows:

Important Strategy

The sample argument is seriously flawed. First of all, the argument is based upon faulty reasoning. The argument consists of a conclusion (stop newspaper recycling) followed by a statistic (no more than 10 percent of recycled newspaper is reused). We don't know how the author got from the statistical statement to the conclusion; the author simply arrives. Additionally, there is almost no use of evidence. The author merely gives the 10 percent figure, but the author makes no attempt whatsoever to explain from whence the 10 percent figure came. Without such an explanation, it is hard to give the 10 percent figure any weight at all.

We are now also in a position to write our conclusory paragraph. In our conclusory paragraph, we decided we would consider:

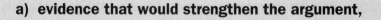

a) **evidence that would strengthen the argument,**

b) **changes that would improve the argument, and**

c) **changes that would help us evaluate the argument.**

For our conclusory paragraph, we might write as follows:

Additional evidence might include the amount of trees that are being saved each year and the amount we are currently spending to save these trees.

To improve the logic of the argument, we need to show how the evidence leads to the conclusion. Such changes would also help us evaluate the argument.

The completed argument would look as follows:

The sample argument is seriously flawed. First of all, the argument is based upon faulty reasoning. The argument consists of a conclusion (stop newspaper recycling) followed by a statistic (no more than 10 percent of recycled newspaper is reused). We don't know how the author got from the statistical statement to the conclusion; the author simply arrives. Additionally, there is almost no use of evidence. The author merely gives the 10 percent figure, but the author makes no attempt whatsoever to explain from whence the 10 percent figure came. Without such an explanation, it is hard to give the 10 percent figure any weight at all.

The argument is weak for many reasons. The first assumption the author makes is that the amount of newspapers that are reused is not a significant savings. This assumption, however, is subject to attack. The author is talking about nationwide recycling. Imagine the number of newspapers that are sold in this country every day. Multiply that number by 365, and a staggering number of newspapers is sold in this country every year. Even if only 10 percent of recycled

Look!

Important Strategy

newspapers is eventually reused, this could still represent an enormous savings of forest.

The second assumption the author makes is that the 10 percent figure will not be significantly increased in the future. If, for example, within the next three years, technology will allow 75 percent of recycled newspaper to be reused, then the author's argument that the entire system be abandoned has been severely weakened.

Look!

Important Strategy

There may be alternate explanations that weaken the conclusion. Perhaps the reason that only 10 percent of recycled newspaper is being reused is that the paper is not getting to the recycling plant in a reusable condition. Perhaps consumers are allowing it to get wet before it is picked up. Or maybe the people picking it up are tossing it into the back of a dirty garbage truck and making the newspapers no longer recyclable.

Counterexamples that weaken the conclusion may also exist. Perhaps there are countries that have recycling programs that use 80 percent of their recycled paper. Or perhaps there are individual states that have figured out ways to use 80 percent of their recycled paper.

There may be plenty of evidence to refute this argument. The argument does not cite any authority for its figure at all. Perhaps the figure is inaccurate. How do we know? How can we judge? A situation such as this, where an entire argument is built upon one statistic and no authority is given for that statistic, must be considered ripe for an attack by additional evidence.

Additional evidence must include the amount of trees that are being saved each year and the amount we are currently spending to save these trees. To improve the logic of the argument, we need much more evidence and we need to show how the evidence leads to the conclusion. Such changes would also help us evaluate the argument.

We will now summarize how you should handle the argument essay.

First, you must understand how the argument has been constructed. (You cannot rip apart an argument until you understand how it has been put together.)

Important Strategy

Second, write the outline for the body of your essay. Look for weak assumptions, possible alternative explanations, possible counterexamples that attack the argument, and additional evidence that would attack the argument.

Third, write the outlines for your introductory and conclusory paragraphs. Finally, write your essay starting with the introductory paragraph and ending with your conclusory paragraph.

Parts of the Essay

The Introduction

If you have made an outline, you should have no problem writing a good introduction. The requirements for the introduction vary slightly depending upon whether you are writing an issue essay or an argument essay. We first consider the issue essay.

An acceptable introductory paragraph to the issue essay need only accomplish two tasks. First, it must be clear. Second, it must state which side of the essay you find more compelling. Anything beyond these requirements is superfluous.

If you look at a sample essay that has been scored 6, you will find that the introductory paragraph usually has three sentences. The first sentence states one side of the issue. The second sentence states the other side of the issue. And the third sentence states the side of the issue that the essayist found the most compelling.

Important Strategy

This is, admittedly, the easiest way to write an introductory paragraph. **We, therefore, recommend that for your introductory paragraph to the issue essay you should clearly state both sides of the issue and then clearly state which side you find more compelling.**

For the argument essay, we again recommend you hasten clearly and quickly to the point. In the introduction, all you seek to do is restate the highlights of what will later be found in the body of your essay.

The Argument

The argument, or body of the paragraph, should take up between one and three paragraphs. It is in this section that you present and develop your ideas. For the most part, we have already discussed the argument section and we will not repeat those ideas at this time.

Important Strategy

If you have made an outline, you should have little trouble translating that outline into the body of the essay. **We wish to remind you, however, that it takes more time to develop an idea than it does to outline it.**

For this reason, before you actually begin to write the body of your essay, you may want to make certain that you are not going to touch on more ideas than you can clearly develop within the time limits of the exam. It is better to clearly express three ideas than to muddle your way through six.

The Conclusion

Once again, if you have written an outline, writing the conclusion should be rather easy. **In the conclusion of the issue essay, you will state the side of the issue that you have chosen to support. You might also choose to support that side with one or two examples from the body of the paper.**

For the argument essay, if you are using the format we have developed, you will use the conclusory paragraph to discuss how the argument could be strengthened. You might discuss what additional information could be presented to make the argument stronger. Or you might discuss how the argument could be altered to make it more logically convincing. You may also discuss how some of the questionable assumptions could be strengthened.

Look!

Important Strategy

Tips for the Analytical Writing Task

If we review the criteria by which you will be scored, we will find the graders to be interested in three areas. First, the graders are interested in what you have to say. Second, the graders are interested in how well you organize what you have to say. Third, the graders are interested in how well you write; that is, how skillful you are in translating your thoughts into standard, written English.

Of these three, the criterion you should probably concern yourself with the least on the day of the exam is the third one. This is not to say that your writing style is unimportant, rather that your writing style is highly unlikely to desert you on the day of the exam.

You are not likely to become so nervous during the exam that you forget how to write complete sentences. Thus, this is an area that you probably need not worry too much about.

There is one point, however, about your writing style that we wish to make. **Be careful not to get into overly complicated sentence structures.** Do not try to do too much with a sentence. It may be a good idea to speak the entire sentence in your head before starting to write it. This method should prevent you from working your way into the middle of a sentence and not being able to figure out how to get to the end of the sentence. This would waste a lot of time and cause your essay to lose clarity and brevity.

The next criterion from the scoring system is organization. We have already mentioned it a number of times, but this cannot be overstressed. **WRITE AN OUTLINE! WRITE AN OUTLINE! WRITE AN OUTLINE!**

Not writing an outline will probably ensure that you will not get above a "4" on the writing sample. If you do not write an outline, your ideas will be all over the place and it will seem as though you do not know what you are talking about.

There are probably two reasons that people do not write outlines. Some people are too lazy. While there is nothing wrong with doing a job in the most efficient manner possible, skipping the outline for this essay is a foolish corner to cut.

The second reason some people will skip the outline is that they believe they do not have time. YOU DO HAVE TIME TO WRITE AN OUTLINE. You have 45 minutes for one essay and 30 minutes for the other. The first 5 or 10 minutes should be spent generating your thoughts and writing your outline. The next 20 or 30 minutes should be spent writing the essay. The remaining 5 minutes should be spent checking for grammatical and spelling errors.

Important Strategy

The last criterion from the scoring guide is the subject matter of your essay. We have discussed this criterion at some length, and there is no reason for another in-depth discussion at this point. For the issue essay, ask yourself what you honestly think and make certain your thinking does not get too complex. A few ideas in a well-organized essay is worth more than the rambling thoughts of a disorganized genius. There is no correct answer to an issue essay; your ideas are appropriate for this essay.

For the argument essay, remember that the first step you must take is to understand the logical structure of the argument you are to critique. After arriving at such an understanding, you may use the template we have outlined. The template will lead you to numerous points you can discuss to critique the argument. If you choose not to use the template, stick close to the issues the directions tell you to discuss. Keep in mind that on the argument essay, they do not want your ideas on the subject; they want you to critique their argument.

Part of the key to doing well on the essays is to be able to handle the time limit. We, therefore, recommend that you do enough practice essays so that you will be confident of producing a quality essay within 45 or 30 minutes, depending on the type of essay you are practicing.

**Important
Strategy**

Practice under actual conditions; give yourself only 45 or 30 minutes. Read the issue or the argument, generate your ideas, create your outline, and then write your essay. Once you get to the point where you know you can write the essay in 45 or 30 minutes, you may want to do one essay each week so that you do not lose your touch.

Remember to keep the structure to your argument simple. You want an introductory paragraph, one to three paragraphs as the body of your essay, and a conclusory paragraph. The introductory paragraph of the issue essay should clearly set forth your position. The introductory paragraph of the argument essay should summarize your critique of the given argument. The conclusory paragraph of the issue essay should restate your position, but it should also tie in some of the facts from the body of the essay. The conclusory paragraph of the argument essay should explain some of the ways that would improve the argument you have analyzed.

Points to Remember

On Target!

✔   *In either type of essay, your first job is to generate ideas. For the issue essays, your thoughts on the subject are fine. For the argument essay, make certain you are critiquing the given argument, which implies you must understand the logic of it.*

✔   *Write an outline.*

✔   *Write an essay having an introductory paragraph, a body, and a conclusory paragraph.*

✔   *You should take 5 or 10 minutes to generate ideas and write your outline, 20 or 30 minutes to write your essay, and 5 minutes to review your essay for grammatical and spelling errors.*

✔   *Do not try to deal with too many ideas in your essay.*

✔   *Avoid complex sentence structures that will cause you to make mistakes.*

✔   *Practice doing essays until you are comfortable with the 45-minute or 30-minute time frame. Then do one essay each week so as not to lose your touch.*

On Target!

Drill: Analytical Writing

DIRECTIONS: Present your perspective on the following issue, using reasons and/or examples to support your opinion.

PERSPECTIVES ON AN ISSUE ESSAY TOPIC

Many new businesses are finding it difficult to survive in modern times without an enormous amount of financial backing. Many people recall "the good old days," when a person with a smart head, an ambitious heart, and a pocketful of change could start a potentially prosperous business. Today, however, larger companies continually swallow up smaller companies, or offer the type of competition against which no small business could ever hope to survive. However, larger corporations provide the country with a certain economic stability that would be lost if the nation were overrun solely with tiny businesses struggling to keep themselves alive.

Sample Essay Scoring 5 to 6

Despite the illusion of financial security offered by large corporations, this country's economy will crumble unless small businesses are given a chance. The fundamental flaw of large corporations' advocates is that they ignore the overwhelmingly negative consequences of the demise of small businesses. The formulating principle of this nation and all capitalistic societies is that every man and woman can pursue a prosperous life without bounds or limitations. However, the rise of the large corporation is turning this country into a place where ambition is discouraged, and competition unthinkable.

clear and effective thesis

good transition

Advocates of large corporations ignore the fact that these businesses did not simply spring out of nowhere. Most of them began as small businesses that, through initiative and sweat, built themselves up into something far beyond their original expectations. Enterprising individuals, in an attempt to better themselves, found in this nation avenues for financial improvement.

good variation in sentence structure

America was famous for being a land of opportunity. For the first time, immigrants from countries with restrictive caste systems could choose their social standing for themselves; they were no longer forced to adopt a role imposed upon them at birth. Now, however, freedom for personal expansion and growth has become extremely limited by the presence of larger corporations. It is much more financially stable and lucrative to become an employee in a large company, and next to impossible to strike out on one's own. The very premises of this country's existence have been undermined by its own successes.

effective use of language

good transition between ideas

Let us imagine that an enterprising individual, Mr. Smith, is very ambitious and eager to make a comfortable living. He lives in a remote neighborhood where there is a need for a grocery store. Years ago, he might have simply found a backer to help him get started or borrowed enough capital from the bank to start a prosperous business. Now, however, in order to start a business with any chance of competing with the larger food store chains, Smith would have to pay a considerably larger fee to become part of a grocery store chain. If he were to strike out on his own, his business would always be jeopardized by the possibility that a Foodtown or an A&P would open up in his area. The only way he could compete with such a store would be to drastically reduce his prices, and this would turn his enterprising skills into a mere struggle for survival.

concrete example strengthens the argument

Of course, there are also advantages to large corporations. Job security and market stability are two important factors that they offer. However, a chain reaction has begun that will certainly end in disaster for this country. If the most ambitious individuals in this country are forced to be underlings in

good transitions

larger corporations, or, at best, buy into large corporations for the sake of competition, then more and more of our nation's outstanding individuals will vanish in the system. <u>The successful ones will be those without initiative, those only willing to take the smooth road laid out by large corporations</u>. Because of this, these corporations will suffer. Top executives will be those "smart" enough to play the game by the rules and squelch ambition in the process.

very clear language

good transition to concluding argument

It is, therefore, imperative that small businesses be given a fairer chance. We have seen how large corporations stifle ambition and initiative, and how they are on the way to creating a society where conformity is the key to success. Perhaps the government can step in and create charters that will lend more advantages to people starting businesses. State budgets should devote portions of tax money to aid small businesses in peril. <u>If not, our country will be sold to corporate giants that will turn our land of promise and dreams into a living nightmare</u>.

strong concluding statement

ANALYSIS OF SAMPLE ESSAY SCORING 5 TO 6

This essay scores highly because of several factors. The writer shows a willingness to take a bold stand and support his or her position with concrete reasons and examples. There is a serious attempt on the writer's part to use descriptive phrases and vary sentence structure to avoid monotony. While his or her views are sometimes generalized and could use some additional support or evidence, they are presented clearly and consistently. There is an overall flow and direction to the essay; each paragraph follows the next in a specific order.

The first paragraph states the writer's perspective and suggests some of his or her reasons for maintaining that position. The second paragraph introduces the premise that large corporations owe their success to having been able to begin as small businesses. The third paragraph provides a reason why smaller businesses are having difficulty surviving in a world filled with large corporations. The fourth paragraph provides a hypothetical example, using "Mr. Smith" to illustrate that ambitious individuals were in a much greater environment in previous years than they are now. The fifth paragraph admits the advantages provided by large corporations but expresses the overwhelming penalties that they impose on society. The sixth paragraph reiterates the writer's position and suggests possible solutions to avert a potential catastrophe.

Sample Essay Scoring 3 to 4

It all boils down to this: is this a country about making money or isn't it? It's quite clear to me that if you aren't making money one way, you should be making it another. — very unspecific If small businesses are failing, then so be it. If they are doing well, then so be it. You've got to go with the flow. There's no question about it. — this is not a thesis

Large corporations have been around for a long time. They provide the nation with many excellent things. — very vague If it weren't for large corporations, we would find it very difficult **fragment** to find the many things that we require in our daily lives. For example, fast food chains. If it weren't for fast food chains, everyone would have only two choices: cook at home or eat out at an expensive restaurant. But fast food chains all over the country (and all over the world for that matter) allow us to choose to pay cheap for a quick meal. Then you can go to the movies, or anywhere else, on time if you have to. — this does not relate to the essay topic

too informal Small businesses are becoming a thing of the past. This is kind of sad, especially if you are fond of nostalgic general stores and such. But in order to survive in a capitalistic society, you've got to do what you must. And that could mean that large corporations are the only way to go for a career. It's just become too hard to survive it on your own. — support for this statement is lacking

There's been a lot of bad press lately about large corporations. But all we have to do is consider the facts. Thousands of jobs are provided by big companies, and now, with all the unions, high salaries come with the job. And you can strike if things are unfair or make you unhappy. This kind of thing would be a little silly in a small business. They'd just rehire your position, but that's not so easy in a large corporation.

clear and precise sentence → ┌ <u>Therefore, large corporations are the key to the future</u>. Small businesses, however nostalgic and cultural, are sinking steadily into the depths of the past. In order to survive in today's world, you have to find a job working for someone else. If you don't find a job, you can try to survive on your own, but you won't find it easy. This isn't a good thing, but there's absolutely nothing that can be done about it. And besides, large corporations provide us with all sorts of things that small companies could never dream of doing, <u>not by a long shot</u>. ← too informal And in order for a small business to become a large business, they have to go against the big shots, the "corporate giants" as it were. And unless they have the luck that David had with Goliath, they don't stand a chance.

ANALYSIS OF SAMPLE ESSAY SCORING 3 TO 4

This essay attempts to establish a firm position: "We have to accept the realistic fact that large corporations are the way of the future. Therefore, to start your own business is brave and praiseworthy, but pointless in today's society." However, it takes the writer a long time to get this message across. There are many vague and unclear statements that can only be deciphered after a good deal of interpretation. The essay often rambles on, restating the same point continually without offering new insight into the idea. It is often difficult to interpret the meaning of certain phrases because of the writer's frequent use of vague pronouns such as "it" and "this," as well as his or her pervasive use of the word "things." The paper demonstrates an effective command of spelling and punctuation, but sentence structure is sloppy, confusing, and monotonous.

The first paragraph attempts to establish the writer's position, but the execution is vague and ambiguous: it is difficult to determine just where the essay is going. The second paragraph demonstrates some of the advantages of large corporations, but uses a very poor example ("fast food chains") to illustrate the point that large corporations provide "the many things that we require in our daily lives." The third paragraph establishes an important point: the writer acknowledges the advantages of small businesses. He or she asserts, however, that the futility of starting such a business outweighs its potential merits. The fourth paragraph again states some of the advantages, such as unions, that are offered by large corporations. The final conclusion offers us no additional insight, and, for the most part, simply repeats the points that have been made previously in the essay.

Sample Essay Scoring 1 to 2

fragment —— Business. That's all we see and hear on T.V. nowadays. It's getting so you can't hear yourself think anymore. It don't ←— subject-verb disagreement matter whether the busness is small or big instead we should wonder whether its good or not good to worry about any of this. lets be frank, there are times when its good to where a ←— wrong word shirt and tie and there's times when its good to kick back and just be yourself.

this is not — a thesis   This country is too concerned with all this stuff; we should be concerned instead with moral issues. When a big company swallows a little company its a moral dilemma, not a social, political, economic dilemma. All those bigwigs in their big desks pushing papers and saying "sign this, sign that; buy this, sell that" when there's a lot of people starving to death ←— poor on the sidewalks of wall street. Its like I said, its a moral spelling dilemma.

←— poor transition between ideas

fragment ——   If I had to make a choice it would be small busnes 99% of the time. No question. Big business dont care about employ- ees or thier famlys. Small busness is run by famlys most of the time. Familys care about each other, big busness don't care about nobody else but thier money. If they have to lay off everybody in the whole city, they'd do it in a flash if it would save them a couple of bucks.

   So what do I think about the whole thing? Well, if you —— too informal must know, I think that we shouldnt worry about these sorts of things. We should just live life happy and not worry about money. Then all those busness, big and little, would be up the creek without a paddle. Thats all I have to say about it.

ANALYSIS OF SAMPLE ESSAY SCORING 1 TO 2

This essay is extremely incoherent and difficult to follow. The inconsistent spelling, punctuation, and grammatical errors are only part of the problem. The more serious flaw of this essay is that it has no direction or flow. It seems, at times, as if the writer is favoring small businesses over large corporations; at other times, he or she seems to be attacking the very idea of organized businesses. There are scattered appeals to contemporary issues to provide emotional support, such as the mention of "people starving to death on the sidewalks of [W]all [S]treet," or the representation of small businesses as primarily family businesses. However, emotional appeals are lost when there is no structure or organization to the essay. The paragraphs drift from one point to the next with no sense of transition or unity. The colloquial expressions that pervade the essay ("good to kick back and just be yourself") also become distracting; their common use in society blinds the reader from what could have been an original and valid argument.

ANALYZE AN ARGUMENT ESSAY TOPIC

> **DIRECTIONS:** Discuss how well reasoned the following argument is.

Television is about to become one of the most important resources of Americans today. With new cellular technology, hundreds of stations from around the world will be available at a user's fingertips. In addition, cellular television users will be able to call specific programs (movies, documentaries, etc.) onto their screens at the touch of a button. An entire world of information will be available to the modern television viewer, who will no longer be a passive "couch potato," but an active student of a global society.

Sample Essay Scoring 5 to 6

This passage makes a number of interesting points about the future of video technology in America. The author anticipates a vast array of resources available "at the touch of a button" for future users of cellular television. There are, however, a few assumptions made by the writer that require additional support. He or she assumes, first of all, that cellular technology will be marketed as an educational tool, and not solely commercialized as a supreme entertainment center. Even granting the assumption that a significant amount of cellular technology users will pool their new resources for the sake of research, we must question whether there is enough activity involved in the process to free these television viewers from the title of "couch potato."

good transition into a critique

very precise

The author identifies two principle uses for cellular television. He or she notes primarily that users will be able to access "hundreds of [television] stations from around the world." There is little doubt that this could indeed be a significant source of educational research. However, it would be ridiculous to assume that this is the avenue that will be pursued by most television viewers. This is clear to anyone with seventy cable stations filled with mindless drivel. The writer might have suggested that some sort of selection process be employed to choose a substantial percentage of research-oriented programming. Without this selection process, there would be "hundreds of stations from around the world" that provided the same commercialistic, mind-wasting rubbish.

close examination of one sentence – very effective

good flow of argument

Users will also be able to call up "specific programs (movies, documentaries, etc.)"; in effect, they will be able to view any known program at any time. This, on the surface, certainly seems to conform to the idea that cellular television users will become "active student[s] of a global society." It

good variation in sentence structure

would be pointless to once again drill the point that such resources could be abused by those with no educational purposes in mind. A more serious concern involves those who would indeed be using this technology for proper research needs. <u>What frightens me is that an unlimited supply of research "at the touch of a button" is not really "research" at all</u>.

— very clear language

effective line of reasoning

This can only be explained by redefining the connotations of the word "research." There is a certain quality of initiative and ambition that builds itself around the "research" conducted by an archaeologist in ancient Egypt as opposed to a high school student examining an encyclopedia to write a history report. It is for this reason that instructors send students to the library to quest for data rather than simply photocopy all the data their students could possibly require. The very act of searching for resources is a significant exercise in our mental development. If all we need to do is punch in a few keys, there will be no challenge to the affair.

Seen in this way, we realize that something of the backbone of humanity will be lost if the connotations of "research" change this drastically. <u>Faced with a seemingly infinite array of information before them, young students of the future will no longer be motivated by that drive which would compel them to seek out and find what humanity has yet to even imagine</u>. Students of the next generation will be blinded by the illusion that all things are already known. Untold discoveries will be lost because that primal urge to explore and discover will be permanently extinguished by this cellular technology.

good variation in sentence structure

this is a solid conclusion – very effective

It would, therefore, be imperative that this technology be carefully utilized. The writer of this passage should have stressed the potential dangers of cellular television, as well as its benefits. For there is no denying that this will indeed be a supreme source of information. But it must be regarded solely as a tool, a way to rediscover that which has already been discovered. Its chief purpose should be to help those in the midst of researching matters unknown to humanity, not simply to appear as a source of infinite knowledge. For there will

never be a time that we will know all. <u>Unfortunately, with the</u> ⎯⎯ *strong*
<u>rise of cellular technology, there may be a tragic time when we</u>   *concluding*
<u>*think* we know all</u>.   *sentence*

ANALYSIS OF SAMPLE ESSAY SCORING 5 TO 6

This essay scores strongly for a number of reasons. Its main strength is that it directly interacts with the passage. The essay shows a distinct understanding of the points made by the author, and reveals a lack of support in the author's assertions that: 1) cellular technology will be used primarily for educational reasons; and 2) cellular research will be an active, not a passive, enterprise. The essay is clear, structurally sound, and easy to follow. Its various criticisms of the main passage are also clearly and firmly supported.

The introductory paragraph clearly states the two assertions with which the essay will contend. The second paragraph explores the first premise (entertainment vs. research) with regard to the author's mention of the many television stations that will be available to users of cellular technology. The third paragraph introduces the second premise (active vs. passive) with regard to cellular television's ability to call up "any known program at any time." The fourth paragraph continues this premise by defining some connotations of the word "research." The fifth paragraph continues this point even further by projecting the dark future that will result if cellular technology is abused in this manner. The sixth paragraph concludes by suggesting that cellular technology can indeed be an excellent source of productive research, as long as it is clearly labelled as a "tool" and not "as a source of infinite knowledge." This conclusion is weakened by the fact that the essayist has lost track of that other, less significant premise (entertainment vs. research). However, the depth of interaction between the essay and the passage more than makes up for this minor flaw.

Sample Essay Scoring 3 to 4

There's no doubt that this will be an excellent part of our society. We will be able to watch any television programs ⎯⎯ *too*
and movies that we desire. We will also be able to watch T.V.   *informal*

in Russia, China, or any other country that we want. This will put video technology into a new place. We will be able to trash our VCR's and rip out our cable wires. Cellular technology is here to stay.

this is an elaboration, not a critique

I couldn't agree more with the writer that "television is about to become one of the most important resources of Americans today." Just imagine coming home from a long day at work and flipping on the television for a little entertainment. You'll be able to call up anything at all, and it will be there in seconds. Or if your a student, and you have to write a report on economics or literature or anything else, and you don't have time to go to the library or you don't have time to go thumbing through your books, then all you have to do is punch some buttons and call up some documentaries or the Discovery channel and you'll have everything before you, right at the proverbial "fingertips."

This will also free television viewers from that abominable label of "couch potato." No one will have time to just sit around all day watching the same old boring stuff. Instead, they'll be punching keys like crazy, calling up all kinds of information and research. <u>They'll be calling up the news from other countries, learning different languages, and just generally using their cellular technology for good things</u>.

too general

good reasoning

There is only one very important critique I can make about the passage. It states that a "world of information will be available to the modern television viewer." If you look at that word, "world," you realize how shallow the idea is. We can't expect the world to be contained in a television screen. This ignores the importance of the outside world, and the experiences that we have outside of our living rooms. The writer of the passage is implying some sort of virtual reality

here is the start of a critique

that will be contained in this cellular technology. She seems to be saying that our entire existence will consist of sitting in front of the television and pressing buttons. Whether she meant to sound that way or not, she should have stressed the fact that cellular technology will only be a part of our lives, not our entire lives in itself.

good transition [In conclusion,] we have a lot to expect out of the cellular technology of the not too distant future. We'll be able to do all kinds of things that we never even dreamt of before. We'll be able to watch television all over the world, and call up movies and programs whenever we want to. But we must also remember that television, no matter how powerful it becomes, can never be allowed to dominate our lives completely.

ANALYSIS OF SAMPLE ESSAY SCORING 3 TO 4

This is a borderline essay for a number of reasons. Although the essayist does make occasional references to the passage, he or she spends too much time on personal tangents. The essayist is more concerned with the general concept of cellular technology than he or she is with the applications for that technology that are implied by the author of the passage. The essayist also fails to make a clear, firm stand regarding the premises of the passage's argument. It merely comments here and there without making definitive assertions. Paragraph order is arbitrary and without direction. Overall, the essay lacks design. It drifts from point to point without a dominating perspective. Key references to the passage are often vague and ambiguous due to a heavy use of vague pronouns such as "it" and "this," and a frequent use of the word "thing."

The first paragraph asserts the essay's overall agreement with the use of cellular technology, but does not even hint at the later misgivings that the essay's writer will portray. The second paragraph states some of the potential advantages and uses of cellular technology. The third paragraph agrees with the passage's assertion that cellular television viewers will be active users, not passive "couch potatoes." The fourth paragraph offers a critique of the argument; it notes that this technology will be abused if it takes the place of all other human experience. The fifth paragraph roughly sums up the essay's main points, offering no additional insight or direction to the essay.

Sample Essay Scoring 1 to 2

here should be an introduction with a clear thesis

First it was celullar telephones. Now its cellullar TV. What will they think of next?

This is where I think the tecknology thing has gotten so out of hand. They keep coming up with new things day in and day out and never once do they think about using that mony for other things. its obvious to me that what we're in for is a bunch of spaced out monkeys sitting in front of the boob tube for the rest of their natural lives.

too informal and vague

very imprecise

They may not be couch potatos any more, but that dont mean their not still lost to the good things in life, like taking walks and being with nature and going on hikes. These are the good things. Watching TV may be good for a little relaxation but its no good for expanding your mind. I dont care what they tell you.

poor spelling

this does not relate to the passage

Its just like this new virtual realty that they keep on making movies about. They want to replace the natural world with a fake one. I cant say I agree with that notion. Thats a bad thing to do. Anyone thats ever been to the beach and then come home to watch TV knows what that theres no comparison no matter whats on the set. It could be your favrite show but you still wish you where down on that beach.

too informal

I also dont buy the idea that it will be a good thing to have lots of TV stations to watch. There's never anything good on TV, not with 50 cable stations, not with 13 network stations, not with nothing. And it might be handy to be able to press a button and get any movie you want, and youll save yourself a trip to the video store, but that dont mean your not missing out, because you coulda been taking a healthy walk on the way to that video store.

run-on sentence

To sum up, all I have to say is that this new technology could do us some good if we use it the right way. But we dont. Thats the plain and simple truth. We dont. Therefor we have to learn the rite way to use it or we're going to lose the one thing that really counts: Mother Erth.

ANALYSIS OF SAMPLE ESSAY SCORING 1 TO 2

This essayist makes very few references to the main passage. He or she barely grasps the general principles of the argument, and rambles continually on matters that are only peripherally related to the passage. There is no organized structure or flow to the essay. It often contradicts itself and makes statements that have nothing to do with its general topic. Spelling, punctuation, and grammar are seriously deficient throughout the essay. The essay is generally incoherent, difficult to follow, and makes very little sense. There are feeble attempts at using illustrations, such as that found in paragraph four, but these are too remote to lend any significant clarity to the essay's overall message.

The GRE Vocabulary Enhancer

You will encounter four types of questions in the Verbal Ability section of the GRE: Sentence Completions; Analogies; Reading Comprehension; and Antonyms. The GRE has one scored Verbal Ability section containing approximately 30 problems, and you will have 30 minutes to solve those problems. There might be an additional unscored Verbal Ability section.

Your success on the GRE Verbal Ability Test begins with one fundamental insight: **these questions have been written and designed to test your vocabulary**. No matter which section you are working in, you will be expected to demonstrate that you have a good command of vocabulary words. Because of this, you should devote as much time as possible to strengthening your vocabulary.

Bust it!

You may be feeling a bit intimidated right now because you may think your vocabulary skills aren't that great. But don't get discouraged. First, remember one of the most important strategies to beating the GRE: Don't be intimidated! Second, there are plenty of ways to build up your vocabulary skills before taking the GRE. The simplest and best way of improving your vocabulary is to READ! It doesn't matter what you read — books, magazines, newspapers — as long as you read!

While you're reading, however, you have to pay attention. You should be asking yourself some questions while reading. These questions include:

Important Information!

- What is the main idea?
- What is the author's purpose?
- How does the author make his or her argument?
- What tone does the author use?

If you keep asking yourself these questions, you'll be surprised how much more you understand while reading. And understanding more will lead to a stronger vocabulary.

Unfortunately, you may not remember all of the words you read. That's why we've provided you with an extremely valuable tool to build your vocabulary: The Vocabulary Enhancer. The Vocabulary Enhancer includes a list of the most frequently appearing vocabulary words on the GRE verbal sections. In addition, the GRE Vocabulary Enhancer has lists of the most important prefixes, roots, and suffixes that you'll need to know to help you recognize more words on the GRE.

What is the Vocabulary Enhancer?

Learning words requires a lot of time and concentration. It's easy to become overwhelmed by looking at the vast number of words that make up the English language. Instead of giving you a list of thousands and thousands of words, we've picked 177 words that are guaranteed to help you on the GRE.

We've given you the words that appear most often on the GRE. Study and know these words and you WILL get a better score.

Important Information!

In addition to learning words, recognizing the **most important prefixes, roots, and suffixes** will give you the skills to understand words that you don't even know. Even though we've provided you with the words that appear the most on the GRE, you will encounter words that you don't know. Fortunately, most English words are based on Greek or Latin words. Studying the meanings of Greek and Latin words will help you "break down" unfamiliar English words so you can understand them. These Greek and Latin words have survived in modern English language as parts of words, such as prefixes, roots, and suffixes. The Vocabulary Enhancer teaches you to recognize these Greek and Latin meanings of prefixes, roots, and suffixes that are used in English so that you can unlock the meaning of unfamiliar words and thereby unlock the answers to the GRE.

How to Use the Vocabulary Enhancer

Important Strategy

The Vocabulary Builder presents a group of words and then presents lists of prefixes, roots, and suffixes. The best way for you to use the Enhancer is to study it one section at a time. Turn to the group of vocabulary words and identify the ones that you don't know or that are defined in unusual ways. Write these words down on index cards with the word on one side and definition on the other. Study these cards and then test yourself by completing the drills that follow the list. Check your answers and review any words that you missed. Then go on to the next group of words.

Once you've gone through the groups of words, turn to the list of prefixes. Review the list and identify the prefixes that are not familiar to you. Write these prefixes down on the front of an index card and their meanings on the back of the card. Study the cards and test yourself by answering the drill questions that follow the list. Check your answers and review any prefixes that you missed. Move on to the roots list and repeat these steps. Then study the suffixes list.

The Vocabulary Enhancer will enable you to attack the GRE Verbal Ability Test with confidence that you never knew you could possess. Like we stated at the beginning of this chapter, to do well on the GRE, you will be expected to demonstrate that you have a good command of vocabulary words. The GRE Vocabulary Enhancer will give you that command of vocabulary. So let's get started!

The GRE Vocabulary Enhancer

The most frequently tested words on the GRE

aberrant – *adj.* – abnormal; straying from the normal or usual path

abstemious – *adj.* – sparing in use of food or drinks

acerbic – 1. – *adj.* – tasting sour or bitter;
              2. – *n.* – harsh in language or temper

alacrity – *n.* – cheerful promptness or speed

allude – *v.* – to refer indirectly to something

allusion – *n.* – an indirect reference (often literary); a hint

altruism – *n.* – unselfish devotion to the welfare of others rather than self

amalgam – *n.* – a mixture or combination (often of metals)

amalgamate – *v.* – to mix, merge, combine

ameliorate – *v.* – to improve or make better

anachronism – *n.* – something out of place in time (e.g., an airplane in 1492)

anomaly – *n.* – an oddity, inconsistency; a deviation from the norm

antipathy – *n.* – a natural dislike or repugnance

apposite – *adj.* – suitable; apt; relevant

arcane – *adj.* – obscure; secret; mysterious

archetype – *n.* – the first model from which others are copied; prototype

arduous – *adj.* – laborious, difficult; strenuous

arid – *adj.* – extremely dry, parched; barren, unimaginative

articulate – *adj.* – clear, distinct; expressed with clarity; skillful with words

articulate – *v.* – to utter clearly and distinctly

ascetic – 1. – *n.* – one who leads a simple life of self-denial
2. – *adj.* – rigorously abstinent

aseptic – *adj.* – germ free

aspersion – *n.* – slanderous statement; a damaging or derogatory criticism

assiduous – *adj.* – carefully attentive; industrious

assuage – *v.* – to relieve; ease; make less severe

astringent – 1. – *n.* – a substance that contracts bodily tissues
2. – *adj.* – causing contraction; tightening; stern, austere

atrophy – *v.* – to waste away, as from lack of use; to wither

attenuate – *v.* – to make thin or slender; to weaken or dilute

autocracy – *n.* – an absolute monarchy; government where one person holds power

autocrat – *n.* – an absolute ruler

baleful – *adj.* – harmful, malign, detrimental

banal – *adj.* – trite; without freshness or originality

beneficent – *adj.* – conferring benefits; kindly; doing good

bilateral – *adj.* – pertaining to or affecting both sides or two sides; having two sides

bombast – *n.* – pompous speech; pretentious words

burgeon – *v.* – to grow or develop quickly

cacophony – *n.* – a harsh, inharmonious collection of sounds; dissonance

cant – *n.* – insincere or hypocritical statements of high ideals; the jargon of a particular group or occupation

caprice – *n.* – a sudden, unpredictable, or whimsical change

catharsis – *n.* – a purging or relieving of the body or soul

chicanery – *n.* – trickery or deception

churlishness – *n.* – crude or surly behavior; behavior of a peasant

circumlocution – *n.* – a roundabout or indirect way of speaking; not to the point

cloture – *n.* – a parliamentary procedure to end debate and begin to vote

cloying – *adj.* – too sugary; too sentimental or flattering

coda – *n.* – in music, a concluding passage

codify – *v.* – to organize laws or rules into a systematic collection (code)

cogent – *adj.* – to the point; clear; convincing in its clarity and presentation

cogitate – *v.* – to think hard; ponder, meditate

cognitive – *adj.* – possessing the power to think or meditate; meditative; capable of perception

cognizant – *adj.* – aware of; perceptive

coherent – *adj.* – sticking together; connected; logical; consistent

cohesion – *n.* – the act or state of sticking together

comeliness – *n.* – beauty; attractiveness in appearance or behavior

commodious – *adj.* – spacious and convenient; roomy

complaisance – *n.* – the quality of being agreeable or eager to please

compliant – *adj.* – complying; obeying; yielding

connotative – *adj.* – containing associated meanings in addition to the primary one

constrain – *v.* – to force, compel; to restrain

contentious – *adj.* – quarrelsome

contiguous – *adj.* – touching; or adjoining and close, but may not be touching

contravene – *v.* – to act contrary to; to oppose or contradict

conundrum – *n.* – a puzzle or riddle

converge – *v.* – to move toward one point (opposite: diverge)

coterie – *n.* – a clique; a group who meet frequently, usually socially

crass – *adj.* – stupid, unrefined; gross; materialistic

debacle – *n.* – disaster; collapse; a rout

debilitate – *v.* – to enfeeble; to wear out

decorous – *adj.* – suitable; proper; seemly

deleterious – *adj.* – harmful; hurtful; noxious

denigrate – *v.* – to defame, to blacken or sully; to belittle

deprecate – *v.* – to express disapproval of; to protest against

deride – *v.* – to laugh at with contempt; to mock

derision – *n.* – the act of mocking; ridicule, mockery

desiccate – *v.* – to dry up

diatribe – *n.* – a bitter or abusive speech

dichotomy – *n.* – a division into two parts

diffident – *adj.* – timid; lacking self-confidence

diffuse – *adj.* – spread out; verbose (wordy); not focused

discourse – *v.* – to converse; to communicate in orderly fashion

discrete – *adj.* – separate; individually distinct; composed of
distinct parts

disingenuous – *adj.* – not frank or candid; deceivingly simple
(opposite: ingenuous)

disinterested – *adj.* – neutral; unbiased (alternate meaning:
uninterested)

disparate – *adj.* – unequal, dissimilar; different

disputatious – *adj.* – argumentative; inclined to disputes

dissemble – *v.* – to pretend; to feign; to conceal by pretense

dissonance – *n.* – musical discord; a mingling of inharmonious
sounds; lack of harmony

dissonant – *adj.* – not in harmony; in disagreement

ebullience – *n.* – an overflowing of high spirits; effervescence

ellipsis – *n.* – omission of words that would make the meaning
clear

elucidate – *v.* – to make clear; to explain

emollient – *adj.* – softening or soothing to the skin; having power
to soften or relax living tissues

encomium – *n.* – high praise

endemic – *adj.* – native to a particular area or people

enervate – *v.* – to weaken; to deprive of nerve or strength

engender – *v.* – to bring about; beget; to bring forth

ephemeral – *adj.* – very short-lived; lasting only a short time

eulogy – *n.* – words of praise, especially for the dead

evanescent – *adj.* – vanishing quickly; dissipating like a vapor

exigent – *adj.* – requiring immediate action; urgent, pressing

extemporize – *v.* – to improvise; to make it up as you go along

extrapolate – *v.* – to estimate the value of something beyond the scale; to infer what is unknown from something known

facetious – *adj.* – not meant to be taken seriously; humorous

feign – *v.* – pretend

gainsay – *v.* – to speak against; to contradict; to deny

garrulous – *adj.* – extremely talkative or wordy

iconoclast – *n.* – one who smashes revered images; an attacker of cherished beliefs

impassive – *adj.* – showing no emotion

imperturbable – *adj.* – calm; not easily excited

impervious – *adj.* – impenetrable; not allowing anything to pass through; unaffected

implacable – *adj.* – unwilling to be pacified or appeased

impugn – *v.* – to attack with words; to question the truthfulness or integrity

inchoate – *adj.* – not yet fully formed; rudimentary

incisive – *adj.* – getting to the heart of things; to the point

incredulous – *adj.* – skeptical

indigenous – *adj.* – native to a region; inborn or innate

inept – *adj.* – incompetent; clumsy

inert – *adj.* – not reacting chemically; inactive

ingenuous – *adj.* – noble; honorable; candid; naive

inherent – *adj.* – part of the essential character; intrinsic

insipid – *adj.* – uninteresting, boring, flat, dull

intractable – *adj.* – stubborn, obstinate; not easily taught or disciplined

intransigent – *adj.* – uncompromising

intrepid – *adj.* – fearless, bold

irascible – *adj.* – prone to anger

laconic – *adj.* – sparing of words; terse, pithy, concise

loquacious – *adj.* – very talkative; garrulous

luminous – *adj.* – emitting light; shining; also enlightened or intelligent

macerate – *v.* – to soften by steeping in a liquid (including softening food by the action of a solvent)

maculate – 1. – *adj.* – spotted, blotched; hence defiled, impure (opposite: immaculate)

2. – *v.* – to stain, spot, defile

magnanimity – *n.* – a quality of nobleness of mind, disdaining meanness or revenge

malevolent – *adj.* – wishing evil (opposite: benevolent)

malign – 1. – *v.* – to speak evil of

2. – *adj.* – having an evil disposition toward others (opposite: benign)

malleable – *adj.* – easy to shape or bend

misanthrope – *n.* – a hater of mankind

obdurate – *adj.* – stubborn

obsequious – *adj.* – servilely attentive; fawning

obviate – *v.* – to make unnecessary

ossify – *v.* – to turn to bone; to harden

palpable – *adj.* – touchable; clear, obvious

panegyric – *n.* – high praise

paradigm – *n.* – model, prototype; pattern

paradox – *n.* – a tenet seemingly contradictory or false, but actually true

parsimonious – *adj.* – very frugal; unwilling to spend

pedantic – *adj.* – overly concerned with minute details, especially in teaching

penurious – *adj.* – stingy, miserly

perfunctory – *adj.* – done in a routine, mechanical way, without interest

petulant – *adj.* – peevish; cranky; rude

placate – *adj.* – to appease or pacify

plethora – *n.* – a superabundance

prevaricate – *v.* – to speak equivocally or evasively, i.e., to lie

pristine – *adj.* – primitive, pure, uncorrupted

propensity – *n.* – an inclination; a natural tendency toward; a liking for

putrefaction – *n.* – a smelly mass that is the decomposition of organic matter

putrefy – *v.* – to decompose; to rot

quiescence – *n.* – state of being at rest or without motion

rancor – *n.* – strong ill will; enmity

recalcitrant – *adj.* – stubbornly rebellious

recondite – *adj.* – hard to understand; concealed; characterized by profound scholarship

redundant – *adj.* – superfluous; exceeding what is needed

sagacious – *adj.* – wise

salubrious – *adj.* – promoting good health

sinuous – *adj.* – full of curves; twisting and turning

specious – *adj.* – plausible, but deceptive; apparently, but not actually, true

spurious – *adj.* – not genuine, false; bogus

squalid – *adj.* – filthy; wretched (from squalor)

subjugate – *v.* – to dominate or enslave

sycophant – *n.* – a flatterer of important people

taciturn – *adj.* – inclined to silence; speaking little; dour, stern

tenuous – *adj.* – thin, slim, delicate; weak

tortuous – *adj.* – full of twists and turns; not straightforward; possibly deceitful

tractable – *adj.* – easily managed (opposite: intractable)

truculent – *adj.* – fierce, savage, cruel

ubiquitous – *adj.* – omnipresent; present everywhere

vacuous – *adj.* – dull, stupid; empty-headed

viscous – *adj.* – thick and sticky (said of fluids)

welter – *n.* – a confused mass; turmoil

Drill 1

<u>DIRECTIONS</u>: Write the word next to its definition.

ABERRANT	ABSTEMIOUS	COGENT
COMPLIANT	CODA	DISSONANCE
ENERVATE	OBVIATE	OSSIFY
PARADIGM		

1. _____ model; example; pattern
2. _____ sparing in eating or drinking
3. _____ obedient; easily managed
4. _____ change or harden into bone
5. _____ abnormal or deviant
6. _____ the concluding section of a musical or literary composition
7. _____ convincing
8. _____ make unnecessary; to get rid of
9. _____ discord; lack of musical agreement
10. _____ to weaken

Drill 2

ATTENUATE   ASSIDUOUS   BANAL
DESICCATE   DIFFIDENCE   EXTEMPORANEOUS
FACETIOUS   INTRANSIGENCE   LACONIC
PREVARICATE

1. _____ to dry up
2. _____ humorous; jocular
3. _____ diligent
4. _____ trite; commonplace
5. _____ unprepared; off the cuff
6. _____ state of stubborn unwillingness to
   compromise
7. _____ to lie
8. _____ make thin; weaken
9. _____ shyness
10. _____ terse; using few words

Drill 3

ASSUAGE   CACOPHONY   DICHOTOMY
DIFFUSION   DISCRETE   EXTRAPOLATION
GAINSAY   INTRACTABLE   PRISTINE
QUIESCENT

1. _____ primitive; unspoiled; having its
   original purity

2. _____ branching into two parts; division into two mutually exclusive groups

3. _____ wordiness; spreading in all directions like a gas

4. _____ projection; conjecture; from what is known to infer what is not known

5. _____ unruly; stubborn; obstinate; not docile

6. _____ ease; lessen (pain)

7. _____ separate and distinct

8. _____ at rest; dormant

9. _____ deny

10. _____ harsh noise

Drill 4

DIRECTIONS: Write the word next to its definition.

ASCETIC	BURGEON	DERISION
DISINTERESTED	DISPARATE	EPHEMERAL
EULOGY	GARRULITY	INGENUOUS
MALLEABLE		

1. _____ capable of being shaped or formed

2. _____ basically different; unrelated

3. _____ to grow quickly; to sprout

4. _____ talkativeness

5. _____ neutral; impartial

6. _____   ridicule
7. _____   short-lived; fleeting
8. _____   naive; young; unsophisticated
9. _____   austere; practicing self-denial
10. _____   praise; often for the dead

Drill 5

DIRECTIONS: Fill in the blanks in the sentences using the words from Vocabulary Drills 1 through 4.

1. The _____ national debt forced the president and Congress finally to take action before the debt grew so large that it overwhelmed us.

2. The school assembly was filled with discord. The fire alarm rang, one band played "Dixie" while another played "The Battle Hymn of the Republic." Dozens of children screamed at each other in several languages while teachers shouted at them to be quiet. It was a moment of pure _____ at P.S. 90.

3. The dispute between the next-door neighbors became so bitter that others on the block urged them to take their disagreement to a _____ arbiter, a third party with no axe to grind, who might help them solve their problem.

4. She was an extremely _____ person. One moment she was going to be a nuclear scientist, the next a fashion model. Even going to lunch was a challenge: she'd change her mind about restaurants a dozen times before finally settling on one.

5. His _____ seemed endless. He just talked and talked and talked and talked and talked and...

6. In the hot, dry desert air, the cut flowers eventually became completely _____. Their fragile beauty was perfectly preserved.

7. She was a Gemini, and there was a real _____ between the two sides of her personality. One side was fun loving and sweet tempered; the other was very hard working and somewhat tense.

8. Jack tried to estimate the height of the house by making a(n) _____ from the height of the garage, which he knew was 15 feet high.

9. He was very _____ in preparing the report. He worked nights and weekends for weeks, checking and double-checking everything.

10. He had a very _____ manner. He constantly kidded around, and it was hard to get him to be serious.

11. At the banquet she was suddenly called upon to make a(n) _____ speech. She was so surprised by the request that all she could say was, "Thanks for everything."

12. The child was so _____ that the teacher could do nothing with him. He was very stubborn and would not cooperate in any way.

13. Her _____ was so great that she never went to parties because she was afraid to meet new people.

14. Steven had a tendency to _____. Even though his father was a shoe salesman, Steve told his classmates stories about his royal ancestry and his weekends spent at luxurious country estates.

15. Looking at the littered beach and garbage-filled water, Joe longed for the _____ beach before the settlers arrived to spoil it.

Prefixes

Prefixes	Meaning	Examples
ab–, a–, abs–	away, without, from	**absent** – away, not present **apathy** – without interest **abstain** – keep from doing, refrain
ad–	to, toward	**adjacent** – next to **address** – to direct towards
ante–	before	**antecedent** – going before in time **anterior** – occurring before
anti–	against	**antidote** – remedy to act against an evil **antibiotic** – substance that fights against bacteria
be–	over, thoroughly	**bemoan** – to mourn over **belabor** – to exert much labor upon
bi–	two	**bisect** – to divide **biennial** – happening every two years
cata–, cat–, cath–	down	**catacombs** – underground passageways **catalogue** – descriptive list **catheter** – tubular medical device
circum–	around	**circumscribe** – to draw a circle around **circumspect** – watchful on all sides
com–	with	**combine** – to join together **communication** – to have dealings with
contra–	against	**contrary** – opposed **contrast** – to stand in opposition
de–	down, from	**decline** – to bend downward **decontrol** – to release from government control

Prefixes	Meaning	Examples
di –	two	**dichotomy** – cutting in two **diarchy** – system of government with two authorities
dis –, di–	apart, away	**discern** – to distinguish as separate **dismiss** – to send away **digress** – to turn aside
epi–, ep –, eph–	upon, among	**epidemic** – happening among many people **epicycle** – circle whose center moves round in the circumference of a greater circle **epaulet** – decoration worn to ornament or protect the shoulder **ephedra** – any of a large genus of desert shrubs
ex –, e –	from, out	**exceed** – go beyond the limit **emit** – to send forth
extra –	outside, beyond	**extraordinary** – beyond or out of the common method **extrasensory** – beyond the senses
hyper –	beyond, over	**hyperactive** – over the normal activity level **hypercritic** – one who is critical beyond measure
hypo –	beneath, lower	**hypodermic** – pertaining to parts beneath the skin **hypocrisy** – to be under a pretense of goodness
in –, il –, im –, ir –	not	**inactive** – not active **illogical** – not logical **imperfect** – not perfect **irreversible** – not reversible
in –, il –, im –, ir –	in, on, into	**instill** – to put in slowly **illation** – action of bringing in **impose** – to lay on **irrupt** – to break in

Prefixes	Meaning	Examples
inter –	among, between	**intercom** – to exchange conversations between people **interlude** – performance given between parts in a play
intra –	within	**intravenous** – within a vein **intramural** – within the walls, as of a town or university
meta –	beyond, over, along with	**metamorphosis** – to change over in form or nature **metatarsus** – part of foot beyond the flat of the foot
mis –	badly, wrongly	**misconstrue** – to interpret wrongly **misappropriate** – to use wrongly
mono –	one	**monogamy** – to be married to one person at a time **monotone** – a single, unvaried tone
multi –	many	**multiple** – of many parts **multitude** – a great number
non –	no, not	**nonsense** – lack of sense **nonentity** – not existing
ob –	against	**obscene** – offensive to modesty **obstruct** – to hinder the passage of
para –, par –	beside	**parallel** – continuously at equal distance apart **parentheses** – sentence or phrase inserted within a passage
per –	through	**persevere** – to maintain an effort **permeate** – to pass through

Prefixes	Meaning	Examples
poly–	many	**polygon** – a plane figure with many sides or angles **polytheism** – belief in the existence of many gods
post–	after	**posterior** – coming after **postpone** – to put off until a future time
pre–	before	**premature** – ready before the proper time **premonition** – a previous warning
pro–	in favor of, forward	**prolific** – bringing forth offspring **project** – throw or cast forward
re–	back, against	**reimburse** – to pay back **retract** – to draw back
semi–	half	**semicircle** – half a circle **semiannual** – half-yearly
sub–	under	**subdue** – to bring under one's power **submarine** – to travel under the surface of the sea
super–	above	**supersonic** – above the speed of sound **superior** – higher in place or position
tele–, tel–	across	**telecast** – to transmit across a distance **telepathy** – communication between mind and mind at a distance
trans–	across	**transpose** – to change the position of two things **transmit** – to send from one person to another
ultra–	beyond	**ultraviolet** – beyond the limit of visibility **ultramarine** – beyond the sea

Prefixes	Meaning	Examples
un–	not	**undeclared** – not declared **unbelievable** – not believable
uni–	one	**unity** – state of oneness **unison** – sounding together
with–	away, against	**withhold** – to hold back **withdraw** – to take away

Drill: Prefixes

DIRECTIONS: Provide a definition for each prefix.

1. pro– _____
2. com– _____
3. epi– _____
4. ob– _____
5. ad– _____

DIRECTIONS: Identify the prefix in each word.

6. efface _____
7. hypothetical _____
8. permeate _____
9. contrast _____
10. inevitable _____

Roots

Root	Meaning	Examples
act, ag	do, act, drive	**activate** – to make active **agile** – having quick motion
alt	high	**altitude** – height **alto** – highest male singing voice
alter, altr	other, change	**alternative** – choice between two things **altruism** – living for the good of others
am, ami	love, friend	**amiable** – worthy of affection **amity** – friendship
anim	mind, spirit	**animated** – spirited **animosity** – violent hatred
annu, enni	year	**annual** – every year **centennial** – every hundred years
aqua	water	**aquarium** – tank for water animals and plants **aquamarine** – semiprecious stone of sea-green color
arch	first, ruler	**archenemy** – chief enemy **archetype** – original pattern from which things are copied
aud, audit	hear	**audible** – capable of being heard **audience** – assembly of hearers **audition** – the power or act of hearing
auto	self	**automatic** – self-acting **autobiography** – a history of a person's life written or told by that person
bell	war	**belligerent** – a party taking part in a war **bellicose** – war-like

Root	Meaning	Examples
ben, bene	good	**benign** – kindly disposition **beneficial** – advantageous
bio	life	**biotic** – relating to life **biology** – the science of life
brev	short	**abbreviate** – make shorter **brevity** – shortness
cad, cas	fall	**cadence** – fall in voice **casualty** – loss caused by death
cap, capit	head	**captain** – the head or chief **decapitate** – to cut off the head
cede, ceed, cess	to go, to yield	**recede** – to move or fall back **proceed** – to move onward **recessive** – tending to go back
cent	hundred	**century** – hundred years **centipede** – insect with a hundred legs
chron	time	**chronology** – science dealing with historical dates **chronicle** – register of events in order of time
cide, cis	to kill, to cut	**homicide** – the act of killing **incision** – a cut
claim, clam	to shout	**acclaim** – to receive with applause **proclamation** – to announce publicly
cogn	to know	**recognize** – to know again **cognition** – awareness
corp	body	**incorporate** – to combine into one body **corpse** – dead body

Root	Meaning	Examples
cred	to trust, to believe	**incredible** – unbelievable **credulous** – too prone to believe
cur, curr, curs	to run	**current** – flowing body of air or water **excursion** – short trip
dem	people	**democracy** – government formed for the people **epidemic** – affecting all people
dic, dict	to say	**dictate** – to read aloud for another to transcribe **verdict** – decision of a jury
doc, doct	to teach	**docile** – easily instructed **indoctrinate** – to instruct
domin	to rule	**dominate** – to rule **dominion** – territory of rule
duc, duct	to lead	**conduct** – act of guiding **induce** – to overcome by persuasion
eu	well, good	**eulogy** – speech or writing in praise **euphony** – pleasantness or smoothness of sound
fac, fact, fect, fic	to do, to make	**facilitate** – to make easier **factory** – location of production **confect** – to put together **fiction** – something invented or imagined
fer	to bear, to carry	**transfer** – to move from one place to another **refer** – to direct to
fin	end, limit	**infinity** – unlimited **finite** – limited in quantity

Root	Meaning	Examples
flex, flect	to bend	**flexible** – easily bent **reflect** – to throw back
fort	luck	**fortunate** – lucky **fortuitous** – happening by chance
fort	strong	**fortify** – strengthen **fortress** – stronghold
frag, fract	break	**fragile** – easily broken **fracture** – break
fug	flee	**fugitive** – fleeing **refugee** – one who flees to a place of safety
gen	class, race	**engender** – to breed **generic** – of a general nature in regard to all members
grad, gress	to go, to step	**regress** – to go back **graduate** – to divide into regular steps
graph	writing	**telegraph** – message sent by telegraph **autograph** – person's own handwriting or signature
ject	to throw	**projectile** – capable of being thrown **reject** – to throw away
leg	law	**legitimate** – lawful **legal** – defined by law
leg, lig, lect	to choose, gather, read	**illegible** – incapable of being read **ligature** – something that binds **election** – the act of choosing
liber	free	**liberal** – favoring freedom of ideals **liberty** – freedom from restraint

Root	Meaning	Examples
log	study, speech	**archaeology** – study of human antiquities **prologue** – address spoken before a performance
luc, lum	light	**translucent** – slightly transparent **illuminate** – to light up
magn	large, great	**magnify** – to make larger **magnificent** – great
mal, male	bad, wrong	**malfunction** – to operate incorrectly **malevolent** – evil
mar	sea	**marine** – pertaining to the sea **submarine** – below the surface of the sea
mater, matr	mother	**maternal** – motherly **matriarch** – government exercised by a mother
mit, miss	to send	**transmit** – to send from one person or place to another **mission** – the act of sending
morph	shape	**metamorphosis** – a changing in shape **anthropomorphic** – having a human shape
mut	change	**mutable** – subject to change **mutate** – to change or alter
nat	born	**innate** – inborn **native** – a person born in a particular place
neg	deny	**negative** – expressing denial **renege** – to deny
nom	name	**nominate** – to put forward a name **nomenclature** – process of naming

Root	Meaning	Examples
nov	new	**novel** – new **renovate** – to make as good as new
omni	all	**omnipotent** – all powerful **omnipresent** – all present
oper	to work	**operate** – to work on something **cooperate** – to work with others
pass, path	to feel	**passionate** – moved by strong emotion **pathetic** – affecting the tender emotions
pater, patr	father	**paternal** – fatherly **patriarch** – government exercised by a father
ped, pod	foot	**pedestrian** – one who travels on foot **podiatrist** – foot doctor
pel, puls	to drive, to push	**impel** – to drive forward **compulsion** – irresistible force
phil	love	**philharmonic** – loving harmony or music **philanthropist** – one who loves and seeks to do good for others
port	carry	**export** – to carry out of the country **portable** – able to be carried
psych	mind	**psychology** – study of the mind **psychiatrist** – specialist in mental disorders
quer, ques, quir, quis	to ask	**querist** – one who inquires **question** – that which is asked **inquire** – to ask about **inquisitive** – inclined to ask questions
rid, ris	to laugh	**ridiculous** – laughable **derision** – mockery

Root	Meaning	Examples
rupt	to break	**interrupt** – to break in upon **erupt** – to break through
sci	to know	**science** – systematic knowledge of physical or natural phenomena **conscious** – having inward knowledge
scrib, script	to write	**transcribe** – to write over again **script** – text of words
sent, sens	to feel, to think	**sentimental** – to feel great emotion **sensitive** – easily affected by changes
sequ, secut	to follow	**sequence** – connected series **consecutive** – following one another in unbroken order
solv, solu, solut	to loosen	**dissolve** – to break up **absolute** – without restraint
spect	to look at	**spectator** – one who watches **inspect** – to look at closely
spir	to breathe	**inspire** – to breathe in **respiration** – process of breathing
string, strict	to bind	**stringent** – binding strongly **restrict** – to restrain within bounds
stru, struct	to build	**strut** – a structural piece designed to resist pressure **construct** – to build
tang, ting, tact, tig	to touch	**tangent** – touching, but not intersecting **contact** – touching **contiguous** – to touch along a boundary
ten, tent, tain	to hold	**tenure** – holding of office **contain** – to hold

Root	Meaning	Examples
term	to end	**terminate** – to end **terminal** – having an end
terr	earth	**terrain** – tract of land **terrestrial** – existing on earth
therm	heat	**thermal** – pertaining to heat **thermometer** – instrument for measuring temperature
tort, tors	to twist	**contortionist** – one who twists violently **torsion** – act of turning or twisting
tract	to pull, to draw	**attract** – to draw toward **distract** – to draw away
vac	empty	**vacant** – empty **evacuate** – to empty out
ven, vent	to come	**intervene** – to come between **prevent** – to stop from coming
ver	true	**verify** – to prove to be true **veracious** – truthful
verb	word	**verbose** – use of excess words **verbatim** – word for word
vid, vis	to see	**video** – picture phase of television **vision** – act of seeing external objects
vinc, vict, vang	to conquer	**invincible** – unconquerable **victory** – defeat of enemy **vanguard** – troops moving at the head of an army
vit, viv	life	**vital** – necessary to life **vivacious** – lively

Root	Meaning	Examples
voc	to call	**vocation** – a summons to a course of action **vocal** – uttered by voice
vol	to wish, to will	**involuntary** – outside the control of will **volition** – the act of willing or choosing

Drill: Roots

DIRECTIONS: Provide a definition for each root.

1. cede _____

2. fact _____

3. path _____

4. ject _____

5. ver _____

DIRECTIONS: Identify the root in each word.

6. acclaim _____

7. verbatim _____

8. benefactor _____

9. relegate _____

10. tension _____

Suffixes

Suffixes	Meaning	Examples
–able, –ble	capable of	**believable** – capable of being believed **legible** – capable of being read
–acious, –icious, –ous	full of	**vivacious** – full of life **delicious** – full of pleasurable smell or taste **wondrous** – full of wonder
–ant, –ent	full of	**expectant** – full of expectation **eloquent** – full of eloquence
–ary	connected with	**disciplinary** – relating to a field of study **honorary** – for the sake of honor
–ate	to make	**ventilate** – to make public **consecrate** – to dedicate
–fy	to make	**magnify** – to make larger **testify** – to make witness
–ile	pertaining to, capable of	**docile** – capable of being managed easily **infantile** – pertaining to infancy
–ism	belief, condition	**Mormonism** – belief in the teachings of the Book of Mormon **idiotism** – utterly foolish conduct
–ist	one who	**artist** – one who creates art **pianist** – one who plays the piano
–ose	full of	**verbose** – full of words **grandiose** – striking, imposing
–osis	condition	**neurosis** – nervous condition **psychosis** – psychological condition
–tude	state	**magnitude** – state of greatness **multitude** – state of quantity

Drill: Suffixes

DIRECTIONS: Provide a definition for each suffix.

1. –ant, –ent _____

2. –tude _____

3. –ile _____

4. –fy _____

5. –ary _____

DIRECTIONS: Identify the suffix in each word.

6. audacious _____

7. expedient _____

8. gullible _____

9. grandiose _____

10. antagonism _____

VOCABULARY ENHANCER ANSWER KEY

Drill: 1

1. paradigm
2. abstemious
3. compliant
4. ossify
5. aberrant
6. coda
7. cogent
8. obviate
9. dissonance
10. enervate

Drill: 2

1. desiccate
2. facetious
3. assiduous
4. banal
5. extemporaneous
6. intransigence
7. prevaricate
8. attenuate
9. diffidence
10. laconic

Drill: 3

1. pristine
2. dichotomy
3. diffusion
4. extrapolation
5. intractable
6. assuage
7. discrete
8. quiescent
9. gainsay
10. cacophony

Drill: 4

1. malleable
2. disparate
3. burgeon
4. garrulity
5. disinterested
6. derision
7. ephemeral
8. ingenuous
9. ascetic
10. eulogy

Drill: 5

1. burgeoning
2. cacophony
3. disinterested
4. ephemeral
5. garrulity
6. desiccated
7. dichotomy
8. extrapolation
9. assiduous
10. facetious
11. extemporaneous
12. intractable
13. diffidence
14. prevaricate
15. pristine

Drill: Prefixes	Drill: Roots	Drill: Suffixes
1. forward	1. to go, to yield	1. full of
2. with	2. to do, to make	2. state
3. upon, among	3. to feel	3. pertaining to, capable of
4. against	4. to throw	4. to make
5. to, toward	5. true	5. connected with
6. e–	6. claim	6. –acious
7. hypo–	7. verb	7. –ent
8. per–	8. ben(e)	8. –ible
9. contra–	9. leg	9. –ose
10. in–	10. ten	10. –ism

Chapter

Attacking Sentence Completion Questions

6

Regardless of the part of the GRE Verbal Ability Test you are working on, all the problem-solving techniques you'll use can be divided into two main categories: skills and strategies. Using these skills and strategies, in addition to the important strategies to beat the GRE that you learned in the beginning of this book, you will successfully attack the Sentence Completion questions and attain a higher score on your GRE Verbal Ability Test.

Bust it!

One of the best ways you can improve your GRE score is to improve your skills of attacking the Sentence Completion questions. The Sentence Completion questions are one of the few places where you can learn a body of knowledge that will help you do better on the GRE. The Quantitative Ability section is another, but we'll discuss those questions later in their respective chapters.

"What body of knowledge can help me on the Sentence Completion questions?" Well, the body of knowledge that the GRE is testing in Sentence Completion questions are the rules of grammar, punctuation, sentence structure, and usage. The best way to improve your score using Sentence Completion questions is to determine your weak areas of grammar and study those areas. You can determine your weak areas by answering the drill questions contained in this section or by taking the practice test we've presented in Chapter 3. Once you've answered the questions, check them against the answer keys, making sure to identify the types of questions you answered incorrectly. Then go and study those areas.

It takes skills and strategies to beat the GRE. We've just discussed the skills you'll need to do well on the Sentence Completion questions, now let's discuss the strategies. In this chapter, you will learn the following strategies to successfully attack the Sentence Completion questions on the GRE:

Bust it!

- **Learning the two types of Sentence Completion questions**

- **Learning the skill of recognizing context clues**

- **Learning how to identify and apply word values**

- **Learning the strategy involved in using the logical structure of Sentence Completion questions**

- **Learning how to use prefixes, roots, and suffixes to answer Sentence Completion questions.**

Now let's get started....

About The Directions

The directions for Sentence Completion questions are relatively straightforward.

> **DIRECTIONS**: Each sentence below has one or two blanks, each blank indicating that something has been omitted. Beneath the sentence are five lettered words or sets of words. Choose the word or set of words that BEST fits the meaning of the sentence as a whole.
>
> Example:
>
> Although the critics found the book _____, many of the readers found it rather _____.
>
> (A) obnoxious . . . perfect
> (B) spectacular . . . interesting
> (C) boring . . . intriguing
> (D) comical . . . persuasive
> (E) popular . . . rare
>
>

About the Questions

You will encounter two main types of questions in the Sentence Completion section of the GRE: One-word completions and Two-word completions.

Important Information!

Question Type 1: ONE-WORD COMPLETIONS

One-Word Completions will require you to fill in one blank. The one-word completion can appear as a Level I (easy), II (average), or III (difficult) question depending on the difficulty of the vocabulary included.

Question Type 2: TWO-WORD COMPLETIONS

Important Information!

Two-Word Completions will require you to fill in two blanks. The correct choice will not only match the sentence in terms of vocabulary, but also on the relationship between the words and between the words and the sentence.

The remainder of this review will provide explicit details on what you will encounter when dealing with Sentence Completion questions, in addition to strategies for correctly completing these sentences.

Answering Sentence Completion Questions

Follow these steps as you attempt to answer each question.

STEP 1 | **Identifying context clues is one of the most successful ways for you to locate correct answers in Sentence Completions. Practicing constantly in this area will help you strengthen one of your main strategies in this type of verbal problem.**

The Sentence Completion question below is an example of a one-word sentence completion question.

Bust it!

Pamela played her championship chess game _____ , avoiding all traps and making no mistakes.

(A)   **hurriedly**   (D)   **imaginatively**
(B)   **flawlessly**   (E)   **aggressively**
(C)   **prodigally**

The **phrase** "avoiding all traps and making no mistakes" is your **context clue**. Notice that the phrase both follows *and* modifies the word in question. Since you know that Sentence Completions are exercises seeking to test your vocabulary knowledge, attack these problems accordingly. For example, ask yourself what word means "avoiding all traps and making no mistakes." In so doing, you discover the answer "flawlessly" (B), which means perfectly or without mistakes. If Pamela played "hurriedly" (A), she might well make mistakes.

An important tip is to look at all of the answer choices in terms of difficulty. Difficult words are seldom the correct answer when the other choices are simpler words. The vice-versa is also true. These difficult words are often magnet words placed by the GRE writers to draw incorrect answers. Therefore, "prodigally" (C) stands out as a suspicious word. This could be a magnet word. However, before you eliminate it, ask yourself whether you know its meaning. If so, does it surpass "flawlessly" (B) in defining the context clue, "making no mistakes"? It does not.

"Imaginatively" (D) is a tempting answer, since one might associate a perfect game of chess as one played imaginatively; however, there is no connection between the imagination and the absence of mistakes. "Aggressively" (E) playing a game may, in fact, cause you to make mistakes. Thus, choice (B) "flawlessly," is the correct answer.

Here is an example of a two-word Sentence Completion question. Try to determine the context clue.

Although most people believe the boomerang is the product of a _____ design, that belief is deceptive; in fact, the boomerang is a _____ example of the laws of aerodynamics.

Bust it!

(A)   foreign . . . modern
(B)   symbolic . . . complex
(C)   practical . . . scientific
(D)   primitive . . . sophisticated
(E)   faulty . . . invalid

The most important **context clue** in this sentence is the opening word "although," which indicates that some kind of antonym relationship is present in the sentence. It tells us there is a reversal in meaning. Therefore, be on the lookout for words which will form an opposite relationship. The phrase "that belief is deceptive" makes certain the idea that there will be an opposite meaning between the missing words. "Primitive . . . sophisticated" (D) is the best answer, since the two are exact opposites. "Primitive" means crude and elementary, whereas "sophisticated" means refined and advanced. "Foreign . . . modern" (A) and "symbolic . . . complex" (B) have no real opposite relationship. Also, "complex" is a magnet word that sounds right in the context of scientific laws, but "symbolic" is not its counterpart. "Practical . . . scientific" (C) and "faulty . . . invalid" (E) are rejectable because they are generally synonymous pairs.

The following is another one-word example, only a little harder. See if you can identify the context clue.

The weekly program on public radio is the most _____ means of educating the public about pollution.

(A)	proficient	(D)	capable	
(B)	effusive	(E)	competent	
(C)	effectual			

The **context clue** in this sentence is "means of educating the public about pollution." "Effectual" (C) is the correct answer. "Effectual" means having the power to produce the exact effect or result. "Proficient" (A) is not correct as it implies competency above the average—radio programs are not described in this manner. "Effusive" (B) does not fit the sense of the sentence. Both "capable" (D) and "competent" (E) are incorrect because they refer to people, not things.

Bust it!

> **STEP 2** Since the Verbal Ability Test of the GRE is fundamentally a vocabulary test, it must resort to principles and techniques necessary for testing your vocabulary. Therefore, certain dynamics like antonyms (word opposites) and synonyms (word similarities) become very useful in setting up a question or word problem.

This idea can be taken one step further by using word values.

Another type of technique that utilizes the tension of opposites and the concurrence of similarities is **word values**. Word values begin with the recognition that most pivotal words in a GRE Sentence Completion can be assigned a positive or negative value. Marking a "+" or "−" next to choices may help you eliminate inappropriate choices. In turn, you will be able to more quickly identify possible correct answers. Using your scrap paper is very helpful while using this technique. Scrap paper will allow you to keep track, remember, and eliminate answer choices by their word values.

Dealing with Positive Value Words

Look!

Important Strategy

Positive value words are usually easy to recognize. They usually convey a meaning which can be equated with gain, advantage, liveliness, intelligence, virtue, positive emotions, conditions, or actions.

The ability to recognize positive and negative word values, however, will not bring you very far if you do not understand how to apply it to your advantage in Sentence Completions. Below you will find examples of how to do this, first with a study of positive value Sentence Completions, then with a study of negative value Sentence Completions.

The following is an example one-word completion question.

An expert skateboarder, Tom is truly _____ ; he smoothly blends timing with balance.

(A) coordinated   (D) supportive
(B) erudite   (E) casual
(C) a novice

As you know, the context clue is the clause after the word in question, which acts as a modifier. Naturally, anyone who "smoothly blends" is creating a *positive* situation. Look for the positive answer.

An expert skateboarder, Tom is truly __+__ ; *he smoothly blends timing with balance.*

+(A)   coordinated   +(D)   supportive

+(B)   erudite   –(E)   casual

–(C)   a novice

"Coordinated" (A), a positive value word that means ordering two or more things, fits the sentence perfectly. "Erudite" (B) is positive, but it is too difficult to be a Level I answer. A "novice" (C) in this context is negative. "Supportive" (D) and "casual" (E) don't fulfill the definition of the context clue, and "casual" is negative, implying a lack of attention. Notice that eliminating negatives *immediately reduces the number of options from which you have to choose.* This raises the odds of selecting the correct answer. (One of the analytic skills you should develop for the GRE is being able to see the hidden vocabulary question in any exercise.)

Bust it!

Here's a two-word completion question. Use it to practice assigning and using word values to answer the question.

Despite their supposedly primitive lifestyle, Australian aborigines developed the boomerang, a ____ and ____ hunting tool that maximizes gain with minimum effort.

(A)   ponderous . . . expensive

(B)   clean . . . dynamic

(C)   dangerous . . . formidable

(D)   sophisticated . . . efficient

(E)   useful . . . attractive

In this case, the context clues begin and end the sentence (in italics below).

Despite their supposedly primitive lifestyle, Australian aborigines developed the boomerang, a __+__ and __+__ hunting *tool that maximizes gain with minimum effort.*

−(A)   ponderous . . . expensive
+(B)   clean . . . dynamic
−(C)   dangerous . . . formidable
+(D)   sophisticated . . . efficient
+(E)   useful . . . attractive

The first context clue (*despite*) helps you determine that this exercise entails an antonym relationship with the word "primitive", which means simple or crude. The second context clue offers a definition of the missing words. Since the meaning of primitive in this context is a negative word value, you can be fairly confident that the answer will be a pair of positive word values. "Sophisticated . . . efficient" (D) is positive *and* it satisfies the definition of the latter context clue. This is the best answer. "Ponderous . . . expensive" (A) is not correct. "Clean . . . dynamic" (B) is positive, but does not meet the definition of the latter context clue. "Dangerous . . . formidable" (C) is negative. "Useful . . . attractive" (E) is positive, but it does not work with the latter context clue.

Bust it!

Here is another example of a one-word completion:

When a physician describes an illness to a colleague, he must speak an _____ language, using professional terms and concepts understood mostly by members of his profession.

(A)   extrinsic   (D)   esoteric
(B)   inordinate   (E)   abbreviated
(C)   ambulatory

Looking at this question, we can see an important context clue. This appears in italics on the following page.

When a physician describes an illness to a colleague, he must speak an __+__ language, *using professional terms and concepts understood mostly by members of his profession.*

+(A)   extrinsic   +(D)   esoteric
–(B)   inordinate   –(E)   abbreviated
+(C)   ambulatory

Bust it!

This clue gives us a definition of the missing word. Begin by eliminating the two obvious negatives, "inordinate" (B) and "abbreviated" (E). This leaves us with three positives. At first, you may be intimidated by the level of vocabulary, but don't be. By using the context clues and the word values you should be able to eliminate at least a couple of the harder words without worrying too much about them.

Note that "esoteric" (D) is the best answer, since it is an adjective that means *inside* or *part of a group.* "Ambulatory" (C) is positive, but it is a trap. It seems like an easy association with the world of medicine. But remember, easy word associations can be magnet words placed there to trap you. *Extrinsic* (A) is positive, but it means "outside of," which would not satisfy the logic of the sentence.

Dealing with Negative Value Words

Here are examples of how to work with negative value Sentence Completion problems. The first example is a two-word completion:

Important Strategy

Although Steve loves to socialize, his fellow students find him _____ and strive to _____ his company.

(A)   generous . . . enjoy

(B)   boring . . . evade

(C)   altruistic . . . accept

(D)   sinister . . . delay

(E)   weak . . . limit

The context clue (in italics) tells us that a reversal is being set up between what Steve thinks and what his fellow students think.

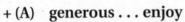

Although Steve loves to socialize, his fellow students find him __⁻__ and strive to __⁻__ his company.

Bust it!

+ (A)   generous . . . enjoy

– (B)   boring . . . evade

+ (C)   altruistic . . . accept

– (D)   sinister . . . delay

– (E)   weak . . . limit

"Boring . . . evade" (B) is the best answer. The words appearing in Level 1 questions are not overly difficult, and they satisfy the logic of the sentence. "Generous . . . enjoy" (A) is positive. "Altruistic . . . accept" (C) is not only positive but contains a very difficult word (altruistic), and it would be unlikely that this would be a Level I answer. The same is true of "sinister . . . delay" (D), even though it is negative. "Weak . . . limit" (E) does not make sense in the context of the sentence.

This next example is a little harder:

Because they reject _____ , conscientious objectors are given jobs in community work as a substitute for participation in the armed services.

(A)	labor	(D)	dictatorships
(B)	belligerence	(E)	poverty
(C)	peace		

Essentially, this example is a synonym exercise. The description of conscientious objectors (in italics on the next page) acts as a strong context clue. Conscientious objectors avoid ("reject") militancy.

Because they reject _____ , conscientious objectors *are given jobs in community work as a substitute for participation in the armed services.*

+ (A)	labor	–(D)	dictatorships
– (B)	belligerence	–(E)	poverty
+ (C)	peace		

Since we are looking for a negative word value (something to do with militancy), "labor" (A) is incorrect since it is positive. "Belligerence" (B) fits perfectly, as this is a negative value word having to do with war. Not only is "peace" (C) a positive value word, it is hardly something to be rejected by conscientious objectors. "Dictatorships" (D), although a negative word value, has no logical place in the context of this sentence. The same is true of "poverty" (E).

Here is a harder two-word completion:

Dictators understand well how to centralize power, and that is why they combine a(n) _____ political process with military _____ .

Bust it!

(A)   foreign . . . victory
(B)   electoral . . . escalation
(C)   agrarian . . . strategies
(D)   domestic . . . decreases
(E)   totalitarian . . . coercion

"Totalitarian . . . coercion" (E) is the best answer. These are difficult words, and both have to do with techniques useful in the centralizing of power by a dictator. "Totalitarian" means centralized, and "coercion" means force.

> *Dictators* understand well how to *centralize power,* and that is why they combine a(n) __–__ political process with military __–__.

> + (A)   foreign . . . victory
> + (B)   electoral . . . escalation
> + (C)   agrarian . . . strategies
> + (D)   domestic . . . decreases
> – (E)   totalitarian . . . coercion

Bust it!

"Foreign . . . victory" (A) are not only easy words, they do not appear to be strictly negative. Remember that easy word answers should be suspect in Level III questions. "Agrarian . . . strategies" (C) is positive. "Domestic . . . decreases" (D) is a positive combination. Since you are searching for two negatives, this answer is incorrect. There will be more about this in the next section.

Dealing with Mixed Value Words

In examples with two-word answers so far, you have searched for answers composed with identical word values, such as negative/negative and positive/positive. However, every GRE Sentence Completion section will have exercises in which two-word answers are found in combinations. On the following page you will find examples of how to work with these.

Despite a healthy and growing environmental _____ in America, there are many people who prefer to remain _____.

(A)   awareness . . . ignorant
(B)   movement . . . enlightened
(C)   bankruptcy . . . wealthy
(D)   crisis . . . unencumbered
(E)   industry . . . satisfied

The context clue *despite* sets up the predictable antonym warning. In this case, the sentence seems to call for a positive and then a negative value word answer.

Despite a healthy and growing environmental __+__ in America, there are many people who prefer to remain __–__.

+/– (A) awareness . . . ignorant
+/+ (B) movement . . . enlightened
–/+ (C) bankruptcy . . . wealthy
–/+ (D) crisis . . . unencumbered
+/+ (E) industry . . . satisfied

Bust it!

"Awareness . . . ignorant" (A) is the best answer. These are logical antonyms, and they fit the meaning of the sentence. Notice that the order of the missing words is positive, *then* negative. This should help you eliminate (C) and (D) immediately, as they are a reversal of the correct order. Furthermore, "industry . . . satisfied" (E) and "movement . . . enlightened" (B) are both identical values, and so are eliminated. Practice these techniques until you confidently can recognize word values *and* the order in which they appear in a sentence.

Here's another example:

Prone to creating characters of _____ quality, novelist Ed Abbey cannot be accused of writing _____ stories.

    (A)   measly . . . drab
    (B)   romantic . . . imaginative
    (C)   mythic . . . mundane
    (D)   sinister . . . complete
    (E)   two-dimensional . . . flat

The best answer is "mythic . . . mundane" (C). "Measly . . . drab" (A) does not make sense when you consider the context clue *cannot,* which suggests the possibility of antonyms. The same is true for "sinister . . . complete" (D), "romantic . . . imaginative" (B), and "two-dimensional . . . flat" (E).

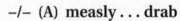

Prone to creating characters of _____ quality, novelist Ed Abbey *cannot* be accused of writing _____ stories.

    –/– (A) measly . . . drab
    +/+ (B) romantic . . . imaginative
    +/– (C) mythic . . . mundane
    –/+ (D) sinister . . . complete
    –/– (E) two-dimensional . . . flat

Bust it!

Notice that the value combinations help you determine where to search for the correct answer. You can easily eliminate three of the five answer choices and have to make your choice from only two.

Here is a harder example for you to practice:

Reminding his students that planning ahead would protect them from _____, Mr. McKenna proved to be a principal who understood the virtues of _____.

(A)   exigency . . . foresight
(B)   grades . . . examinations
(C)   poverty . . . promotion
(D)   deprivation . . . abstinence
(E)   turbulence . . . amelioration

The best answer is "exigency . . . foresight" (A). The first context clue tells us that we are looking for a negative value word. The second context clue tells us the missing word is most likely positive. Furthermore, "exigency . . . foresight" is a well-suited antonym combination. "Exigencies" are emergencies, and "foresight" helps to lessen their severity, if not their occurrence.

Reminding his students that planning ahead would *protect them* **from __−__, Mr. McKenna proved to be a principal who understood the** *virtues* **of __+__ .**

Bust it!

−/+ (A) exigency . . . foresight
0/0 (B) grades . . . examinations
−/+ (C) poverty . . . promotion
−/− (D) deprivation . . . abstinence
−/+ (E) turbulence . . . amelioration

"Grades . . . examinations" (B) are a trap, since they imply school matters. Furthermore, they are neutrals. There will be more on neutrals in the next section. "Poverty . . . promotion" (C) is an easy word answer and should be immediately suspect, especially if there are no difficult words in the sentence completion itself. Also, this answer does not satisfy the logic of the sentence. "Turbulence . . . amelioration" (E) is a negative/positive combination, but it does not make sense in this sentence. Even if you are forced to guess between this answer and "exigency . . . foresight" (A), you have narrowed the field to two. These are excellent odds for success.

Dealing with Neutral Value Words

Important Strategy

Bust it!

There is another category of word values that will help you determine the correct answer in a Sentence Completion problem. These are **neutral word values**. Neutral words are words that convey neither loss nor gain, advantage nor disadvantage, etc. Consider our previous example:

Reminding his students that planning ahead would *protect them* from ___⁻___ , Mr. McKenna proved to be a principal who understood the *virtues* of ___+___ .

–/+ (A) exigency . . . foresight
0/0 (B) grades . . . examinations
–/+ (C) poverty . . . promotion
–/– (D) deprivation . . . abstinence
–/+ (E) turbulence . . . amelioration

Notice that "grades . . . examinations" (B) is rated as neutral. In fact, in this case, both words are considered of neutral value. This is because neither word conveys a usable value. Grades in and of themselves are not valued until a number is assigned. Examinations are not significant until a passing or failing value is implied or applied.

Neutral word values are significant because they are *never* the correct answer. Therefore, when you identify a neutral word or combination of words, you may eliminate that choice from your selection. **You may eliminate a double-word answer even if only one of the words is obviously neutral.**

Neutral words are rare, and you should be careful to measure their value before you make a choice. Here is another example from an exercise seen previously (Note: The answer choices have been altered.):

> *Dictators* understand well how *to centralize power,* and that is why they combine a(n) _[−]_ political process with military _[−]_.

0/+ (A) foreign . . . victory
0/+ (B) electoral . . . escalation
0/+ (C) agrarian . . . strategies
0/0 (D) current . . . jobs
−/− (E) totalitarian . . . coercion

Bust it!

Here, "current . . . jobs" (D) is an obvious neutral word combination, conveying no positive or negative values. You may eliminate this choice immediately. There is no fixed list of words that may be considered neutral. Rather, you should determine *from the context* of a word problem whether you believe a word or word combination is of a neutral value. This ability will come with practice and a larger vocabulary. As before, the correct answer remains "totalitarian . . . coercion" (E).

STEP 3 | Another way to determine the correct answer is by using etymology. Etymology is the study of the anatomy of words. The most important components of etymology on the GRE are prefixes and roots. GRE vocabulary is derived almost exclusively from the etymology of Greek and Latin word origins, and that is where you should concentrate your study.

In this section, you will learn how to apply your knowledge of prefixes and roots to Sentence Completion problems.

Etymological skills will work well in conjunction with other techniques you have learned, including positive/negative word values. Furthermore, the technique of "scrolling" will help you understand how to expand your knowledge of etymology.

Important Information!

Scrolling is a process whereby you inspect a list of known related words, roots, or prefixes to help you discover the meaning of a word. As an example, consider the common GRE word "apathy." The prefix of apathy is *a.* This means "without." To scroll this prefix, think of any other words that may begin with this prefix, such as *a*moral, *a*typical, or *a*symmetrical. In each case, the meaning of the word is preceded by the meaning "without."

At this point, you know that "apathy" means without something. Now try to scroll the root, *path,* which comes from the Greek word "pathos." Words like pathetic, sympathy, antipathy, and empathy may come to mind. These words all have to do with feeling or sensing. In fact, that is what "pathos" means: feeling. So apathy means without feeling.

With this process you can often determine the fundamental meaning of a word or part of a word, and this may give you enough evidence with which to choose a correct answer. Consider the following familiar Level I (easy) example:

An expert skateboarder, Tom is truly _____⁺___; he smoothly blends timing with balance.

+ (A) coordinated   + (D) supportive

+ (B) erudite   – (E) casual

– (C) a novice

Bust it!

As you should remember, the correct answer is "coordinated" (A). The prefix of this word is *co–*, meaning together, and the root is *order*. Something that is "ordered together" fits the context clue perfectly. Combining that with the knowledge that you are looking for a positive value word certifies "coordinated" (A) as the correct answer.

Here is another familiar example:

Because they reject __−__ , conscientious objectors *are given jobs in community work as a substitute for participation in the armed services.*

+ (A) labor   – (D) dictatorships
– (B) belligerence   – (E) poverty
+ (C) peace

Bust it!

From working with this example previously, you know that the correct answer is "belligerence" (B). The root of this word is *bellum*, Latin for war. Belligerence is an inclination toward war. Other words that may be scrolled from this are bellicose, belligerent, and antebellum, all of which have to do with war. Study your roots and prefixes carefully. A casual knowledge is not good enough. Another root, *bellis,* might be confused with *bellum. Bellis* means beauty. Is it logical that a conscientious objector would reject beauty? Know when to use which root and prefix. This ability will come with study and practice.

Here is yet another familiar example:

When a physician describes an illness to a colleague, he must speak an __+__ language, *using professional terms and concepts understood mostly by members of his profession.*

+ (A) extrinsic   + (D) esoteric

– (B) inordinate   – (E) abbreviated

+ (C) ambulatory

Bust it!

Recalling this example, you will remember that the context clue defines the missing word as one meaning language that involves a special group of people, i.e., "inside information." The correct answer is "esoteric" (D). *Eso–* is a prefix that means "inside." The prefix of "extrinsic" (A) is *ex–,* which means "out", the opposite of the meaning you seek. "Inordinate" (B) means "not ordered." In this case, the prefix *in–* means "not." This is Level III, so beware of easy assumptions! The root of "ambulatory" (C) is *ambulare,* which means "to walk." "Abbreviated" (E) breaks down to *ab,* meaning *"to"*; and *brevis,* Latin for brief or short.

In many Level III words you may not be able to scroll or break down a word completely. However, often, as in the example above, a partial knowledge of the etymology may be enough to find the correct answer.

Now, take what you have learned and apply it to the questions appearing in the following drill. If you are unsure of an answer, refer back to the review material for help.

Points to Remember

On Target!

✔   *Most GRE Sentence Completion questions contain "magnet words," answer choices that look good but are designed to draw the student* away from the correct answer. Magnet words can effectively mislead you, so always watch for them.

✔   Deductive reasoning is a tool that will be of constant assistance to you as you work through Sentence Completion questions. To deduce means to derive a truth (or answer) through a reasoning process.

✔   Sentence Completion questions are puzzles, and they are put together with a certain amount of predictability. One such predictable characteristic is the structure of a Sentence Completion question. Since there are always five possible answers from which to choose, you must learn to see which answers are easy to eliminate first. Use the process of elimination.

On Target!

✔   Most Sentence Completion questions are designed around a "three-two" structure. This means that there are three easier answers to eliminate before you have to make the final decision between the remaining two.

✔   Learn how to identify the context clues of Sentence Completion questions and use these clues to point you to the correct answer choice.

✔   Word values are an invaluable tool for attacking Sentence Completion questions. Learn how to identify and apply positive, negative, mixed, and neutral word values.

On Target!

✔   *Remember that any choice with a neutral word value is to be eliminated. If a two-word question presents an answer choice with one or two neutral values, immediately eliminate that choice.*

✔   *Use word prefixes, roots, and suffixes to find the meanings of words you do not know.*

Now, take what you have learned and apply it to the questions appearing in the following drill. If you are unsure of an answer, refer back to the review material for help.

Drill: Sentence Completion

DIRECTIONS: Each sentence below has one or two blanks, each blank indicating that something has been omitted. Beneath the sentence are five lettered words or sets of words. Choose the word or set of words that BEST fits the meaning of the sentence as a whole.

Example:
Although the critics found the book _____, many of the readers found it rather _____.

(A) obnoxious . . . perfect
(B) spectacular . . . interesting
(C) boring . . . intriguing
(D) comical . . . persuasive
(E) popular . . . rare

1. A careful reading of the text is _____ his argument. On the one hand, scarcely anything can be adduced in support of it, and on the other hand, a great deal can be produced in disproof.

(A) supportive of   (D) neutral toward
(B) unrewarding toward   (E) indicative of
(C) fatal to

2. Their mutual _____ seemed clear, but in fact they had a long-standing _____ toward each other.

(A) admiration...fondness
(B) dislike...hatred
(C) aptitude...antipathy
(D) attraction...animosity
(E) enchantment...affection

3. In recent years, the notion that Columbus discovered America has been caught in the _____ between those who believe this to be an example of white racism and those who _____ the Norsemen as discoverers.

(A) symposium...question
(B) discussion...substitute
(C) interplay...support
(D) crossfire...advocate
(E) paradox...prefer

4. The strength of a perceptive biography lies not just in its factual accuracy or in the biographer's prose style, but in his skill in creating the moments that reveal the most _____ psychological truths—the motivations, transformations, and points of conflict—in the life of the subject.

(A) appealing   (D) trivial
(B) amazing   (E) fascinating
(C) profound

5. Dryden has no equal in prayers, objurations, politic addresses, and speeches of defiance; he wears the robes that he has borrowed from the orator with a splendid assurance; his accents, although they, too, are borrowed, ring _____. But in poetic narrative his limits are _____.

(A) musically...interesting
(B) hollow...substantial
(C) false...nonexistent
(D) splendidly...peerless
(E) true...firmly fixed

6. Once again the president reaffirmed his _____ the treaty. Moreover, he indicated that his negotiators were engaged in _____ bargaining.

(A) neutrality toward...serious
(B) opposition to...useful
(C) support of...responsible
(D) conditional support of...diplomatic
(E) antagonism toward...good faith

225

7. The numerous _____ of the project do not include popularity. The public has traditionally been _____ such projects.

(A) highlights...enamored of
(B) features...interested in
(C) advantages...skeptical of
(D) innovations...misled by
(E) enticements...wary of

8. A mentally deficient person who has special talents or gifts is correctly referred to as _____; an extraordinary child is referred to as _____.

(A) proselyte...a progeny
(B) tainted...prodigious
(C) a stapes...a progenitor
(D) a lithographer...portentous
(E) an idiot savant...a prodigy

9. The domineering male gorilla usually appears _____ in its mating ritual in the wild.

(A) subjugated
(B) vanquished
(C) subdued
(D) surmounted
(E) imperious

10. She never took aspirin for her headaches; classical music was a more effective _____.

(A) antidote
(B) anodyne
(C) accolade
(D) analogy
(E) anomaly

11. Many professors find it necessary to warn their students against _____ when assigning research papers.

(A) probity
(B) clarity
(C) calumny
(D) plagiarism
(E) umbrage

12. He was chosen as club treasurer because he has always been _____ about repaying his debts.

(A) scrupulous
(B) munificent
(C) prodigious
(D) impervious
(E) incorrigible

13. Use of the company limousine is just one of the _____ of being executive vice president.

(A) tenets
(B) prerequisites
(C) perogatives
(D) perquisites
(E) precepts

14. The overall effect of the plangent music, dim lighting, and subdued colors was overwhelmingly _____.

(A) parsimonious
(B) froward
(C) lachrymose
(D) quotidian
(E) ignominious

15. The secret agent's taking the one sheet of _____ had an _____ on the lives of many of her companions.

(A) vellum...edict
(B) stationary...affect
(C) stationery...effect
(D) parchment...obligation
(E) bond...effigy

16. The weekly program on public radio is the most _____ means of educating the public about pollution.

(A) proficient
(B) effusive
(C) effectual
(D) capable
(E) competent

17. The accused appeared _____, since she felt certain the male witness would _____ her alibi.

(A) sanguine...corroborate
(B) meddlesome...substantiate
(C) conjugal...revoke
(D) garbled...authenticate
(E) concupiscent...abolish

18. The _____ habits of the wild hawk caused a serious _____ to develop for the chicken farmer.

(A) marauding...emergency
(B) parasitic...malady
(C) saprophytic...insurrection
(D) predatory...predicament
(E) meticulous...tête-à-tête

19. Louis Phillipe, so far as was practical, _____ the citizens of foreign states for losses caused by Napoleon.

(A) repartitioned   (D) subscribed
(B) apportioned   (E) subsidized
(C) indemnified

20. Anti-machine groups, such as the nineteenth-century Chartists, flat-Earth societies, and, more recently, anti-computer groups, are all examples of _____.

(A) paranoia   (D) misogynism
(B) xenophobia   (E) eccentricity
(C) misoneism

21. The governor was impeached for gross _____, although embezzlement charges were never filed.

(A) multifariousness   (D) malfeasance
(B) negligence   (E) recidivism
(C) malediction

22. Fear persisted, and with it persisted an animosity toward the sister; undoubtedly this was the psychological _____ of the incest taboo.

(A) antithesis   (D) variance
(B) impression   (E) correlate
(C) resemblance

23. The sociologist interpreted _____ as being socially shared ideas about what is right and _____ as specific models of behaviors for a surrounding environment.

(A) culture...laws
(B) mores...technologies
(C) class...caste
(D) sanctions...folkways
(E) values...norms

24. Soulé is five feet five inches tall and inclines toward stoutness, but his erect bearing and quick movements tend to _____ this.

(A) emphasize   (D) camouflage
(B) conceal   (E) disavow
(C) negate

25. A man may be moral without being _____, but he cannot be _____ without being moral.

(A) devout...pious
(B) altruistic...veracious
(C) chaste...precise
(D) pious...religious
(E) iniquitous...contrite

26. He was eagerly interested and wanted to experiment on himself, although ultimately _____ on account of his age.

(A) deterred   (D) dissuaded
(B) accommodated   (E) acclimated
(C) reconciled

27. The enthusiastic teacher described the talented student's clever display as _____.

(A) ingenuous   (D) adroit
(B) incongruous   (E) prosaic
(C) indolent

28. The practiced _____ displayed with _____ three pastes which he represented as costly gems to the buyers.

(A) charlatan...diffidence
(B) mountebank...self-possession
(C) empiric...concern
(D) swindler...aplomb
(E) imposture...assurance

29. Not all persons whose lives are _____ remain provincial; some have the intellectual and personal characteristics which enable them to develop a/an _____ orientation to life.

(A) confined...philanthropic
(B) limited...progressive
(C) circumscribed...enterprising
(D) restricted...cosmopolitan
(E) restrained...hedonistic

30. Committees are ineffective when they cannot agree upon what to do or just how to go about accomplishing it; this situation is a/an _____ of faulty _____ of committee responsibility.

(A) factor...acceptance
(B) cause...guidelines
(C) result...specifications
(D) part...guidelines
(E) example...direction

31. The cook prepared a particularly rich shellfish purée, or _____, for the honored guests.

(A) pottage   (D) bouillon
(B) bisque   (E) soufflé
(C) broth

32. The work of those government officials who must live in hostile foreign countries is full of perils–_____ for their families and _____ for themselves.

(A) moderate...hazardous
(B) hazardous...moderate
(C) perils...also
(D) minimal...dangerous
(E) dangerous...moderate

33. Increasing specialization on the part of workers results in better communication and higher degrees of achievement of goals in relation to the immediate work group or department, but decreases effectiveness of communication among groups or departments and the focus on institutional goals; this presents managers with the problems of increasing _____ and providing _____.

(A) coordination...vision
(B) supervision...mission
(C) support...direction
(D) retraining...articulation
(E) relationship...orientation

34. She was a perfect receptionist for the complaint department because with her _____ temperament she was not easily aroused.

(A) impassive   (D) apathetic
(B) stoic   (E) stolid
(C) phlegmatic

35. As an ardent _____ of parental leave benefits, James had few _____ among the women at the meeting.

(A) opponent...supporters
(B) supporter...friends
(C) activist...foes
(D) foe...enemies
(E) advocate...backers

36. The sustenance was given so _____ that it did not _____ the patient with new life and vigor.

(A) infrequently...imbue
(B) uncommonly...infuse
(C) scarcely...suffuse
(D) sporadically...inoculate
(E) rarely...leaven

37. Ages of fierceness have suppressed what is naturally kindly in the _____ of ordinary men and women.

(A) condition   (D) disposition
(B) character   (E) evolution
(C) phenomenon

38. His life was described as a lonely bachelor life spent in caring for his property and in adding to it by _____ living.

(A) parsimonious   (D) paltry
(B) exorbitant   (E) prudent
(C) prodigal

39. The taxi driver saved a man from a burning car, proving himself a _____ of the human race.

(A) paragon   (D) subjugated
(B) amoral   (E) officious
(C) malfeasant

40. The effect of the internal strain and instability on his system was, over time, _____.

(A) invidious   (D) abhorrent
(B) compatible   (E) congenial
(C) alluring

Sentence Completion Drill
ANSWER KEY

1. (C)	21. (D)
2. (D)	22. (E)
3. (D)	23. (E)
4. (C)	24. (D)
5. (E)	25. (D)
6. (C)	26. (D)
7. (C)	27. (D)
8. (E)	28. (D)
9. (E)	29. (D)
10. (B)	30. (C)
11. (D)	31. (B)
12. (A)	32. (C)
13. (D)	33. (A)
14. (C)	34. (C)
15. (C)	35. (A)
16. (C)	36. (A)
17. (A)	37. (D)
18. (D)	38. (A)
19. (C)	39. (A)
20. (C)	40. (A)

Attacking Analogy Questions

Bust it!

Before we begin, you should understand exactly what an analogy is. **An analogy is a comparison between items that are different, but that also have some similarities**. We know that may sound confusing, but if we give you an example you'll see what we mean.

Look at this analogy:

GALAXY : UNIVERSE :: STATE : COUNTRY

At first you may think that what you just read was gibberish. That may be because you need to **learn how to *read* an analogy**. The above analogy can be read as "Galaxy is to Universe as

State is to Country." The way to *translate* an analogy is to substitute "is to" for all single colons and "as" for all double colons. Pretty simple, right?

"But," you might ask, "what do these words have in common?" Well, as we said, analogies are comparisons between items that are different but are also similar in some way. Because of these similarities, terms in an analogy may share a common bond or relationship that is the key to understanding the analogy.

Let's look at our example again:

GALAXY : UNIVERSE :: STATE : COUNTRY

Ask yourself, what do the terms have in common? You may note that a galaxy is much smaller than the universe and that states are smaller than their country. This is one way to understand the analogy. You may also conclude that there are many galaxies in the universe as there are many states in a country. This is an equally acceptable way to *read* this analogy.

Important Strategy

For each Analogy question on the GRE, you must compare a sample pair of words with five other pairs, and then pick the pair that best matches the relationship between the words in the sample pair. That's all there is to it!

Now that you understand what an analogy is, how to *read* one, and how to answer an Analogy question, you're ready to start preparing to attack them on the GRE. This chapter will teach you to excel on Analogy questions through:

- Learning the eight different types of analogy patterns.

- Identifying the meanings of the words in the analogy.

- Identifying the pattern of the analogy.

- Eliminating any answer choice that does not match the sample analogy's pattern.

- Comparing the differences of answer choices with the sample analogy to eliminate wrong choices.

On Target!

This review for analogies assumes that you have an adequate vocabulary; it therefore does not employ any special word-building exercises. However, that does not mean that you can ignore vocabulary. Reading, of course, develops vocabulary. You are urged to build your vocabulary to improve on the verbal skills you will need to successfully attack the Analogy questions of the GRE.

Important Strategy

About the Directions

Important Information!

As with all sections of the GRE, it is important that you know the directions before the day of the test. That way you won't waste valuable time while taking the actual test.

The directions for Analogy questions will appear similar to the following:

> **DIRECTIONS:** Each question below consists of a related pair of words or phrases, followed by five lettered pairs of words or phrases. Select the lettered pair that best expresses a relationship similar to that expressed in the original pair.
>
> Example:
>
> **SMILE : MOUTH ::**
> (A) wink : eye   (D) tan : skin
> (B) teeth : face   (E) food : gums
> (C) voice : speech
>
>

About the Questions

The following is an overview of the different types of analogy questions you will encounter on the GRE, along with strategies for solving them quickly and accurately.

Question Type 1: PART-TO-WHOLE

One frequent pattern is a part of an item or concept to the whole idea or concept. Examples are:

SONG : REPERTORY   **CHAPTER : BOOK**

If we assume that a singer has a repertory of songs, we see that a "song" is a part of a whole "repertory." A "chapter" is also a part of a whole "book." So, the pattern is Part-to-Whole, and the answer choice to look for will have the same pattern.

Look!

Important Strategy

This pattern can also be reversed, as indicated below:

BANK : VAULT   **ZOO : CAGE**

Now the pattern is Whole-to-Part. For example, if we assume that a "bank" is the whole building or organization, then a "vault" is a smaller part of it. Also, "zoo" is the whole organization, and a "cage" is a part of this whole.

Question Type 2: CAUSE-AND-EFFECT

Another frequent pattern is the relationship of the Cause to its Effect. Look at these examples:

BACTERIA : DISEASE   **SUN : HEAT**

In the first example, "bacteria" are the cause of the result, "disease." In the second example, "sun" is the cause of the result "heat." In each case so far, you will look for a pattern with nouns.

Look!

Important Strategy

The reverse pattern is Result-to-Cause. Examples are:

FOOD : AGRICULTURE   **LAUGHTER : JOKE**

Here, "food" is the result of "agriculture," which causes it to be produced. And "laughter" is the result that follows (or *should* follow) a "joke."

Question Type 3: USER-TO-TOOL

These are examples of a third pattern, the relationship of the User-to-Tool:

DENTIST : DRILL   **GARDENER : RAKE**

A "dentist" uses a "drill" as a tool, and a "gardener" uses a "rake" as a tool.

The reversal of this pattern is Tool-to-User. For example:

COMPUTER : PROGRAMMER   **HAMMER : CARPENTER**

The "computer" is the tool, and the "programmer" is the user. The "hammer" is the tool, and the "carpenter" is the user.

A variation of this pattern might be the Instrument-to-Application, or Tool-to-Application, and its reversal. For example:

COMPUTER : WRITING   **TROWEL : GARDENING**

Examples of the reverse are:

OVEN : BAKING   **PIANO : CONCERT**

In these examples, too, the words are nouns.

Question Type 4: GROUP-TO-MEMBER

A fourth common pattern is the Group-to-Member. Examples are:

PRIDE : LION　　　　**SENATE : SENATOR**

A "pride" is the group to which a "lion" belongs. The "Senate" is the group to which a senator belongs.

The reversal, then, is Member-to-Group. For example:

WOLF : PACK　　　　**WITCH : COVEN**

The "wolf" is a member of a group called a "pack." And a "witch" is a member of a group called a "coven."

There are other variations of this basic pattern, such as Members-to-Group and the reverse.

Look!

Important
Strategy

Question Type 5: TRAIT-TO-EXAMPLE

Another pattern is a Trait or Characteristic to an Example of this Trait or Characteristic. For example:

DISHONESTY : LIE　　　　**BRILLIANCE : DIAMOND**

Note that "dishonesty" is a character trait, and one example of this trait is a "lie." Also, "brilliance" is a physical trait and "diamond" is an example. Reversals of this pattern are common as well.

A variation of this pattern is a **Greater Degree of a Characteristic in relation to the Characteristic Itself**. For example:

INGENIOUS : INTELLIGENT　　　　**BRAZEN : EXTROVERTED**

Look!

Important
Strategy

In these examples, "ingenious" is a greater degree of the trait "intelligent," and "brazen" is a greater degree of the trait "extroverted." Note, too, that all four words here are adjectives.

One variation of the pattern is **Lesser Degree of a Trait in relation to the Trait Itself**. Another variation might be a **Trait to an Opposite Trait**, as here:

VALOR : COWARDICE   COURAGEOUS : PUSILLANIMOUS

The words in the first example are nouns; in the second example they are adjectives.

At times, you may not know the exact meanings of all the words. In that case, you will have to make some educated guesses. For example, you probably know words that bear resemblance to "valor" and "cowardice," such as "valiant" and "coward." So, "valor" must be a trait resembling courage, whereas "cowardice" is the opposite trait. And don't give up on the second example because of "pusillanimous." You already know what "courageous" means. If you did not know what "pusillanimous" meant, you will know what it means from now on: it means "cowardly," or the trait opposite to "courageous." However, on the GRE, you will know that you are looking for an adjective either opposite in meaning to "courageous" or having the same meaning. That narrows your options considerably. If you should see the answer choice "brave : fearful," you can be reasonably sure that it is the correct answer choice.

Bust it!

Question Type 6: OBJECT-TO-MATERIAL

The pattern of Object-to-Material creates an analogy between an object and the material from which it is made. This type of question is quite common, as is its reversal. For example:

Important
Strategy

SKIRT : GABARDINE   or   COTTON : SHIRT

The "skirt" is the object made of the material "gabardine," and "cotton" is the material of which the object "shirt" is made.

Question Type 7: WORD-TO-DEFINITION, SYNONYM, OR ANTONYM

These patterns are heavily dependent on their dictionary meanings. Examples include:

✔ **Word-to-Definition**

SEGREGATE : SEPARATE

✔ **Word-to-Synonym**

VACUOUS : EMPTY

✔ **Word-to-Antonym**

DESOLATE : JOYOUS

Important
Strategy

In the first example, the word "segregate" means "separate"—it is both a definition and a synonym. Next, a synonym and definition for the word "vacuous" is "empty." Finally, a word opposite in meaning to "desolate" is the word "joyous."

Question Type 8: SYMBOL-TO-INSTITUTION

Important Strategy

These are examples of the pattern Symbol-to-Institution:

FLAG : GOVERNMENT   **CROWN : MONARCHY**

In the first case, "flag" is a symbol of the institution "government"; "crown" is the symbol of "monarchy."

These are the most commonly occurring patterns. However, many other types may appear including Plural-to-Singular, Creator-to-Creation, Male-to-Female, or Broad-Category-to-Narrow-Category (for example, FISH : SALMON).

Points to Remember

On Target!

✔   *If you do not know the meanings, try to recall in what context you have heard the words used. This might provide some clues. However, keep in mind that you are looking for a match with the same relationship as the capitalized sample pair. You are not looking for a pair that matches in meaning.*

✔   *Check that the parts of speech used in both pairs of the analogy are consistent.*

INAUGURATE : PRESIDENT :: CORONATION : KING

would not be correct because "inaugurate" is a verb and "coronation" is a noun. The two words are not the same part of speech.

✔   Sometimes, two answer choices exhibit the same pattern and have the same grammatical form. This means they are the same parts of speech, and they are the same in number—that is, both are singular or both are plural. In this case, you can eliminate them both, because they cannot both be right. One of the other choices must be right—one that refines the pattern.

✔   While the correct answer choice may be of the same class, type, or species as the pair in the example, this isn't always the case.

For example, in the analogy

PUPPY : DOG :: SAPLING : TREE

the first pair of words refers to an animal, whereas the second pair refers to a plant. However, the link between the words in both pairs is the same: the "immature subject" to the "mature subject."

✔   Sometimes, two answer choices have a pattern that is the same as the sample except that one choice shows the pattern in reverse. For example, assume that the sample exhibits the pattern Part-to-Whole. One choice shows this pattern, and another shows Whole-to-Part. In that case, one of these two choices is probably right. The one that is right, of course, is presented in the same order as in the sample.

On Target!

Answering Analogy Questions

The recommended strategy for completing an analogy is to examine the two sample words; then, from the meanings of these words, trace the pattern or relationship between them. It is also helpful to identify the grammatical form of the words. Once you can identify the pattern and form, you can forget the meanings and search the five answer choices for the same pattern.

You will not be looking for a match of dictionary meanings, although you will certainly need to use the dictionary meanings as clues. The match you want is the choice whose members resemble one another in the same way the words of the sample pair are related. For example, if the relationship between the same pair is "part-to-whole," you will look for the answer choice showing "part-to-whole." If the link between the same pair is "cause-to-effect," then the matching choice must also be "cause-to-effect."

There are four basic steps to answering any analogy question:

Look!

Important Strategy

STEP 1	Identify the meanings of both words in the sample.

STEP 2	From the meanings, identify the pattern of the sample. Also identify the part of speech and the number (singular or plural) of each word.

STEP 3   Ignoring the meanings of the words in the sample, now look over the answer choices. Use the meanings of the words in each choice ONLY to identify its pattern. Eliminate any choices that do not match the pattern in every way, including the order of presentation and grammatical form.

STEP 4   If one answer choice remains, it is the exact match. If two choices remain, examine them to see what is different about them. Compare these differences with the sample. Eliminate the answer choice that does not match the sample perfectly.

Look!

Important Strategy

For example, suppose the original pair is

AUTOMOBILE : BRAKE;

an "automobile" is a whole and the "brake" is a part. The answer choices are:

(A) **doer : thinker**   (D) **carburetor : choke**

(B) **man : conscience**   (E) **society : detergent**

(C) **horse : ride**

Bust it!

We can eliminate (A), since the two words have opposite meanings, and also (C), since "horse" is the doer and "ride" is what is done. We can also eliminate (E), since "society" is a whole, or producer, and "detergent" is a soap—what is produced by society.

Two choices remain: (B) and (D). In (D), a "carburetor" is the part of an automobile that supplies the fuel, and "choke" is a part that restricts the amount of fuel flowing to the engine. Since these are two separate parts, we can eliminate (D). What is left is (B), the perfect match, since "conscience" is a part of the whole "man." Besides, a conscience restrains a man just as the brake restrains an automobile.

Important Strategy

Always look for answer choices to eliminate. However, occasionally you can save a lot of time if you just happen to note the perfect match from the start. In that case, though, you should review the other choices, just to be sure your hunch was correct. For example:

CLOCK : SECOND ::

(A) ruler : millimeter   (D) product : shelf life

(B) sundial : shadow   (E) quart : capacity

(C) arc : ellipse

Right from the start, choice (A) looks right. The pattern seems to be an instrument and one of its measures, and choice (A) fits nicely. A cursory look at the other options shows that no other choice would be even tempting to select.

Bust it!

Not all the analogies are so simple. In the previous example, suppose the original pair and all choices except for choice (B) remained the same. Then assume that choice (B) is replaced by "scale : pounds." The pattern again is an instrument and one of its measures. Now we must choose between two options:

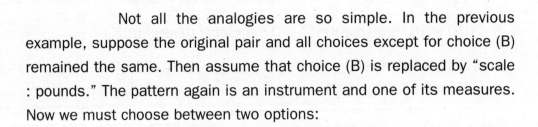

(A) ruler : millimeter   (B) scale : pounds

What is different about them? A ruler is calibrated in centimeters first and then millimeters. A scale is calibrated in pounds and then ounces. There's the difference: a millimeter is the smaller measure, but a pound is the larger measure. How is a clock calibrated? By minutes and then seconds. Obviously, the matching choice should show the smaller measure—choice (A).

Let's try an example in which you may need to refine the pattern you first identify. For example, suppose the original pair is

Important Strategy

SHELL : WALNUT.

The five choices are:

(A) coating : candy   (D) loaf : bread

(B) peel : banana   (E) root : tree

(C) icing : cake

Our first assumption seems obvious here: Part-to-Whole. Looking more closely, we see this pattern won't work because it fits all the options except (D), loaf : bread. So, we need a more specific pattern. One possibility is "Covering-to-What-is-Covered." A "shell" covers a "walnut." Now we can eliminate (E), since the root doesn't cover the tree, and also (C), since icing doesn't cover the bottom of the cake. That leaves options (A) coating : candy and (B) peel : banana. So, what is different about a coating for a candy and the peel of a banana? The difference is that coating on candy is edible, but the peel on a banana is not. Since the shell of a walnut is not edible, we can eliminate (A). This means that choice (B) is the exact match.

Bust it!

Completing the following drill questions will help you learn to apply the information you have just studied. When you complete the drill, make sure to check your answer. Refer back to the review material if you are unsure of an answer. Keep in mind that speed is important. Try to correctly answer each question in a minute or less.

Drill: Analogies

DIRECTIONS: Each question below consists of a related pair of words or phrases, followed by five lettered pairs of words or phrases. Select the lettered pair that best expresses a relationship similar to that expressed in the original pair.

EXAMPLE :
SMILE : MOUTH ::
(A) wink : eye   (D) tan : skin
(B) teeth : face   (E) food : gums
(C) voice : speech

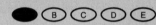

1. SCULPTOR:CHISEL::

    (A) artist:paint
    (B) writer:pen
    (C) librettist:songwriter
    (D) physician:stethoscope
    (E) conductor:baton

2. LUMBER:ELEPHANT::

    (A) soar:eagle
    (B) scamper:mice
    (C) circumambulate:hippopotamus
    (D) dive:seal
    (E) waddle:duck

3. BANALITY:TRITE::

    (A) stereotype:racial
    (B) genius:intelligent
    (C) politician:bromide
    (D) aphorism:apt
    (E) hackneyed:cutting

4. PLUMP:OBESE::

    (A) lean:emaciated
    (B) adipose:turgid
    (C) large:expanded
    (D) narrow:elongated
    (E) corpulent:swollen

5. ABSTEMIOUS:ASCETIC::

    (A) starving:hungry
    (B) gourmand:gourmet
    (C) dogma:iconoclast
    (D) unrestrained:libertine
    (E) beneficent:donor

6. LACONIC:PRATE::

    (A) sagacious:think
    (B) ascetic:indulge
    (C) despot:rule
    (D) authoritative:administer
    (E) inquisitive:inquire

7. CULPABLE:CENSURE::

    (A) moral:penance
    (B) meritorious:reward
    (C) laughable:abuse
    (D) admirable:judgment
    (E) affable:praise

8. PESSIMISTIC:BENEVOLENT::

    (A) miscellaneous:assorted
    (B) hemlock:herb
    (C) minimize:derogate
    (D) mien:demeanor
    (E) suspicious:innocent

9. AFFABLE:FRIENDLY::

    (A) fun:smile
    (B) amicable:congenial
    (C) hilarious:delight
    (D) speak:conversation
    (E) outspoken:taciturn

10. BANDAGE:GAUZE::

    (A) labyrinth:confusion
    (B) cement:gravel
    (C) meter:prosody
    (D) timbre:sound
    (E) metal:gold

11. COURAGE:GALLANTRY::

(A) cowardice:timidity
(B) poltroonery:fortitude
(C) chivalry:pusillanimity
(D) anxiety:solicitude
(E) agitation:perturbation

12. PRIDE:HAUGHTINESS::

(A) arrogance:submission
(B) abasement:crestless
(C) affability:supercilious
(D) vainglory:pomposity
(E) diplomatic:inconsonant

13. CALORIE:HEAT::

(A) sand:cement
(B) succumb:yield
(C) metronome:music
(D) calipers:diameter
(E) retaliation:forgiveness

14. FICTION:NON-FICTION::

(A) skies:roads
(B) novel:textbook
(C) television:telephone
(D) vitamins:food
(E) oxygen:breath

15. WANT:NEED::

(A) indigence:exigency
(B) crave:deprive
(C) thirst:hunger
(D) desire:lust
(E) coveted:necessary

16. ALLUDE:HINT::

(A) shy:conspicuous
(B) boisterous:obstreperous
(C) intelligent:sagacious
(D) self-conscious:assertive
(E) infer:deduce

17. SOCIABILITY:SOCIOPATH::

(A) delusion:schizophrenic
(B) sensitivity:psychic
(C) space:claustrophobic
(D) illusion:psychotic
(E) calm:neurotic

18. SAND:DUNE::

(A) tree:forest
(B) rock:boulder
(C) shower:deluge
(D) clamor:tumult
(E) twig:log

19. VARIABLE:EQUATION::

(A) oxygen:water
(B) paramecia:amoeba
(C) analysis:summary
(D) clay:sculpture
(E) furnace:heat

20. DECODE:UNDERSTAND::

(A) detonate:explode
(B) study:research
(C) destroy:build
(D) skill:practice
(E) sow:reap

21. CIRCULATORY:HEART::

(A) excretory:sweat
(B) neurological:skeleton
(C) lungs:respiratory
(D) digestive:kidney
(E) reproductive:testes

22. QUART:LITER::

(A) yard:acre
(B) yard:meter
(C) ounce:kilowatt
(D) liter:gallon
(E) mile:kilogram

23. QUILL:FOUNTAIN PEN::

(A) rural:urban
(B) young:old
(C) truce:peace
(D) solo:quartet
(E) mangle:iron

24. EXPURGATE:CENSOR::

(A) expunge:wash
(B) conceal:secrete
(C) frenetic:french
(D) phrenetic:phoneme
(E) wrought:excited

25. RIB:UMBRELLA::

(A) leg:table
(B) stud:wall
(C) shelf:closet
(D) hinge:door
(E) knob:drawer

26. SOLID:LIQUID::

(A) oxygen:air
(B) ice:water
(C) dirt:water
(D) grass:wood
(E) fire:air

27. LEAVE:RETURN::

(A) dry:wet
(B) black:white
(C) open:close
(D) down:up
(E) left:right

28. FEALTY:LORD::

(A) patriotism:country
(B) tax:government
(C) fidelity:spouse
(D) money:creditor
(E) belief:religion

29. LINEN:FLAX::

(A) chintz:silk
(B) madras:linen
(C) rayon:plastic
(D) coal:nylon
(E) chamois:leather

30. PUGILISM:FISTS::

(A) lexicographer:animals
(B) gynecology:genes
(C) nepotism:relatives
(D) archeology:fossils
(E) pediatrics:aged

31. DOOR:KEY::

(A) gem:ring
(B) perfume:aroma
(C) enigma:clue
(D) effort:achievement
(E) mold:gelatin

32. EDIFICE:FACADE::

(A) dorsal:ventral
(B) turtle:shell
(C) anachronism:chronologic
(D) body:skeleton
(E) counterfeit:fraudulent

33. DEFICIT:PECULATION::

(A) attire:dress
(B) hunger:abstinence
(C) appear:manifest
(D) drought:famine
(E) magistrate:judge

34. UNCTUOUS:BRUSQUE::

(A) gauche:suave
(B) abstruse:recondite
(C) bumptious:deleterious
(D) lustrous:luminous
(E) vitriolic:caustic

35. CATAPULT:PROJECTILE::

(A) glacier:ice
(B) precipice:cliff
(C) transmit:message
(D) prototype:replica
(E) perspiration:emit

36. VITAMIN C:SCURVY::

(A) sun:skin cancer
(B) niacin:pellagra
(C) goiter:iodine
(D) rickets:calcium
(E) plague:rats

37. CONVEY:DUCT::

(A) transport:transfer
(B) pollute:filter
(C) decipher:key
(D) autograph:biography
(E) falsify:fabricate

38. BENEVOLENCE:PHILANTHROPY::

(A) tolerance:bigotry
(B) lenity:virulence
(C) haunt:sporadic
(D) amiability:complaisant
(E) penurious:hoard

39. VORACIOUS:HUNGER::

   (A) penchant:partiality
   (B) supineness:propensity
   (C) disdain:inattention
   (D) aspire:seek
   (E) avaricious:want

40. PHYLUM:CLASSIFICATION::

   (A) cat:feline
   (B) commitment:vow
   (C) lie:deceit
   (D) medal:honor
   (E) control:harness

Analogies Drill
ANSWER KEY

1. (B)	21. (E)
2. (E)	22. (B)
3. (B)	23. (C)
4. (A)	24. (B)
5. (D)	25. (B)
6. (B)	26. (B)
7. (B)	27. (C)
8. (E)	28. (C)
9. (B)	29. (E)
10. (E)	30. (C)
11. (A)	31. (C)
12. (D)	32. (B)
13. (D)	33. (B)
14. (B)	34. (A)
15. (A)	35. (C)
16. (E)	36. (B)
17. (E)	37. (C)
18. (A)	38. (E)
19. (A)	39. (E)
20. (E)	40. (D)

Attacking the Reading Comprehension Questions

The Reading Comprehension questions test your ability to read a passage and answer questions based on that passage. It is crucial, however, to note that you are to answer questions based upon the information in the passage. You are not to answer questions based upon information you have gathered outside of the test itself.

Reading Comprehension questions present you with reading passages followed by six to eight questions. There are two basic Reading Comprehension subjects on the GRE: Science passages and Non-Science passages.

Science passages deal with specific details and facts about science. Science passages can also deal with general scientific

Important Information!

themes such as the scientific method. Non-Science passages contain information about humanities or social science topics. **Regardless of the subject of the passage, every Reading Comprehension questions that you will encounter on the GRE will be able to fall into one of six types. We will teach you these six types of questions and how to attack them.**

In this section, you'll learn how to:

Important Information!

- **Identify the six different types of reading questions.**

- **Read the passages to best answer the questions.**

- **Read the questions to get the correct answers faster and more consistently.**

About the Directions

<u>DIRECTIONS</u>: Each passage in this group is followed by questions based on its content. After reading a passage, choose the best answer to each question and fill in the corresponding oval on the answer sheet. Answer all questions following a passage on the basis of what is stated or implied in that passage.

There are two points about the directions that we'd like to make. **First, you must answer questions based upon what is stated or implied in the passage.** As we mentioned before, these questions are not meant to test knowledge that you have acquired outside of the test itself. Answering questions based upon your outside knowledge can quickly lead to incorrect answers. Stick like glue to the passage itself.

Second, you are to choose the best answer for each question. It may be that none of the answers provided is overly impressive. Nonetheless, it is your job to choose the best answer from the possible choices.

Important Information!

Additionally, if you must choose the best answer provided, it is necessary that you read all of the answer choices. Choice (A) may be a good answer, but it will not be the correct answer if choice (E) is better. This is extremely important: When answering a Reading Comprehension question, always read and consider every answer choice. There are no exceptions to this rule.

About the Reading Comprehension Questions

As we previously mentioned, there are six types of Reading Comprehension questions:

*Important
Information!*

TYPES OF QUESTIONS

- **Main Idea**
- **Specific Detail**
- **Implied Idea**
- **Logical Structure**
- **Further Application**
- **Tone**

We will now discuss each of these question types.

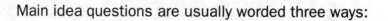

Question Type 1: MAIN IDEA QUESTIONS

Main idea questions are extremely common on the GRE. Often, the first question after the passage is a main idea question. Also, other questions may be directly or indirectly based upon the main idea of the passage.

*Important
Information!*

Main idea questions are usually worded three ways:

a. The main idea of the passage is . . .

b. The primary purpose of the passage is . . .

c. The best title of the passage is . . .

Main idea questions can be worded in other ways, but the three just mentioned are the most common.

What are the GRE writers looking for as an answer to a main idea question? **The correct answer to a main idea question is considered by the GRE writers to be the answer choice that most accurately describes what the author wrote about in the passage.** Here's an example of how to determine the main idea of a passage:

Let's assume we have a reading comprehension passage. Each paragraph of that passage discusses the economic, social, and foreign policies of one of the following presidents: Truman, Eisenhower, Kennedy, Johnson, Nixon, Ford, Carter, Reagan, Bush, and Clinton.

Let's assume that question number one asks for the best title of the passage. Choice (A) for this question is, "A Discussion of the Economic, Social, and Foreign Policies of the Presidents of the United States."

Setting aside, for the moment, the requirement that you always read all of the answer choices to a reading comprehension problem, do you think choice (A) is likely to be the correct answer or do you think choice (A) is likely to be incorrect? Take a moment and think about the question before going on.

You probably surmised that choice (A) is not likely to be correct. By using the phrase "of the Presidents," choice (A) implies a discussion of all of the presidents. The passage, however, only discusses presidents in the post-World War II era. Thus, choice (A) is probably too broad in its scope to be the correct answer.

Suppose choice (B) states, "A Comparison of the Social Policies of Presidents Nixon and Clinton." Because of the narrowness of this answer choice, it is also unlikely to be the correct answer.

From just these two example answer choices, we can see that correct answer choices to main idea questions are those answer choices that correctly describe the subject matter discussed in the passage.

Although the main idea of the passage can best be found by considering all of the passage, if the author is going to sum up the main idea in one or two sentences, those sentences are likely to be in the first or last paragraphs. **Try not to look beyond the first or last paragraph for the main idea.** It is often dangerous to look for the answer to a main idea question in the body of the passage. This is true because, very often, incorrect answers to main idea questions will be facts stated in the body of the passage. The GRE writers place these facts as incorrect answer choices as traps. These facts are usually too narrow in scope to be the correct answer to a main idea question. Unfortunately, under the time pressures of the test, such answers may *appear* to be correct. Because of this, the test writers tend to go out of their way to give you an answer choice that corresponds almost word for word with a portion of the passage.

Also, truthfulness is not the sole component of a correct answer to a main idea question. **Correct answers to main idea questions proportionally represent how time was spent in the passage.** Facts gleaned from the body of the passage are unlikely to do so, and, thus, despite their **attractiveness**, are likely to be incorrect.

At this point, we will look at a typical reading comprehension passage so that you can more clearly see what we are discussing and how it applies to the GRE Reading Comprehension questions.

PASSAGE

The words "organic," "chemical," "natural," and "health" are among the most misunderstood, misused, and maligned in our vocabulary, especially when they are applied to our food.

All organic materials are complex combinations of chemicals and contain one chemical element in common—carbon. But not all chemicals occur in the form of organic material. All of our food supply is in organic form because it has come from animal or plant sources. Most man-made foods are also in organic form.

Today, our chief concern about things organic and chemical relates to how foods are grown and processed. Our greatest concern is about the substances used in growing and processing our food.

Bust it!

Organic fertilizers used in growing the plants we eat directly, or which are fed to the animals that furnish our meat, are all made by the living cells in animal or plant tissues. They contain nutrients such as nitrogen, phosphorus, potassium, sulfur, magnesium, and other essential minerals in complex combinations with carbon, hydrogen, and usually oxygen.

Inorganic or commercial fertilizers contain the same chemical nutrients, but in simpler forms, and not always in combination with carbon. It is inaccurate to refer to inorganic fertilizers as "artificial" just because they have not been made from living cells.

A plant is unaware of the type of fertilizer—organic or inorganic—that is furnishing the chemicals for its growth. It does demand that these building blocks be in inorganic form. Plant cells synthesize the complex materials needed for growth rather than absorbing them ready-made from the soil.

Organically-raised animals are fed on organically grown grasses and feed. They are not given growth hormones, antibiotics, or synthetic materials. But it is unlikely that an animal's cells are aware of whether the many essentials for their growth are being furnished by feed in the organic or inorganic form.

The primary purpose of the passage is to

(A)   analyze a frequent source of disagreement.
(B)   define terms.
(C)   explain a theory.
(D)   eliminate a misunderstanding by defining.
(E)   explore the implications of a finding.

Bust it!

The correct answer to the question is choice (D). Choice (D), however, is by no means a perfect answer choice. It is correct because it is less flawed than the other choices.

Choice (A) is incorrect because we don't know of any disagreement and we don't know that this disagreement arises frequently. You could only have selected choice (A) had you made certain assumptions based on the passage. Making assumptions of this nature is likely to lead to incorrect answers on main idea questions. Again, we want to emphasize that you should answer the question based on information given in the passages, not on outside knowledge.

Choice (B) is incorrect because it is too narrow in its scope. The author does more than simply define terms. He or she uses those definitions to make points and reach conclusions.

Choice (C) is incorrect because the passage does not explain a theory.

Choice (E) is incorrect for at least two reasons. First, there is no "finding" in the passage. Second, even if one could find evidence of a finding in this passage, there is still no exploration of such a finding.

This brings us to choice (D). Choice (D) is correct because the purpose of the passage is to eliminate a misunderstanding. We know that the author is concerned with misunderstandings because he or she sets this forth in the first paragraph. We also know that the author makes frequent use of definitions in the paragraph. Hence, choice (D) is the best. (NOTE: The information provided in the first paragraph was useful in arriving at the correct answer.)

To be honest, however, we must admit that choice (D) is by no stretch of the imagination a great answer choice. The flaws in choice (D), however, are not so much caused by the answer choice itself as they are by the rambling nature of the passage.

The passage begins by telling us that certain words are "misunderstood, misused, and maligned in our vocabulary." Without telling us how these words have been misunderstood or misused, the passage then launches into a rather abbreviated and elementary discussion of organic chemistry and some of its applications. The passage concludes by telling us "it is unlikely that an animal's cells are aware of whether the many essentials for their growth are being furnished by feed in the organic or inorganic form."

Bust it!

Bust it!

The problem with choice (D) is that, because we have never been precisely told in what manner certain words have been "misunderstood, misused, or maligned," it is extremely difficult for us to know whether this "misunderstanding" has been "eliminated."

That being said, choice (D) is, nevertheless, the best of the lot because it is clear that the passage spends much of its time defining terms and that the author is concerned with misunderstandings.

As mentioned before, we are not so much concerned with finding a great answer, or a perfect answer, as we are with finding the best answer.

The techniques of working from the answer choices is of paramount importance in answering Reading Comprehension problems. You must work from the answer choices; there is no other way. To attempt to formulate your own answer to a Reading Comprehension question would only waste time.

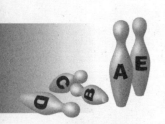

Eliminating Answer Choices

Similarly, when answering Reading Comprehension problems, **you must use the process of elimination**. By the process of elimination we mean that, in the problem above, choice (D) must be the best answer because it is less flawed than choices (A), (B), (C), or (E). With all reading comprehension questions, you could always create a "better" answer. But you are to choose the best from the answer choices that have been provided, and that implies eliminating the rest of the answer choices.

Question Type 2: SPECIFIC DETAIL QUESTIONS

Specific detail questions, as the name implies, ask questions based upon narrow points found in the passage. Specific detail questions will often be introduced with language similar to the following:

a. According to the passage, ...

b. Which of the following is stated in the passage?

To answer a specific detail question, read the question and go through the answer choices, eliminating any that are clearly incorrect. This technique utilizes the process of elimination. This initial pass through the answer choices should eliminate two or three answer choices.

Important Information!

Once you've eliminated the obvious wrong choices, it is usually necessary to go back to the line or lines of the passage giving rise to the question. For this reason, **it is always a good idea to pay attention to paragraphs with important points in the passage and note the function of those paragraphs within the passage. This will decrease the amount of time it takes you to find these paragraphs when answering specific detail questions.**

Do not attempt to complete a specific detail question without going back to the passage. The passages are much too dense, and the remaining two or three answer choices are always close in terms of their relative correctness. After having gone back to the passage, return to the answer choices, eliminate one or two answer choices, and choose the best answer choice.

If you are still not sure which is the correct answer choice, do not go back to the passage another time. You will only

waste time by doing so. If you have eliminated one or more of the answer choices, even if you are not certain which of the remaining choices is correct, choose the answer choice you think is the best and go on to the next question.

Here's an example using the same passage used for main idea questions:

EXAMPLE

According to the passage, nearly all of man's food supply

(A)   has been organically processed.
(B)   has been organically grown.
(C)   is both organic and inorganic because it comes from both plants and animals.
(D)   has been contaminated by artificial additives.
(E)   is in organic form because it is the product of living cells.

Bust it!

While answering this question, your thought processes may run along the following lines: Choice (A) is probably not correct because the idea of organic processing seems to be a contradiction in terms. Choice (B) seems better than choice (A), but much of man's food supply comes from animals and fish, and we don't usually speak in terms of animals being grown. We grow plants, but we raise animals.

Choice (C) seems wrong because it implies that either plants or animals is an inorganic source. Choice (D) seems too strong to be correct and is not supported by the passage. Choice (E) seems good because we remember some tie-in between organic things being products of living cells.

At this point, however, it would not be wise to answer the question without going back to the passage. Having seen the answer choices once, you are now in a good position to return to the passage.

Skimming quickly through the passage and remembering where important points were made, we come across the words "food supply" in the third sentence of the second paragraph. We are told that "all of our food supply is in organic form because it has come from animal or plant sources."

Returning again to the answer choices, we can now quickly toss out choices (A), (B), and (D) because the paragraph concerning the food supply has nothing to do with how things are processed or grown. Nor does that paragraph deal with artificial additives.

Choices (C) and (E) remain. Choice (C), although seemingly incorrect at first glance, is very tempting (as the second best answer choice usually is), but it must be eliminated because it says that man's food supply is "both organic and inorganic." When you returned to the passage, you found that it clearly states, "all of our food supply is in organic form." If all of the food supply is organic, then none of it is inorganic, so we must eliminate choice (C).

This leaves choice (E), which is the correct answer. Note that choice (E) states, "is in organic form because it is the product of living cells." The paragraph states that "our food supply is in organic form because it has come from animal or plant sources." Note that the phrases "is the product of living cells" and "has come from animal or plant sources" are not identical.

Whether these two phrases are close enough in meaning to make this a great answer choice will cast a certain level of doubt upon choice (E). But, as we have stated before, even though we cannot

Bust it!

be absolutely sure that choice (E) is not flawed, it is not as clearly flawed as choice (C), which incorrectly proclaims that man's food supply is partially inorganic. Thus, by working closely with the answer choices and using the process of elimination, we see that we must select choice (E) as the best answer choice for the question.

Bust it!

There is a variation on the specific detail question which comes up with sufficient regularity on the GRE. Consider this question based on the same passage:

The passage contains information that would answer all of the following questions EXCEPT:

(A)   Why is organic fertilizer superior to inorganic fertilizer?

(B)   What are organic materials?

(C)   Do plants require nutrients in organic or inorganic form?

(D)   What is the common chemical in all organic materials?

(E)   Why is it inaccurate to call inorganic fertilizers "artificial"?

We will call this type of problem a reverse specific detail problem. Instead of asking which is a specific detail of the problem, this type of problem asks which is <u>not</u> a specific detail.

The best answer is choice (A). We are not given any information that helps us know why organic fertilizer is superior to inorganic fertilizer. To the contrary, the first sentence of paragraph four indicates that organic fertilizer is not superior.

Remembering the key points in the passage will help you eliminate some of these choices without second thought. But some of

Bust it!

the choices may seem correct. To eliminate all the incorrect answer choices you must go back to the passage and look for specific sentences that will answer the questions posed in the answer choices:

The first sentence of the second paragraph provides information that would help us answer the question posed in choice (B). The second sentence of the sixth paragraph helps us to answer the question found in choice (C). That sentence says a plant demands that these building blocks be in inorganic form. "These" refers to the chemicals needed for growth, noted in the previous sentence. And the chemicals, listed at the end of the fourth paragraph, are also termed "nutrients." The first sentence of the second paragraph tells us that carbon is the common chemical in all organic materials, thus answering choice (D). And the second sentence of the fifth paragraph tells us why it is inaccurate to call inorganic fertilizers "artificial," thus eliminating choice (E).

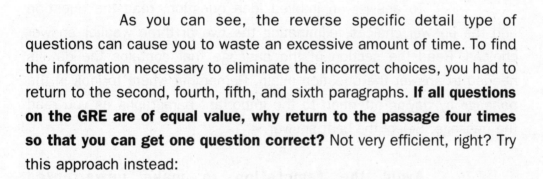

As you can see, the reverse specific detail type of questions can cause you to waste an excessive amount of time. To find the information necessary to eliminate the incorrect choices, you had to return to the second, fourth, fifth, and sixth paragraphs. **If all questions on the GRE are of equal value, why return to the passage four times so that you can get one question correct?** Not very efficient, right? Try this approach instead:

Upon spotting a reverse specific detail question, read all of the answer choices and eliminate any that you know are not the correct answer choice. (Do not go back to the passage to perform this operation.) If you can eliminate two or three of the answer choices, make your best guess at the correct answer. This will save you a lot of time. Only if you cannot eliminate at least two of the answer choices should you return to the passage to look for information to eliminate answer choices. Even then, only return to the passage once. Use the information you found in the passage to eliminate any incorrect answer choices and then make your best guess from the remaining answers.

Question Type 3: IMPLIED IDEA QUESTIONS

Implied idea questions test your ability to recognize information that is not explicitly stated in the passage, but is strongly implied. Such questions can refer to specific details or more general ideas and are usually worded in one of the following ways:

      a. It can be inferred . . .

      b. The passage suggests . . .

      c. The author probably considers . . .

      d. The author implies that . . .

Important Information!

To answer an implied idea question, read the question and the answer choices, eliminating the two or three weaker answer choices. Read the section of the passage that contains the details needed to answer the question again. Remember where to look in the passage by paying attention to the important paragraphs as you read the passage. Select the best answer.

Avoid the temptation to make unwarranted assumptions. The majority of wrong answer choices in implied idea questions try to draw you into making assumptions for which you do not have sufficient facts. Be careful of your assumptions. Avoid using your outside knowledge. Use only the information in the passage.

Here's an example using the organic fertilizer passage previously presented:

EXAMPLE

It can be inferred from the passage that

(A)   animals must convert synthetic fertilizers to organic form to benefit from them.

(B)   organically raised animals are more likely to be disease-free than those raised inorganically.

(C)   organically raised animals process chemical nutrients in the same way as organically raised plants.

(D)   organically raised animals tend to be smaller than animals raised inorganically.

(E)   animals can use chemical nutrients for growth in either organic or inorganic form.

Upon our first pass through the answer choices, we can eliminate choices (B), (C), and (D). Choice (B) is not correct because there is no mention whatsoever of which type of feeding is likely to produce disease-free animals. We are told that organically fed animals are not given antibiotics, but cannot draw any conclusions concerning the likelihood of disease from a barren statement about antibiotics. Choice (C) is not correct because there is nothing in the passage that would lead us to believe that animals process nutrients in the same way that plants do. And, in choice (D), there is no mention in the passage that the type of feeding can affect the size of the animal.

We are now down to choices (A) and (E). Remembering that the last paragraph dealt with animals, we return to that paragraph. The last sentence tells us it is unlikely that an animal's cells are aware of whether the nutrients are furnished in organic or inorganic form.

Bust it!

If the animal's cells are likely to be unaware of the form of the nutrients, then it is not likely that synthetic fertilizers must be converted to organic form. Thus, we eliminate choice (A).

Additionally, if the animal's cells are unaware of the form of the nutrients, then it is likely, as stated in choice (E), that animals can use nutrients for growth in either organic or inorganic form. Choice (E) is correct.

Question Type 4: LOGICAL STRUCTURE QUESTIONS

Logical structure questions test your ability to analyze the organization of the author's argument. These questions focus on the organization of the passage as a whole, the organization of a paragraph, or the role of a particular detail in the structure of the argument.

If a logical structure question concerns the entire passage, the key to answering the question is to select the answer choice that fully and precisely describes the structure of the passage. **Therefore, some logical structure questions are similar to main idea questions. You must search for an answer choice that is neither too broad nor too narrow.**

If a logical structure question concerns either a paragraph or a section of a paragraph, your focus must be more narrow. You must ask yourself one of two questions. First, what is the function of this paragraph within the passage? To answer this question, it may be helpful to get an idea of the purpose of the other paragraphs of the passage. Again, you should be paying attention to key paragraphs and their function in the structure of the passage as you read it.

*Important
Information!*

Second, what is the function of this sentence within the paragraph? To answer this question, it is a good idea to keep in mind the function of the paragraph housing the sentence in question. **The sentence in question will usually do one of three things. It will support the main idea, contradict the main idea, or serve as a stepping-stone to ideas conveyed in the next paragraph.**

Very often, logical structure questions concerning paragraphs or specific sentences will make specific references to those paragraphs or sentences. An example of such a question might be, "In line 34, the author cites Newton because . . ."

If confronted with such a question, line 34 must be the place you begin your inquiry. You should, however, remember to ask yourself what the purpose of the paragraph that contains line 34 is.

Additionally, simply because you are referred to line 34 does not automatically mean the answer to the question will be found in line 34 or even in the paragraph containing line 34. **When a question refers to a line in the passage, that line is the beginning of your inquiry. Realize, however, that you may well have to go very far from that line to discover the correct answer. This is a trap placed by the GRE writers to make you waste time.**

Because of the possibility of wasting time when faced with a logical structure question (as with all Reading Comprehension questions), you should eliminate as many answer choices as you can before going back to the passage. Once you've eliminated at least two answer choices, go back to the passage and find information to eliminate the other choices. Don't spend too much time, and only go back to the passage once. When you cannot eliminate any further choices, make your best guess at the correct answer and move on.

Bust it!

Here's an example of a logical structure question based on the same passage we've been using for other examples:

EXAMPLE

Which of the following statements best describes the organization of the passage?

(A)   A dispute is presented and resolved.

(B)   A problem is outlined and a solution is proposed.

(C)   A misunderstanding is underscored and clarifying definitions are presented.

(D)   A critique is made and supporting evidence is presented.

(E)   A current hypothesis is examined and an alternative is suggested.

Note that, in terms of scope, this question is similar to a main idea question. Both questions look at the entire passage. To answer this question, we must work from the answer choices and use the process of elimination.

Choice (A) appears weak because there is neither a dispute nor a resolution of a dispute.

Choice (B) is weak for a similar reason. We don't really have a problem. Even if we stretch the definition of a "problem" (and it is always a bad idea to stretch the definition of a word on the GRE) to include the population's misuse of certain words (organic, chemical), we still do not have a solution to that problem. That the people who read this passage might not misuse the relevant words does not mean the problem has been cleared up for the general population.

Bust it!

Upon initial consideration, choice (C) looks reasonable. The first paragraph does mention a misunderstanding, and the rest of the passage does contain numerous definitions.

Choice (D) is weak because we have neither a critique nor supporting evidence.

Choice (E) is also incorrect. We do not have a hypothesis, nor do we have an alternative.

Bust it!

Having read all of the possible answers, choice (C) is the correct answer. Once again, note that the correct answer tied into the main idea: the logical structure of the passage was related to the main idea.

Question Type 5: FURTHER APPLICATION QUESTIONS

Further application questions require you to relate the ideas presented in the passage to a broader context or a context that is not the same as the one found in the passage. Further application questions take on forms similar to the following:

a. The passage most likely appeared in a . . .

b. The passage is most relevant to which field of study . . .

To answer a further application problem, keep in mind the main idea of the passage. It is also helpful to pay attention to how details have been used in the passage. Finally, look at the tone the author used in the passage. Here's an example of a further application problem using the passage on organic fertilizer:

Important Information!

EXAMPLE

The passage most likely appeared in a(n)

(A)   nutrition textbook.
(B)   encyclopedia.
(C)   popular science magazine.
(D)   medical journal.
(E)   college chemistry textbook.

Once again, we must work from the answer choices and use the process of elimination. As to choice (A), a nutrition textbook would be designed to tell us what kinds of food to eat and why we should eat those foods. Some nutrition books might also discuss using vitamins. Much of our passage concerns the requirements for fertilizers or the types of fertilizers required by plant life. Such paragraphs are out of place in a nutrition book, making choice (A) inappropriate.

As to choice (B), the purpose of an encyclopedia is to give the reader straightforward information concerning a topic. An encyclopedia does not usually get involved in clearing up misunderstandings between different topics. Hence, choice (B) is incorrect.

Choice (D) is incorrect. Most articles in medical journals report the latest findings of scientific studies that might be helpful to the medical profession. For example, there might be a study on the rate of skin cancer of polar bears that were exposed to 16 hours of sun a day after having been given 200 grams of vitamin C a day. The language of the medical journal is likely to be much more technical than that of the passage. Most doctors would have learned the context of the passage in their science courses in college.

Bust it!

Choice (E) is incorrect because our passage is outside the scope of a chemistry textbook. Chemistry textbooks are concerned with the molecular or atomic make-up of cells and how certain cells interact with other cells. Chemistry textbooks spend a lot of time on formulas. Also, a chemistry textbook would present the information in a much more technical and complex language.

This leaves choice (C), which is the correct answer. The scope of a popular science magazine would be quite broad and, therefore, this passage is not outside the realm of a popular science magazine. Second, this passage (with its great reliance on definitions) has been written for a broad audience, all of whom may not be familiar with the subject matter. You should determine that the passage was written for a broad audience because of its simple language and lack of technical terminology. The audience of a popular science magazine is likely to be the average reader as well as scientists. Thus, choice (C) is correct.

Bust it!

Choice (C) is the correct answer, not because it is absolutely certain that the passage would appear in a popular science magazine, but because choice (C) is better than the rest of the answer choices. Once again, you must work from the answer choices given and use the process of elimination.

Question Type 6: TONE QUESTIONS

Tone questions test your ability to answer questions concerning the tone of the author. A tone question can be based on the entire passage, or just a part of a passage. **As you read passages, try to be sensitive to the tone of the author.**

To answer tone questions of a general nature, you must first ask yourself whether the tone of the author is positive, negative, or

neutral. **A positive tone would present support of a topic or action. A negative tone would present disapproval of a topic or action. A neutral tone would present both sides of a topic or action and neither support nor disapproval.** After answering this question, go through the answer choices. You will probably be able to eliminate two or three answer choices.

To work your way down to the correct answer choice, ask yourself to what degree the author is positive, negative, or neutral. Is the author extremely positive, or only slightly positive? Look at the remaining answer choices and think about the connotations and implications of the remaining answer choices. Tone questions rely to a certain degree upon your knowing the meanings of words. Select the answer choice that best reflects the author's tone and intensity.

When answering a tone question which concerns the entire passage, it is usually a good idea not to go back to the passage. You do not have time to read the entire passage again and focusing on a portion of the passage could lead you astray.

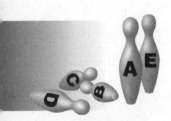

Eliminating Answer Choices

If the tone question is only based on a portion of the passage, read the answer choices, eliminating any obviously incorrect answers. Then go back and read the relevant portion of the passage. After having read the relevant portion of the passage, try to judge the tone. Then eliminate any other choices that are incorrect. Next, try and identify the intensity of the author's tone. Is it very negative? Slightly negative? Once again, pay attention to the connotations of the words. Finally, select the best answer choice.

EXAMPLE

The author's attitude toward inorganic fertilizers can best be described as

(A)   extremely biased.

(B)   hostile.

(C)   mildly critical.

(D)   objective or neutral.

(E)   enthusiastically supportive.

Because this is a tone question based on only part of the passage, you must first eliminate any obviously wrong choices. Once you've done that, go back to the passage and read the fifth paragraph of the passage again. The overall tone of the paragraph is somewhat neutral. The author is simply relating facts about inorganic fertilizers.

This eliminates choices (A), (B), and (E). These choices are much too intense to fit the paragraph. You can eliminate choice (C) because the second sentence of the paragraph is, if anything, defends the use of inorganic fertilizers. So, by the process of elimination, choice (D) is the correct answer.

Bust it!

Reading the Passages

The first point we wish to discuss concerns how you will use your time on the Reading Comprehension questions. It is clear that there are two tasks that must be performed during Reading Comprehension questions: First, you must read the passage. Second, you must answer the questions.

Look!

Important Strategy

How do you want to use the limited time you have for this section? Do you want to spend more time reading the passage than answering the questions? Should you spend more time answering the questions than reading the passage? Should you spend equal amounts of time on each?

As we showed you throughout our explanation of the types of Reading Comprehension questions you'll encounter on the GRE, you should spend most of your time answering the questions. Spending most of the time answering the questions probably runs counter to what you would think is the preferred method. Let's examine the issue in greater detail:

You might think that a total understanding of the passage would make the questions very easy to answer. This assumption is wrong. Even if you had a perfect knowledge of the passage, the questions would still be difficult.

The difficulty arises because there will not be much difference between two or three of the answer choices presented. You should be able to eliminate at least two or three answer choices without going back to the passage. This leaves you with two or three choices to choose from. **A perfect understanding of the passage is not going to help you to notice the distinction between the shades of meaning of the two or three best answer choices remaining. To notice the difference between the remaining answer choices, you are going to need to go back to the passage.** If you know you will have to go back to the passage to find the best answer, why spend a lot of time trying to gain a perfect understanding of the passage? **Time spent carefully and completely reading the passage (this doesn't mean reading for perfect understanding) is time that you won't have to go back to the passage to consider and eliminate the second-best answer choices.**

We don't mean to imply that you should ignore or disregard the passage. **We are only suggesting that you spend more time on the answer choices and less time actually reading the passage**. Keep in mind that you get credit for answering the questions, not for understanding the passage.

How then should you read the passage? **You should read the passage fairly quickly and without stopping.** This does not mean you should "speed read" the passage. Nor does it mean you should skip sentences or words. It means you should read through the passage at a brisk pace, understanding it as best you can. Don't re-read complex sentences over and over until you understand them. Read them just once, paying strict attention to the points being made as well as to transitions.

What should you be trying to get out of the passage during your initial reading? We've pointed these items out in our discussion of the types of Reading Comprehension questions. Here are the three items you should be concerned with:

Look!

Important Strategy

- **The main idea of the passage**

- **The organization of the passage**

- **The tone the author uses in the passage**

First of all, and most importantly, you should be trying to understand **the main idea of the passage**. The main idea will almost always be a topic of one of the questions you'll have to answer, and the main idea is the cornerstone upon which the rest of the passage is built. Keep in mind that in a passage of about 400 words, the main idea is likely to control most of the passage.

Second, you should formulate some idea as to **how the passage is organized**—the logical structure of the passage. Third, you want to pick up **the tone of the passage**. If you get these three things out of the passage, you will be in good shape to answer the questions.

Concerning the actual reading of the passage, we make one final point. Each time that you see a new paragraph, the author is probably introducing a new idea. Thus, whenever you see a new paragraph, you should ask yourself: What is the new idea introduced by this paragraph?

We don't expect you to be able to remember the new idea introduced by each new paragraph. But we do believe it would help if you are aware that a new idea is on the way.

To justify the manner in which we are suggesting you read the passage, we return to the various kinds of questions. If you recall, some of the questions force you to look at the "big picture": main idea questions or tone questions. Other questions focus in on part of passage: specific detail and implied idea questions.

Important
Strategy

For "big picture" questions, a three-minute reading of the passage will usually suffice. Your task is not so much grasping the main idea, but determining which answer choices best express the main idea.

For more focused questions, you are going to have to return to the passage to answer the questions. **Why spend time attempting to memorize the details of the passage when you will refer back to those details to answer questions concerning those details? The most important thing is to have an idea of where those details are so that you can quickly find those details when needed.**

Reading the Questions

After you finish reading the passage, proceed immediately to the questions. Be prepared to face the natural temptation of immediately choosing between (A) and (B) if they represent reasonable answers. Resist that temptation and go on to choices (C), (D), and (E) to see if they meet the "reasonableness" standard. During this first reading of the answer choices, you do not want to spend too much time with any one of the answer choices. You only want to get an idea whether each answer choice is in the ballpark or out of the ballpark.

Additionally, at this time you want to avoid the temptation to compare any two of the answer choices. If choice (A) is decent and choice (B) is decent, there is a natural temptation to immediately want to decide between them. The problem with such a comparison at this stage of the game is that choice (E) may be clearly better than either choices (A) or (B). **Any effort spent comparing choices (A) and (B) would, therefore, clearly have been a waste of time.**

Important Strategy

After the first reading of the answer choices, you should have been able to eliminate two or three answer choices. Focus very carefully on the remaining choices. It's now crunch time. Be careful of the language of these remaining answer choices. Try to be sensitive to the nuances of these answer choices.

If the type of question being asked is of a focused nature, now is the time to return to the appropriate section of the passage. **Do not attempt to do a question of a focused nature without returning to the passage!** The passages are crammed with details. Relying on your memory for such details is ill-advised.

Important Strategy

Important Strategy

Once you've read the pertinent section of the passage, return to the answer choices and read again the ones you haven't eliminated. Think about each answer choice for a few seconds and select the one you think is the best answer choice. **Do not return a second time to the passage for further information. Repeated trips to the passage for any given question are unlikely to enlighten you. They will only waste time.**

Choosing the Best Answer Choice

It is an unfortunate truth that the line between the best and the second-best answer choice is a fine line indeed. Put another way, **the best answer choice is not always all that much better than the second-best answer choice.**

Important Strategy

What are you to do, then, when you are not sure?

Before we answer that question, we feel it necessary to appropriately frame the question. By the very nature of the test, with regard to the verbal questions, even if you understand the question, you will not be absolutely certain of the correct answer in more than 80 percent of the questions.

The questions have been deliberately designed to leave you with a high degree of uncertainty at the moment you enter your selection. The GRE has been designed to measure how well you can function when you are "intellectually weightless" — in other words, when the choices before you can't be pinned down as absolutely correct or incorrect.

The GRE rewards people who can efficiently make decisions based upon imperfect knowledge. The test punishes people who have a hard time making up their minds. It is unclear why the GRE has been set up in this manner. Perhaps the GRE tests in this fashion because uncertainty is a very real component of graduate school.

Look!

Important Strategy

On all the Verbal Ability sections of the GRE, you must narrow down the answer choices as far as you can with any degree of certainty (usually there will be two, sometimes three, choices left), then pick the one you think is correct. **Dwelling on each answer until you're 100% sure will risk damaging your performance on the entire test. Good time management is its own reward.**

You must narrow down the field, make your decision, and then go on to the next question. The more you practice making decisions within the time frame allotted by the test, the better you will do on the test.

Practicing for the Reading Comprehension Questions

One of the major problems you may have with Reading Comprehension questions are the passages themselves. You may find the passage quite difficult. The reason for the difficulty is that the passage is usually outside the primary field of your study.

Look!

Important Strategy

For example, if you had majored in biology, you probably would have had an easier time reading a passage about genetics than if you had majored in music. **But, we'd like to reiterate, you are being** tested on your ability to understand information presented in the passage, not on your outside knowledge. If you find you are having trouble understanding the reading passages, you must hone your skill of reading and understanding unfamiliar material.

To sharpen your skills in this area, get in the habit of reading the editorials in a good daily newspaper (e.g., the *Miami Herald, Des Moines Register, Philadelphia Inquirer*, or *Toronto Sun*). Editorials may prove useful to you for many reasons, but here are two biggies.

First, newspaper editors tend to write on a wide range of topics. They write on music, art, foreign policy, Medicaid, taxes, sports, elections, economic policy, and the environment. The list goes on and on. Reading the editorial column of a good newspaper will help you to gain skills at reading in fields outside of your own.

Second, the editors tend to make their points in writings that are almost the same length as a GRE passage: about 450 words. There are not too many places where writers regularly develop ideas so concisely. Reading the editorial column of a good newspaper will also help you become acclimated to reading passages where the theme is developed in a short space.

Important
Strategy

If you are going to follow this suggestion, try to read the editorial without having read the title of the editorial. One of the reasons that Reading Comprehension passages are difficult is that they come without a title. The absence of a title places the burden on you of figuring out what the passage is all about, in effect forcing you to figure out the main idea.

Almost everything you read or see comes with a title: books, movies, newspaper articles, magazine articles. If you are reading it, it probably came with a title. Now look at a GRE Reading Comprehension passage: no title. Thus, if you are going to read editorial columns, we recommend you try not to look at the title. Developing your ability to pick out the main idea of a writing when it has not been given to you is a skill that may come in handy on the GRE.

Points to Remember

✔   *Read the passage in no more than three minutes.*

✔   *While reading the passage, try to pick out the main idea, logical structure, and tone.*

✔   *Do not try to pick out or remember the details of the passage.*

✔   *Read the question, then read all of the answer choices. Eliminate the two or three poorer answer choices.*

✔   *If the question concerns detailed information from the passage, return to the section of the passage where those details can be found.*

✔   *Read very carefully the remaining two or three answer choices. Pay attention to the nuances of each answer choice.*

On Target!

On Target!

✔   Remember to answer Reading Comprehension questions based on the information provided in the passage. Do not base your answers upon prior knowledge.

✔   Do not make repeated trips to the passage to answer any one question.

✔   After you have given yourself an allotted amount of time to answer, select the answer you think is the best. Then go on to the next question.

✔   Memorize the directions for the Reading Comprehension questions before you take the test so that you don't waste time reading them while taking the actual GRE.

Drill: Reading Comprehension

The major debilitating symptoms of Alzheimer's disease include serious forgetfulness — particularly about recent events — and confusion. At first, the individual experiences only minor and almost imperceptible symptoms that are often attributed to emotional upsets or other physical illnesses. Gradually, however, the person becomes more forgetful and this may be reported by anxious relatives. The person may neglect to turn off the oven, may misplace things, may recheck to see if a task was done, may take longer to complete a chore that was previously routine, or may repeat already answered questions. As the disease progresses, memory loss and such changes in personality, mood, and behavior as confusion, irritability, restlessness, and agitation, are likely to appear. Judgment, concentration, orientation, writing, reading, speech, motor behavior, and naming of objects may also be affected. Even when a loving and caring family is available to give support, the victim of Alzheimer's disease is most likely to spend his or her last days in a nursing home or long-term care institution. At this time, there is no cure.

1. The author's purpose for writing this passage is

(A) to demonstrate how forgetfulness is the first stage of Alzheimer's disease.
(B) to illustrate how the family of an Alzheimer's patient is affected.
(C) to document the typical progression of Alzheimer's disease.
(D) to warn that emotional upsets can lead to the development of Alzheimer's disease.
(E) to prove the importance of finding a cure for Alzheimer's disease.

2. This passage implies that victims of Alzheimer's disease will probably

(A) have only sporadic memories of childhood events.
(B) retain their cognitive functions.
(C) lose their cognitive functions without incurring personality and behavioral changes.
(D) spend their last days at home with their families.

(E) retain the ability to perform those skills learned prior to the onset of the disease.

3. Serious forgetfulness is described as being debilitating due to

(A) the length of time needed to complete a task.
(B) a loss of judgment and concentration.
(C) the loss of sensory functions.
(D) the extreme amount of care needed for the patient.
(E) the inability to read and write.

4. The passage supplies information for verifying which of the following assumptions?

(A) The Alzheimer's patient has a specific illness at the onset of the disease.
(B) Skill mastery is retained after cognitive functioning is diminished.
(C) Personality changes may be a major symptom of the disease.
(D) Senility and Alzheimer's disease are synonymous.
(E) Long-term care is necessary for all patients.

A submarine was first used as an offensive weapon during the American Revolutionary War. The *Turtle*, a one-man submersible designed by an American inventor named David Bushnell and hand operated by a screw propeller, attempted to sink a British man-of-war in New York Harbor. The plan was to attach a charge of gunpowder to the ship's bottom with screws and explode it with a time fuse. After repeated failures to force the screws through the copper sheathing of the hull of HMS *Eagle*, the submarine gave up and withdrew, exploding its powder a short distance from the *Eagle*. Although the attack was unsuccessful, it caused the British to move their blockading ships from the harbor to the outer bay.

On 17 February 1864, a Confederate craft, a hand-propelled submersible, carrying a crew of eight men, sank a Federal corvette that was blockading Charleston

Harbor. The hit was accomplished by a torpedo suspended ahead of the Confederate Hunley as she rammed the Union frigate *Housatonic*, and is the first recorded instance of a submarine sinking a warship.

The submarine first became a major component in naval warfare during World War I, when Germany demonstrated its full potentialities. Wholesale sinking of Allied shipping by the German U-boats almost swung the war in favor of the Central Powers. Then, as now, the submarine's greatest advantage was that it could operate beneath the ocean surface where detection was difficult. Sinking a submarine was comparatively easy, once it was found — but finding it before it could attack was another matter.

During the closing months of World War I, the Allied Submarine Devices Investigation Committee was formed to obtain from science and technology more effective underwater detection equipment. The committee developed a reasonably accurate device for locating a submerged submarine. This device was a trainable hydrophone, which was attached to the bottom of the ASW ship, and used to detect screw noises and other sounds that came from a submarine. Although the committee disbanded after World War I, the British made improvements on the locating device during the interval between then and World War II, and named it ASDIC after the committee.

American scientists further improved on the device, calling it sonar, a name derived from the underlined initials of the words <u>so</u>und <u>n</u>avigation and <u>r</u>anging.

At the end of World War II, the United States improved the snorkel (a device for bringing air to the crew and engines when operating submerged on diesels) and developed the Guppy (short for greater underwater propulsion power), a conversion of the fleet-type submarine of World War II fame. The superstructure was changed by reducing the surface area, streamlining every protruding object, and enclosing the periscope shears in a streamlined metal fairing. Performance increased greatly with improved electronic equipment, additional battery capacity, and the addition of the snorkel.

5. This passage is organized to best show

(A) the invention of the submarine.
(B) how engineers realized the importance of streamlined submarine design.
(C) the evolution of the submarine.
(D) events leading to the development of the snorkel.
(E) how the submarine was used in WWII.

6. According to the passage, the submarine's success was due in part to its ability to

(A) strike and escape undetected.
(B) move swifter than other vessels.
(C) remain underwater for longer periods of time.
(D) submerge to great depths while being hunted.
(E) run silently.

7. The passage implies that one of the most pressing modifications needed for the submarine was to

(A) streamline its shape.
(B) enlarge the submarine for accommodating more torpedoes and men.
(C) reduce the noise caused by the submarine.
(D) modify for staying submerged longer.
(E) add a snorkel.

8. The passage states that, in the first submarine offensive, the submarine

(A) encountered and sank German U-boats.
(B) sank a ship belonging to its own nation.
(C) torpedoed a British man-of-war.
(D) sank nothing and exploded its powder away from its target.
(E) was detected and was itself destroyed.

9. It is implied that

(A) ASDIC was formed to obtain technology for underwater detection.
(B) ASDIC developed an accurate device for locating submarines.
(C) the hydrophone was attached to the bottom of the ship.
(D) the technology of the hydrophone is being used currently.
(E) ASDIC was formed to develop technology to defend U.S. shipping.

10. All of the following are true EXCEPT

(A) The first underwater vehicle was designed for only one person.
(B) Submarines were hand propelled until the German U-boats of WWII.
(C) In WWI, the Allied Submarine Devices Investigation Committee sought to obtain a means for locating submersed vehicles.
(D) SONAR was developed by British and American scientists.
(E) A Guppy is a modification of a WWII fleet submarine.

11. From the passage, one can infer

(A) David Bushnell was indirectly responsible for the sinking of a Federal corvette in Charleston Harbor.
(B) David Bushnell invented the *Turtle*.
(C) the *Turtle* was a one-man submarine.
(D) the *Turtle* sank the *Eagle* on February 19, 1864.
(E) the design of the *Turtle* was a response to science fiction.

Our heritage is richer because of the men and women of France who came to this continent and explored and settled the wilderness. The breadth of their achievements and the depth of the heritage they bequeathed to the United States transcends their small numbers. A substantial part of this heritage was mixed into the mainstream of America through 6,000 unhappy Acadians, who were expelled in 1755 from Acadia (Nova Scotia) by the British, its new rulers under the terms of the Treaty of Utrecht. The Acadians at first scattered throughout the British colonies, from Maine to Georgia, but most of them finally settled in Louisiana. Henry Wadsworth Longfellow's poem *Evangeline*, an epic about the Acadian odyssey, is the most widely known tribute to the French heritage in the United States.

Other persecuted Huguenots, also seeking refuge and religious freedom, contributed another equally important segment of our French heritage. They settled in clusters from Rhode Island to South Carolina, especially in Charleston, and enriched the cultural patterns evolving in the colonies. Therefore, much of the flavor of France in the United States today stems not from areas that once were French colonies but from French settlers in the British colonies.

12. The author gives primary emphasis to

(A) racial persecution by the British.
(B) those French who settled in Louisiana.
(C) those French who settled in the wilderness.
(D) an epic of the French odyssey.
(E) French heritage in America.

13. It can be inferred that the Acadians were
(A) British.   (D) unhappy.
(B) persecuted.   (E) reclusive.
(C) gypsies.

14. The author viewed the coming of the French to America as

(A) auspicious.   (D) unlikely.
(B) unfortunate.   (E) foreboding.
(C) inevitable.

Pennsylvania was the most successful of the proprietary colonies. Admiral Sir William Penn was a wealthy and respected friend of Charles II. His son, William, was an associate of George Fox, founder of the Society of Friends—a despised Quaker. When the senior Penn died, in 1670, his Quaker son inherited not only the friendship of the Crown but also an outstanding unpaid debt of some magnitude owed to his father by the King. As settlement, in 1681 he received a grant of land in America, called "Pennsylvania," which he decided to use as a refuge for his persecuted coreligionists. It was a princely domain, extending along the Delaware River from the 40th to the 43rd parallel. As Proprietor, Penn was both ruler and landlord. The restrictions on the grant were essentially the same as those imposed on the second Lord Baltimore: colonial laws had to be in harmony with those of England and had to be assented to by a representative assembly.

Penn lost little time in advertising his grant and the terms on which he offered settlement. He promised religious freedom and virtually total self-government. More than 1,000 colonists arrived the first year, most of whom were Mennonites and Quakers. Penn himself arrived in 1682 at New Castle and spent the winter at Upland, a Swedish settlement on the Delaware that the English had taken over; he renamed it Chester. He founded a capital city a few miles upstream and named it Philadelphia — the City of Brotherly Love. Well situated and well planned, it grew rapidly. Within two years, it had more than 600 houses, many of them handsome brick residences surrounded by lawns and gardens.

Shiploads of Quakers poured into the colony. By the summer of 1683, more than 3,000 settlers had arrived. Welsh, Germans, Scotch-Irish, Mennonites, Quakers, Jews, and Baptists mingled in a New World utopia. Not even the great Puritan migration had populated a colony so fast. Pennsylvania soon rivaled Massachusetts, New York, and Virginia. In part its prosperity was attributable to its splendid location and fertile soils, but even more to the proprietor's felicitous administration. In a series of laws — the Great Law and the First and Second Frames of Government — Penn created one of the most humane and progressive governments then in existence. It was characterized by broad principles of religious toleration, a well-organized bicameral legislature, and forward-looking penal code.

Another reason for the colony's growth was that, unlike the other colonies, it was not troubled by the Indians. Penn had bought their lands and made a series of peace treaties that were scrupulously fair and rigidly adhered to. For more than half a century, Indians and whites lived in Pennsylvania in peace. Quaker farmers, who were never armed, could leave their children with neighboring "savages" when they went into town for a visit.

By any measure, Penn's "Holy Experiment" was a magnificent success. Penn proved that a state could function smoothly on Quaker principles, without oaths, arms, or priests, and that these principles encouraged individual morality and freedom of conscience. Furthermore, ever a good businessman, he made a personal fortune while treating his subjects with unbending fairness and honesty.

15. Which of the following statements would the author most likely agree with?

(A) The King of England imposed severe restrictions on Penn's land grant.
(B) Penn was an opportunistic businessman.
(C) The Indians of Pennsylvania were savages.
(D) Penn was too friendly with the King of England.
(E) Indians didn't bother the settlers because they were permitted to practice their own religion.

16. The author mentions the "Holy Experiment" as an example of

(A) English-Colonial collaboration.
(B) an early bicameral.
(C) a treaty with Indians.
(D) religious toleration.
(E) a reason for establishing a proprietary colony.

17. Which of the following was NOT true of Pennsylvania's colony?

(A) Rapid settlement
(B) Refuge for religious non-conformists
(C) Tolerant state religion
(D) Proprietary government
(E) Laws in harmony with those of England

18. It can be inferred from the selection that

(A) all other colonies would have grown more rapidly if they had been organized in a manner similar to Pennsylvania.
(B) all colonies should have been in harmony with the laws of England and had a representative assembly.

(C) those colonies that were awards for service from the crown were better-administered.
(D) the Pennsylvania Colony was the first colony to experience a tolerance for a number of nationalities and varied religious groups.
(E) life with the Indians would have been much easier in other colonies if land had been purchased and treaties adhered to.

19. The "Great Law" and the "First and Second Frames of Government"

(A) established Penn's political reputation.
(B) created treaties with the Indians.
(C) became the basis of a progressive republic form of government.
(D) placed restrictions on immigration.
(E) had to be overturned when they became inefficient.

20. After the summer of 1683 the Pennsylvania colony could be referred to as

(A) a "melting-pot" colony.
(B) a Quaker colony.
(C) the largest American colony.
(D) a Colonial Republic.
(E) the first "democratic" colony.

21. According to the selection, as religious freedom was guaranteed, all of the following religious sects were mentioned as settlers in Pennsylvania except

(A) Catholics.   (D) Mennonites.
(B) Jews.   (E) Quakers.
(C) Baptists.

22. The author uses which of the following writing techniques?

(A) Syllogistic form
(B) Development of an analogy
(C) Literary allusion
(D) Direct quotation
(E) Supporting facts

Cacti and other succulent plants originate in areas where water is only occasionally available and are, therefore, conditioned to deal with long periods of drought. They possess structural modifications enabling them to store moisture for use in times of scarcity.

Such adaptations may be similar in both groups. (All cacti are succulents, but not all succulents are cacti.) Storage areas include thickened leaves, stems, and corms. Leaves, which transpire precious moisture, may be eliminated altogether (with the stem taking over the process of photosynthesis), or the moisture in the leaves may be protected from evaporation by a leathery surface or covered with wiry or velvety hairs, thick spines, or even with a powdery coating.

The very shape of many succulents provides the same protection; globular and columnar forms offer the least exposed area to the drying effects of sun and wind.

Many times there are "look-alikes" in the two groups. Certain cacti coming from the New World closely resemble counterparts in the Euphorbias of Africa.

How do we then differentiate between cacti and other succulents? It is not always easy. Presence or absence of leaves can be helpful; size and brilliance of flowers are also helpful, but the real test comes by learning to recognize the areole.

The areole is possessed by cacti alone, and consists of cushion-like modifications on the body of the cactus from which arise spines, hairs (and the barbed hairs or spines of *Opuntia*), flowers, fruit, and often new growth.

The flowers of cacti are usually more conspicuous and most often appear from areoles near the top of the plant. In other succulents they are inclined to be less showy and more likely to emerge from between the leaves or from the base.

In addition, with a very minor possible exception (a form of *Rhipsalis*), all cacti are native to the Western Hemisphere. It is sometimes hard to believe this because of the vast areas of escaped cacti in many parts of the world today.

The majority of other succulents (excluding *Agave*, *Echeveria*, *Sedum*, *Sempervivum* and a few others) are indigenous to Africa and a few scattered areas in the Eastern Hemisphere.

Both cacti and other succulents are excellent subjects for the outdoor garden, greenhouse, or windowsill. They require a minimum of care, provided that they have a requisite amount of sunlight and that their condition of hardiness is respected.

23. Which one of the following is the best title for the passage?

(A) Succulents and Non-Succulents
(B) Regions of the World and their Vegetation
(C) Distinguishing Between Succulents and Cacti

(D) Subjects for the Outdoor Garden
(E) Characteristics of Cacti and Other Succulents

24. Which features from the list below best distinguish cacti from other succulents?

(A) Absence of leaves; presence of areoles; large, brilliant flowers; nativity to the Western Hemisphere
(B) Presence or absence of leaves; showy flowers which always appear at the top of the plant; indigenous to Africa and a few scattered areas in the Eastern Hemisphere
(C) The areole; presence of leaves; flowers which are likely to emerge from between the leaves or from the base
(D) The flowers of cacti are usually more conspicuous and most often appear near the top of the plant; the areole is possessed by cacti alone.
(E) The majority of other succulents are indigenous to Africa and a few scattered areas in the Eastern Hemisphere.

25. Which one of the following statements best describes the attitude of the author toward cacti and succulents?

(A) Cacti are to be chosen over succulents for the home.
(B) Either are excellent subjects to study in the wild, but to preserve their beauty they should not be removed to the home.
(C) Both are excellent subjects for botanists to study.
(D) Both feature interesting adaptations; the cacti is the preferred.
(E) Both are excellent subjects for the outdoor garden, greenhouse, or windowsill.

26. According to the information given in the passage, which one of the following statements is NOT true?

(A) Cacti and other succulents have evolved in areas where there is little water available.
(B) Leathery or hairy surfaces, thick spines, and even powdery coatings have evolved to help retard the transpiration of moisture from the leaves of cacti.
(C) Because of the vast areas of escaped cacti, it is difficult to believe that almost all cacti are native to the Eastern Hemisphere.
(D) The globular and columnar forms of cacti

offer a smaller exposed area to the sun; therefore, drying is reduced and more moisture is retained.
- (E) Both cacti and other succulents are excellent subjects for the outdoor garden, greenhouse, or windowsill since they require minimal care.

27. It could logically follow that the first line of the next paragraph would begin with which one of the following?

- (A) The size and brilliance of the flowers of the cacti are interesting subjects for further attention.
- (B) Cacti and other succulents are generally able to withstand rapid changes in temperature.
- (C) The globular and columnar shapes of cacti have been frequent topics of study for artists–particularly those of the American Midwest.
- (D) Disney's "The Living Desert" is a full-length feature which focuses on cacti.
- (E) A study of the flowers can tell the researcher much about the original location and structural modifications of the cacti.

28. The most compelling reason for choosing cacti over other succulents for a windowsill would be which one of the following?

- (A) Cacti require less care than do other succulents.
- (B) The shape of the cacti is more appealing than that of the other succulents.
- (C) Succulents from the Eastern Hemisphere do not adapt well to the Western Hemisphere.
- (D) The flowers of cacti are usually more conspicuous and most often appear between the leaves or at the base.
- (E) The flowers of cacti are usually more conspicuous and most often appear from areoles near the top of the plant.

29. According to the passage, which of the following statements are true?

- I. The areole distinguishes cacti from other succulents.
- II. Cactus flowers are more conspicuous and tend to emerge from between the leaves or near the base.
- III. The adaptations to conserve moisture are not very similar in cacti and other succulents.

- (A) I only.
- (B) II only.
- (C) I and II only.
- (D) III only.
- (E) I and III only.

30. Which one of the following would probably best describe the author's reaction to the many laws being enacted to protect the cacti and to prevent their being removed from desert areas or vandalized?

- (A) Apathy
- (B) Confusion
- (C) Despair
- (D) Distaste
- (E) Understanding

The Jefferson nickel was executed by Felix Schlag, whose design was chosen from among 390 artists' sketches submitted to the government. This national competition carried with it a prize for $1,000. The Director of the Mint, with the approval of the Secretary of the Treasury, had suggested that Thomas Jefferson's likeness be placed on a U.S. coin as a tribute to his outstanding statesmanship and his record of public service. Schlag's splendid portrayal of our third President appears on the obverse. The reverse has an illustration of Monticello, the magnificent home Jefferson built for himself near Charlottesville, Virginia. The mintmark was on the reverse at the right side of Monticello until 1968. After that date, it was moved to the right of Jefferson's wig, beside the date on the obverse.

Jefferson began building Monticello, his dream house, at the age of 20 and finally finished it 40 years later in the twilight of his life. Monticello, pictured in careful detail on the reverse of the nickel, is not an ordinary kind of house. It is rather a revolutionary house for his day. Jefferson was a gadgeteer—a man of creative and inventive genius who put his ideas to practical use. Monticello has an observatory in which Jefferson studied the stars and planets with a telescope. The clock in the main hall not only tells the hour but the days of the week as well, and the gears that drive the hands pass through the wall to a duplicate clock over the porch outside. The house has dozens of other amazing conveniences that have to be seen to be appreciated.

No matter what his talents, Jefferson is remembered as a defender of the human rights of man. He spoke to the world through his pen, preferring to put his thoughts in writing rather than in public speech. In a time when revolution was commonplace in America, Jefferson was asked to write The Declaration of Independence, the ageless announcement of Colonial freedom. His words inspired people and sent out to the world a call to arms in the precious name of liberty:

"We hold these Truths to be self-evident, that all men are created equal, that they are endowed by their Creator with certain unalienable Rights, that among these are Life, Liberty and the Pursuit of Happiness."

31. Which one of the following best describes the organization of the information in the passage?

   (A) The passage begins with a description of the Jefferson nickel, then discusses Jefferson's contributions to the Treasury system.

   (B) The passage begins with a discussion of the work of Felix Schlag on the Jefferson nickel, and continues with a discussion of Jefferson's architectural studies.

   (C) The passage begins with a description of the contest for the design of the Jefferson nickel, then continues with a discussion of Jefferson's role as author of The Declaration of Independence.

   (D) The passage begins with a description and brief history of the Jefferson nickel, and continues with a sketch of Jefferson's architectural interests and his role as a statesman.

   (E) The passage begins with a description and brief history of the Jefferson nickel, and continues with a discussion of Jefferson's political beliefs.

32. Where would the mintmark appear on a 1969 nickel?

   (A) On the obverse side to the right of Monticello

   (B) On the reverse side to the right of Monticello

   (C) On the obverse side to the right of Jefferson's wig

   (D) On the reverse side to the right of Jefferson's wig

   (E) Mintmarks do not appear after 1968.

33. Which one of the following words would be the best substitute for the word "revolutionary" in the passage?

   (A) Creative   (D) Political

   (B) Unusual   (E) Innovative

   (C) Expensive

Père Claude Jean Allouez explored Lake Superior from 1665 to 1667. At his little mission station near the western end of the lake, he heard from the Indians of a great river to the west. Père Jacques Marquette determined to investigate. In 1673, accompanied by Louis Jolliet and five others, he left St. Ignace Mission and ascended the Fox River, which flows into Green Bay, crossed over to the Wisconsin River, and followed it to the upper Mississippi. The party then descended the Mississippi to the mouth of the Arkansas. These Frenchmen were not the first Europeans to sight or travel the Mississippi; De Soto and Moscoso had done so a century and a half before.

The report of the exploration was rushed back to Quebec, where, in 1672, Count Frontenac had arrived as Governor of the province. He and his friend, the remarkable La Salle–who earlier may have penetrated the Ohio River Valley–listened with deep interest. Prior to that time, the two men had been involved in projects to open the Western Lake country to French trade.

34. The author's attitude toward Allouez and Marquette is best described as

   (A) admiring and speculative.

   (B) critical and biased.

   (C) objective and positive.

   (D) interested and analytical.

   (E) inconclusive and tentative.

35. Through his exploration, Marquette discovered

   (A) he needed to travel north to reach his southern destination.

   (B) a river he had not expected to find.

   (C) he was not the first Frenchman to travel the river.

   (D) a new route for transporting French settlers to the West.

   (E) French settlements already existed.

36. Frontenac and La Salle had been involved in projects for opening the lake country. The passage implies the projects were related to

   (A) missionary work.

   (B) agriculture.

   (C) fur trading.

   (D) surveying and exploring.

   (E) water transportation.

37. All of the following are either stated or implied in the passage EXCEPT:

(A) Allouez explored the western end of Lake Superior.
(B) Marquette and his party were the first Frenchmen to travel the Mississippi River.
(C) La Salle explored the Mississippi River valley.
(D) Marquette had to follow the Wisconsin River to reach the Mississippi.
(E) Marquette did not travel past the Arkansas River.

Dr. Robert H. Goddard, at one time a physics professor at Clark University in Worcester, Massachusetts, was largely responsible for the sudden interest in rockets in the 1920s. When Dr. Goddard first started his experiments with rockets, no related technical information was available. He started a new science, industry, and field of engineering. Through his scientific experiments, he pointed the way to the development of rockets as we know them today. The Smithsonian Institute agreed to finance his experiments in 1920. From these experiments he wrote a paper titled "A Method of Reaching Extreme Altitudes," in which he outlined a space rocket of the step (multistage) principle, theoretically capable of reaching the moon.

Goddard discovered that with a properly shaped, smooth, tapered nozzle he could increase the ejection velocity eight times with the same weight of fuel. This would not only drive a rocket eight times faster, but 64 times farther, according to his theory. Early in his experiments he found that solid-fuel rockets would not give him the high power or the duration of power needed for a dependable supersonic motor capable of extreme altitudes. On 16 March 1926, after many trials, Dr. Goddard successfully fired, for the first time in history, a liquid-fuel rocket into the air. It attained an altitude of 184 feet and a speed of 60 mph. This seems small as compared to present-day speeds and heights of missile flights, but instead of trying to achieve speed or altitude at this time, Dr. Goddard was trying to develop a dependable rocket motor.

Dr. Goddard later was the first to fire a rocket that reached a speed faster than the speed of sound. He was the first to develop a gyroscopic steering apparatus for rockets. He was the first to use vanes in the jet stream for rocket stabilization during the initial phase of a rocket flight. And he was the first to patent the idea of step rockets. After proving on paper and in actual tests that a rocket can travel in a vacuum, he developed the mathematical theory of rocket propulsion and rocket flight, including basic designs for long-range rockets. All of this information was available to our military

men before World War II, but evidently its immediate use did not seem applicable. Near the end of World War II we started intense work on rocket-powered guided missiles, using the experiments and developments of Dr. Goddard and the American Rocket Society.

38. Which one of the following questions does the passage best answer?

(A) How did Dr. Goddard become interested in rocket science?
(B) How did Dr. Goddard develop the new field of rocket science?
(C) How is a multistage rocket capable of reaching the moon?
(D) Why is liquid fuel more dependable than solid fuel?
(E) How did the American Rocket Society get its start?

39. One can assume from the article that

(A) all factors being equal, the proper shape of the rocket nozzle would increase the ejection velocity and travel distance.
(B) solid-fuel rockets would give higher power and duration.
(C) a blunt nozzle would negatively affect speed and distance.
(D) supersonic motors are needed for extreme altitudes.
(E) the first successfully fired liquid fueled rocket was for developing a dependable rocket motor.

40. The first step in Dr. Goddard's development of a feasible rocket was

(A) the mathematical theory of rocket propulsion and rocket flight.
(B) the development of liquid rocket fuel.
(C) the development and use of vanes for rocket stabilizing.
(D) the development of the gyroscope.
(E) his thesis for multistage rocket design.

Reading Comprehension Drill
ANSWER KEY

1. (C)	21. (A)
2. (A)	22. (E)
3. (C)	23. (E)
4. (C)	24. (D)
5. (C)	25. (E)
6. (A)	26. (C)
7. (C)	27. (B)
8. (D)	28. (E)
9. (D)	29. (A)
10. (B)	30. (E)
11. (A)	31. (D)
12. (E)	32. (C)
13. (B)	33. (E)
14. (A)	34. (C)
15. (B)	35. (A)
16. (B)	36. (C)
17. (C)	37. (C)
18. (E)	38. (B)
19. (C)	39. (C)
20. (A)	40. (E)

Attacking Antonym Questions

In keeping with the rest of the GRE Verbal Ability Test, the Antonym questions test your vocabulary skills. If your vocabulary skills are well honed, you will be able to do well on the Antonym questions. This is true because Antonym questions often require you to make fine distinctions between words. Thus, a strong vocabulary is an asset.

Since the Antonym questions test your vocabulary skills, your first step in preparing for them is to make sure you carefully studied Chapter 4, the Vocabulary Enhancer. If, even after studying Chapter 4, you are still worried about your vocabulary skills, you're in luck. We say this because there are other ways to attack the Analogy questions.

Important Information!

But before we get into the specifics of how to attack Antonym questions, you should learn a little more about antonyms. **An antonym is opposite in meaning to a given word.** For example, the antonym of *hot* is *cold*. Another example: *dry* is the antonym of *wet*. Unfortunately, the GRE will not be testing you on such simple words!

*Important
Information!*

The Antonym questions on the GRE will give a word and then you must choose the best antonym from the five choices. The words used in Antonym questions will be nouns, verbs, or adjectives. It is very important to know that the form of the word must match its antonym. If the word you are given is a noun, the correct antonym will also be a noun. We will show you how to use this to your advantage later in this chapter.

About the Directions

*Important
Information!*

Take time to learn the directions for the Antonym questions of the Verbal Ability Test. Learning them now will save you valuable time when you take the GRE.

> **DIRECTIONS:** Each question below consists of a word printed in capital letters, followed by five words or phrases. Choose the word or phrase that is most nearly opposite in meaning to the word in capital letters. Since some of the questions require you to distinguish fine shades of meaning, be sure to consider all the choices before deciding which one is best.

Tips for Answering Antonym Questions

When you sit back and think, there are only three types of Antonym questions that you'll encounter on the GRE:

- **Words you know**
- **Words you think you know**
- **Words you don't know**

Important Strategy

Luckily for you, we have some great strategies to attack each type!

Attacking Words You Know

When you get a question that presents a word that you definitely know, don't immediately jump at the first choice that you think is correct. Even the GRE writers warn you against this. Remember the directions. The last sentence of the directions explicitly tells you to consider every choice before making your decision.

Important Strategy

This warning is extremely critical. **Even if you know the definition of the capitalized word, not all words have clear opposites (antonyms).** For example, suppose you're given the word *corrugated*. What its opposite? Visualize a corrugated box. Seeing the grooves and ridges in your mind's eye will help you find the right the choice: *smooth* or, perhaps, *seamless*.

Important Strategy

To avoid being confused by the choices, we suggest the first step you take with Antonym questions is to read the capitalized word and NOT look at the choices yet. **First, let's work with the capitalized word alone. Now, since you know what the word means, come up with an antonym on your own.**

> **STEP 1** | Look at the capitalized word, and before you even check the choices, come up with an antonym on your own.

We suggest you take this preliminary step to avoid becoming confused by the choices (we'll explain ourselves better in a minute, just trust us for now). Let's continue and work with an example:

FRENZIED:

Remember we aren't looking at the answer choices yet. What's the opposite of *frenzied*? You probably would come up with a word that is close to *calm*, since *frenzied* means to be frantic or in an excited state.

Bust it!

Your next step is to take the antonym you've come up with (*calm*) and look at the answer choices. **Since you already have an antonym to the capitalized word, you are now looking for a synonym**

(a similar word) for that antonym in the answer choices. Now do you see why we suggest coming up with an antonym of your own?

The human brain works much faster and with less chance for error when comparing similar things, which is why the GRE tests you on antonyms. The writers of the GRE want to push your brain to its limits. But if you simply come up with an antonym before looking at the choices presented, you are no longer working with opposites. Now you are looking for synonyms, which is much easier and faster!

Bust it!

| STEP 2 | In the answer choices, look for a synonym to the antonym you've come up with on your own. |

Here are the answer choices for our example:

FRENZIED:

(A) solid   (D) taciturn

(B) wild   (E) imperturbable

(C) hyperactive

Remember that you are now looking for a word that is similar to the antonym you came up with on your own (*calm*). Of the choices, (B), *wild*, and (C), *hyperactive*, are clearly not correct since they are opposites of *calm*. Choice (A), *solid*, is defined as "powerful or robust." Choice (A) is different from *wild*, but is not synonomous with *calm*, so it should be eliminated. This leaves choices (D), *taciturn*, and (E), *imperturbable*.

Look!

Important Strategy

Now, let's pause for a minute and look back at what you just did. Recognize the pattern. That's right! You used the process of elimination to narrow the choices down to the best answer. **This is the third step to answering an Antonym question: use the process of elimination to find the best answer.**

> **STEP 3** | Use the process of elimination to find the best answer.

Important Strategy

So far, you've eliminated choices (A), (B), and (C). This leaves (D) and (E). You might recognize choice (D), *taciturn*, which means "inclined to speak very little," but not (E) *imperturbable*. At this point it doesn't matter that you don't know what *imperturbable* means since you recognize that (D) *taciturn* is not a synonym for *calm*. Thus, using the process of elimination, choice (E) must be the correct answer.

Attacking Words You Think You Know

Important Strategy

The second type of Antonym question you'll encounter involves a capitalized word that you aren't absolutely sure about, but think you know what it means. This situation can occur if you can use the capitalized word in a sentence but can't come up with a dictionary-type definition for it.

There are a few techniques to help you out in this situation. Let's look at them:

Word Values

You should remember the strategy of using word values from the Sentence Completion review. To refresh your memory, positive words convey a meaning which can be equated with gain, advantage, liveliness, intelligence, virtue, and positive emotions, conditions, or actions. Negative words convey a meaning which can be equated with loss, defeat, dullness, evil, and negative emotions, conditions, or actions.

At this point you might be asking, "How does word value help me with Antonym questions?" The answer to that can be found when approaching capitalized words when you only think you might know their meanings.

Important Strategy

If you can't define a capitalized word in a question, you can probably give it a positive or negative value. Taking this one step further, **if the capitalized word has a positive word value, its antonym will have a negative value! Conversely, if the capitalized word has a negative value, its antonym will have a positive value.**

Let's look at an example:

SARDONIC:

(A) ironic   (D) profitable

(B) benevolent   (E) spiteful

(C) sarcastic

The capitalized word, *sardonic*, may not be familiar to you, but you recognize it. Think of where you have heard or read this word. In your experience, *sardonic* has probably only been used to convey negative emotions. Since the capitalized word has a negative value, you are looking for an antonym that has a positive word value and can eliminate any choices with negative values.

Bust it!

Looking at the answer choices, you can immediately eliminate the negative value choices: (A), *ironic* (meaning the contrary to what is expressed); (C), *sarcastic* (sneering or caustic); and (E), *spiteful* (annoying or malicious). This leaves you with (B), *benevolent*, and (D), *profitable*; both positive value words.

While you may not know the exact definition of *sardonic*, you've probably never seen it used in the context of financial or money matters. This casts a serious doubt on choice (D), *profitable* (yielding profit, gain, or benefit). You probably know that choice (B), *benevolent*, means being inclined to do good. You've used word values to narrow the choices from five to two. Now you must choose between *profitable* and *benevolent*. In your experience, you've never seen *sardonic* used in terms of loss or financial ruin, thus choice (D), *profitable*, could be eliminated. This leaves choice (B), *benevolent*, as your best choice.

Using the Choices to Define the Capitalized Word

Look!

Important Strategy

If you sort of recognize the capitalized word, but can't come up with a concrete definition, and assigning word values doesn't help you to narrow the choices, you can try and use the choices by themselves to work out the question.

Let's look at an example:

FRAUDULENT:

(A) **willful**   (D) **tricky**

(B) **honest**   (E) **legal**

(C) **immaculate**

It is not that difficult to assign a negative value to *fraudulent* if you think about how you've seen it used in context. So you are looking for a choice that has a positive value. Reviewing the choices, you probably would assign four choices with positive values: (A), *willful*; (B), *honest*; (C), *immaculate*; and (E), *legal*. The only negative value choice you can eliminate is (D), *tricky*. So assigning word values won't help you very much to eliminate many choices.

Remember the first step when attacking an Antonym question when you are sure what the capitalized word means. You should come up with an antonym of the capitalized word on your own. This is the same step you should take here, only you should come up with your own antonyms for the CHOICES instead of the capitalized word and work from the choices.

Bust it!

Looking at the choices in our example, can you think of some antonyms for them (excluding choice (D), *tricky*, since you've already been able to eliminate that because of its negative word value):

(A)   *willful* would have an antonym of *involuntary* since it means being done of one's own free will.

(B)   *honest* would have an antonym of *dishonest* or *deceptive* since it means to do something in a respectable or creditable manner.

(C)   *immaculate* would have an antonym of *flawed, messy* or *dirty* since it means perfectly clean, without error, or spotless.

(E)   *legal* would have an antonym of *illegal* or *criminal* since it means something that conforms to the law or rules.

It's a good idea to write down these antonyms on your scrap paper so you don't forget or confuse them. Having them written down on scrap paper will also enable you to cross each off as you eliminate them.

Now take each antonym you've thought of for the choices and compare them to the capitalized word. When comparing them, think "could this antonym I've thought of mean the same thing as the capitalized word?"

(A)   does *fraudulent* mean *involuntary*?

(B)   does *fraudulent* mean *dishonest* or *deceptive*?

(C)   does *fraudulent* mean *flawed, messy,* or *dirty*?

(E)   does *fraudulent* mean *illegal* or *criminal*?

Bust it!

After comparing your choices' antonyms, you should be able to eliminate some more choices. Always keep in mind the ways in which you've seen the capitalized word *fraudulent* used. Using the capitalized word in context will help you very much.

You should have been able to eliminate choices (A), *willful*, and (C), *immaculate*, right away since the antonyms and the capitalized words aren't even close in meaning. This leaves you with choices (B), *honest*, and (E), *legal*.

Thinking back to how you've seen *fraudulent* used in context, you might lean more towards choice (B), *honest*, since you might remember *fraudulent* being used in a context outside of legal or criminal references. You would be correct since *honest* is a better antonym for *fraudulent* than the more narrow definition of *legal*. Thus, choice (B), *honest*, is the correct answer.

Even if you couldn't make a strong decision between choices (B) and (C), by thinking of antonyms for the choices you were able to eliminate all but two of the possible answers. That gives you a 50 percent chance of answering correctly. Not bad when you started with only a 20 percent chance of picking the correct choice.

Bust it!

It should be extremely clear to you now that you must choose the BEST answer among the choices, not simply the correct answer. Both *honest* and *legal* are acceptable antonyms for *fraudulent*. But *honest* is the BETTER choice. The GRE will require you to make some fine distinctions between words. So make sure you look at all the choices very carefully.

Eliminate Words That Don't Have Antonyms

Earlier, we mentioned the possibility of words that don't have antonyms. The example we used was *corrugated*. But some word choices have no opposites at all. When these words appear as answer choices, simply eliminate them!

"How can there be a word without an antonym?" you might ask. Think about that. Here are some examples:

**Important
Strategy**

> **pink**
> **bee**
> **golf**
> **planet**

See what we mean? When you encounter an answer choice that has no clear antonym, eliminate it and go on to the next choice.

The Parts of Speech Should Match

The antonym to the capitalized word will always be the same part of speech as the capitalized word. We mentioned this earlier and it is very important to remember.

Important Strategy

The antonym to a noun is always a noun. The antonym to a verb is always a verb. Eliminate any answer choices whose part of speech does not match the capitalized word. For example:

QUARTER:

(A) imbibe   (D) eliminate

(B) house   (E) defend

(C) unite

All the choices given are verbs; therefore, *quarter* must also be used here as a verb. (Yes, *house* is a verb as in "to house the homeless.") Since *quarter* means "to divide," our choice here would be (C), *unite*. *House* could easily have misled us if we were thinking about *quartering* (housing) soldiers. But, of course, *house* would then have been a synonym, not an antonym.

Look Out for Multiple Meanings

Always keep in mind that English words often have multiple meanings, even when the part of speech remains the same. Read the example below carefully to see what meaning is needed.

PRIDE:

(A) one   (D) arrogance

(B) magistrate   (E) self-esteem

(C) immodesty

If this question caused you difficulty, think of *pride* as "a pride of lions" (a group). Used in this way, the antonym of *pride* would be choice (A), *one*.

Important Strategy

Use Word Parts and Foreign Languages to Assist You

If you do not know the meaning of a word, look at its prefix, suffix, or root to help you (remember the lists in Chapter 4, the Vocabulary Enhancer?).

Knowing that *mal-* means *bad* may help you figure out *maladroit* can be defined as "someone who is unskillful." Also, use any knowledge you have of foreign languages to help you with vocabulary. For instance, if you know that *cantar* means "to sing" in Spanish, then you can decipher the meaning of the English word *canticle* (a song or hymn).

Important Strategy

Attacking Words You Don't Know

If you look at the capitalized word and cannot figure out what it means and, after trying all of the techniques we've described in this chapter so far, cannot even get a vague idea of what the capitalized word means, you are truly stuck.

Since you cannot skip questions on the GRE CBT, you must make a choice and move on to the next question. But, an educated guess is much better than a blind guess. So there is one last technique that can help you.

Look!

Important Strategy

If you have no idea of the meaning of the capitalized word, look at the choices to see if you can find a pattern. If three of the choices seem to indicate *dryness*, then maybe the capitalized word means *wet*. You can think in this manner because the writers of the GRE probably placed answer choices that are synonyms with the capitalized word to confuse people who might know the definition of the capitalized word.

This is not, of course, a foolproof strategy, but it may help (in combination with the other techniques we've taught you) if you are totally at a loss. Just make the best choice you can and move on.

Here's an example:

QUERCINE:

(A) cow

(B) oaken

(C) treed

(D) wooden

(E) aquatic

Wow! You might have never seen or heard this word before. And trying to break *quercine* down to its prefix, root, or suffix doesn't help much either. The next technique you should use is to look at the choices and try to determine a pattern.

You should immediately see that choices (B), *oaken*, (C), *treed*, and (D), *wooden*, all are adjectives associated with trees. *Oaken* means having to do with oak trees. *Treed* means provided or planted with trees. *Wooden* means made of wood from trees.

Taking this pattern into consideration, you might assume that *quercine* is an antonym of something to do with trees. Looking at the remaining choices, find the word that is opposite of *tree-like*.

Remember that the parts of speech must match. Since you've determined that the capitalized word is probably an adjective for *tree*, the correct answer will be an opposite adjective for *tree*. This eliminates choice (A), *cow*, since that word is a noun, not an adjective.

Bust it!

By working through this question using all of the techniques we've previously described, and by looking at the pattern of the choices, you should have been able to eliminate all but one choice: (E) *aquatic*. This is the best answer since it is the only choice that is an adjective and also opposite in meaning to *tree-like*.

By the way, *quercine* is an adjective meaning "of the oak tree."

While using the pattern of the answer choices will not work all the time, it usually can help you eliminate at least three of the choices. If you can eliminate three of the choices, you are left with a 50 percent chance of guessing the correct answer. Those are pretty good odds for getting a question right when you can't even define the capitalized word!

Points to Remember

On Target!

✔   *There are only three types of Antonym questions on the GRE: words you know; words you think you know; and words you don't know.*

✔   *Make up your own antonym for the capitalized word and look among the choices for a synonym to the antonym you thought of.*

✔   *Use the process of elimination to narrow down the possible correct answer choices.*

✔   *Choose the word or phrase that is most nearly opposite in meaning to the capitalized word.*

✔   *Carefully consider all choices before picking your answer.*

✔   *Use word values to eliminate answer choices that do not have opposite values from those of the capitalized word.*

✔   *Use the choices to define the capitalized word and then work the problem out.*

✔   *Eliminate answer choices that don't have clear antonyms.*

✔   *Eliminate any answer choices whose part of speech does not match the capitalized word. The antonym to a noun is always a noun. The antonym to a verb is always a verb.*

✔　　　　If you do not know the meaning of a word, look at its suffix, prefix, or root for clues.

✔　　　　Use any foreign language knowledge you might have to decipher word meanings.

✔　　　　Look for any patterns among the choices that might give you a clue if you are unsure of the meaning of the capitalized word.

On Target!

Drill: Antonym Questions

1. AMELIORATE:
(A) decline
(B) pause
(C) aggravate
(D) arrest
(E) amputate

2. CLOYING:
(A) bland
(B) flattering
(C) saccharine
(D) boring
(E) acerbic

3. EUPHONY:
(A) eulogy
(B) cacophony
(C) lethargy
(D) verbosity
(E) brevity

4. EPHEMERAL:
(A) constant
(B) perennial
(C) eternal
(D) brief
(E) durable

5. COGENT:
(A) lucid
(B) pedagogical
(C) abstruse
(D) inerrant
(E) inane

6. DEARTH:
(A) sufficiency
(B) paucity
(C) voluminous
(D) parsimony
(E) cornucopia

7. CONTUMACIOUS:
(A) obdurate
(B) sinuous
(C) facetious
(D) malleable
(E) spurious

8. NESCIENCE:
(A) lack of conviction
(B) remote thought
(C) keen awareness
(D) disinterest
(E) naiveté

9. ENCOMIUM:
(A) aphorism
(B) epitaph
(C) euphemism
(D) diatribe
(E) emendation

10. DESICCATE:
(A) wet
(B) humidify
(C) baptize
(D) immerse
(E) dehydrate

11. PAUCITY:
(A) dearth
(B) loquacious
(C) sanative
(D) plethora
(E) lugubrious

12. CONSONANCE:
(A) conscience
(B) conscious
(C) coalesce
(D) contention
(E) consign

13. TILT:
(A) incline
(B) align
(C) list
(D) pitch
(E) slant

14. VENIAL:
(A) hedonic
(B) ineffable
(C) peccadillo
(D) implacable
(E) heinous

15. PRODIGAL:
(A) wandering
(B) tarrying
(C) spendthrift
(D) frugal
(E) lavish

16. VIABLE:
(A) remnant
(B) viands
(C) subsistence
(D) vestige
(E) moribund

17. RECUMBENT:
(A) prone
(B) obligatory
(C) vertical
(D) supine
(E) level

18. VOLATILE:
(A) explosive
(B) impulsive
(C) mercurial
(D) deliberate
(E) transitory

19. FACTIOUS:
(A) bellicose
(B) desultory
(C) fortuitous
(D) fractious
(E) felicitous

20. PROBITY:
(A) aesthetics
(B) perfidy
(C) abeyance
(D) predilection
(E) complementary

21. FACTITIOUS:
(A) authentic
(B) travesty
(C) pedantic
(D) mordant
(E) rapacious

22. PROCLIVITY:
(A) penchant
(B) deflection
(C) dilatory
(D) diminish
(E) procedure

23. REMOTE:
(A) foreign
(B) proximate
(C) parallax
(D) inapposite
(E) propinquity

24. TREPIDATION:
(A) apprehension
(B) sagacity
(C) perturbation
(D) agitation
(E) courage

25. ABYSS:
(A) zenith
(B) profundity
(C) interval
(D) interstice
(E) depression

26. CORPULENT:
(A) portly
(B) vociferate
(C) becoming
(D) anorexic
(E) adverse

27. ABJECT:
(A) caring
(B) joyful
(C) empathetic
(D) objective
(E) rational

28. RESERVED:
(A) chivalrous
(B) affable
(C) ingratiating
(D) cultivated
(E) well-bred

29. CALORIC:
(A) fervor
(B) modicum
(C) temperature
(D) zero
(E) frigidity

30. FERAL:
(A) voracious
(B) unconscientious
(C) savage
(D) exacting
(E) cultivated

31. UNCTUOUS:
(A) scrupulous
(B) morose
(C) ravenous
(D) agitated
(E) ingratiating

32. DISSEMBLE:
(A) betray
(B) express sincerely
(C) reassemble
(D) dissolve
(E) resolve

33. ADULTERATED:
(A) ribald
(B) defiled
(C) chaste
(D) infantile
(E) vicious

34. AUGMENTATION:
(A) constriction
(B) accession
(C) expansion
(D) perturbation
(E) satiation

35. TACITURN:
(A) reticent
(B) appeased
(C) reserved
(D) inveigled
(E) effusive

36. HELICAL:
(A) spiral
(B) coiled
(C) curved
(D) straight
(E) round

37. ASININE:
(A) fatuous
(B) cunning
(C) idiosyncratic
(D) eccentric
(E) antithetic

38. SAGACIOUS:
(A) shrewd
(B) astute
(C) procumbent
(D) ductile
(E) incapable

39. DISPUTATIOUS:
(A) tending to be dissimilar
(B) bursting apart
(C) unfocused
(D) anxious
(E) agreeable

40. BEATIFIC:
(A) animalistic
(B) melancholy
(C) urbane
(D) civilized
(E) similitude

Antonym Drill
ANSWER KEY

1. (C)	21. (A)
2. (E)	22. (B)
3. (B)	23. (B)
4. (C)	24. (E)
5. (C)	25. (A)
6. (E)	26. (D)
7. (D)	27. (B)
8. (C)	28. (B)
9. (D)	29. (E)
10. (A)	30. (E)
11. (D)	31. (D)
12. (D)	32. (B)
13. (B)	33. (C)
14. (E)	34. (A)
15. (D)	35. (E)
16. (E)	36. (D)
17. (C)	37. (B)
18. (D)	38. (E)
19. (E)	39. (E)
20. (B)	40. (B)

Attacking the Problem Solving Questions

You will encounter two types of questions in the Quantitative Ability section: Problem Solving and Quantitative Comparisons. The GRE has one scored Quantitative section containing approximately 28 problems, and you will have 45 minutes to solve those problems. There might be an additional unscored Quantitative Ability section.

Approximately 12 to 16 of the Quantitative Ability questions will be Problem Solving questions and the other half will be Quantitative Comparison questions. Regardless of which type of question you are working on, however, the Quantitative Ability section of the GRE will only test your knowledge of the following four areas:

Bust it!

- **Arithmetic**

- **Algebra**

- **Geometry**

- **Data Analysis**

That's all. You don't need to worry about calculus. You don't need to worry about trigonometry. **All you are being tested on is the basic mathematical rules and formulas.** Don't worry about all of the advanced math you may have taken in college!

Some bad news is that it may have been a while since you've used the basic math skills you'll need to do well on the GRE. When was the last time you reduced a fraction? To help you remember things like fractions, solving equations, and the Pythagorean Theorem, we'll review these basic math principles. **Some good news is that you've already learned these basic math skills. Although you'll need to refresh your knowledge of these skills (since you haven't used them recently), it won't take long to become comfortable using them again. So, your mission during this review is to refresh your memory and then learn how to use these basic math skills quicker and with more ease!**

Since the Problem Solving questions on the GRE are simply multiple-choice math questions, we've integrated our basic math skills review with the review for the Problem Solving questions. In the next chapter, we'll introduce and prepare you for the Quantitative Comparison questions you'll encounter on the GRE.

Importance of Math on the GRE

If you're trying to improve your GRE score by the most number of points in the shortest amount of time, the math sections are the first places you should look.

There are a number of reasons for this. **First, by studying Problem Solving questions you are also studying Quantitative Comparison questions.** The building blocks of both Quantitative Comparison and Problem Solving questions are arithmetic, algebra, geometry, and data analysis. Much of the knowledge needed to do well on Problem Solving questions is, therefore, transferable to Quantitative Comparison questions.

The second reason you can improve greatly on the math sections is that you are able to review and/or learn the material being tested. For example, **if you review arithmetic, algebra, and geometry, and understand your strengths and weaknesses, you will do much better on the Quantitative Ability section**. But you will be unable to review the material for the Analogies, Antonyms, or Reading Comprehension questions. You can certainly get a better understanding of the question types and you can improve through studying them, but because the questions are based solely on what you read on the day of the test, you cannot get as much of an advantage over these sections of the test as you can over the math sections.

You might be wondering why we didn't include the Sentence Completion questions in that last statement. That's because Sentence Completion questions are somewhat similar to the math questions. There is a body of knowledge that the GRE is testing in Sentence Completion questions: the rules of grammar, punctuation, sentence structure, and so on. So, there is a great deal you can learn to improve your Sentence Completion score. For now, let's concentrate on the math questions to help you increase the "body of knowledge" you have about basic math principles.

Multiple-Choice Math

*Important
Information!*

There are a number of advantages and disadvantages associated with multiple-choice math tests. **The greatest advantage of a multiple-choice test is that the right answer is always given to you.** This means that you may be able to spot the right answer even if you don't understand a problem completely or don't have time to finish it. It means that you may be able to pick the right answer by simply guessing intelligently. It also means that you may be saved from answering a question incorrectly if the answer you obtain is not among the answer choices.

Unfortunately, there are also disadvantages. **One of the biggest disadvantages is that every question presents you with four wrong answers.** These wrong answers are not randomly chosen numbers—they are the answers that you are most likely to get if you make certain mistakes. **These wrong answers also tend to be choices that "look right" if you don't know how to solve the problem.** Thus, on a particular question, you may be relieved to find "your" answer among the answer choices, only to discover later that you fell into a common error trap. Wrong answer choices can also distract or confuse you when you are attempting to solve a problem correctly, causing you to question your answer even though it is right. Here's an example:

What number's square is 35% greater than 60?

(A) 81

(D) 40.5

(B) 12

(E) 95

(C) 9

You may or may not consider this a difficult math question, but that doesn't matter. What matters is that the GRE writers have deemed this a hard question and will try and trap you into selecting the wrong answer choice.

Eliminating Answer Choices

Let's look at choice (A). Even if you knew how to answer this question, you may still have fallen victim to this trap. Yes, choice (A) is a trap answer choice. It's a trap because if you pick this choice you didn't work the problem through to its completion. To illustrate, let's take the problem step by step:

To answer this question, you should know that the first step is to reword the problem to make it easier to understand: "What number's square is 35% greater than 60?" can be thought of as "What number's square is 21 greater than 60?" Why? Because 35% of 60 is 21:

$$35\% \times 60 = 21$$

or

$$.35 \times 60 = 21$$

So, you must determine what is 21 greater than 60. Right, 81! Simply add 21 and 60 to get 81.

Now if you had stopped there and selected choice (A), you would have fallen into the trap because you didn't complete the question. Notice that you are being asked "What *number's square* is

21 greater than 60?" You need to determine the square root of 81 to find the correct answer. What's the correct answer? That's right, choice (C), because the square root of 81 is 9.

But choice (A) is not the only trap in this question! Let's say you know how to answer this type of question up to getting the number 81, but didn't know how to determine a square root. You might have known you had to find its square root, but incorrectly thought that the square root is the number divided by 2. Well, there's the trap waiting for you! Answer choice (D), 40.5, was placed there by the GRE writers exactly because of the chance that test-takers might mistakenly think that the square root of a number is its half. They've placed two traps into this question.

And it's not over yet! If you didn't know how to answer this type of question, but were determined to figure it out through the answer choices, you might pick choice (E), 95, because 35 plus 60 equals 95. A hasty decision on your part, in addition to not knowing how to solve the problem, may place you directly in the path of this trap.

So you can see that it is extremely simple for the writers of the GRE to write hard questions with a high level of difficulty and include multiple traps to trick you into selecting the wrong answer. **To avoid these traps, pay attention and thoroughly read the questions. Once you understand the question, try and find the answer as carefully and quickly as you can.**

Now that you know how the GRE writers can create traps for you in the Quantitative Ability section and you realize how important it is to do well on the Quantitative Ability section of the GRE, you're ready to begin preparing yourself.

Problem Solving Questions

Mastering Problem Solving Questions: STAGE 1

Doing well on the GRE Problem Solving questions involves two separate tasks: mathematical knowledge and understanding the types of problems.

You must have a firm grasp of the mathematical knowledge needed to complete the Problem Solving questions. Without such knowledge, it's almost impossible for you to do well on the GRE. This review will help you meet this requirement. For most people, refreshing their knowledge of basic math on the GRE is the hardest part of preparing to take the test.

Mastering Problem Solving Questions: STAGE 2

The second task required to do well on the GRE Problem Solving questions is to understand as many types of problems as possible. **The more problems you understand, the better off you will be.** And this means practice, practice, practice.

Important Information!

The math on the GRE is fundamentally different from the math you did in high school. In high school, your teacher would teach you something, do a few problems on the board, and then give you a few problems for homework. Usually, the homework problems were the same problems you did in class, with different numbers.

A few weeks would go by, a few more topics would be covered, and your teacher would give you a test. Of course, the problems on the test would be remarkably similar to those you had done in class or for homework. The numbers would, of course, be changed. This is how you learned math in high school. High school math is not designed to test your ability to use mathematical concepts in new ways.

Math on the GRE is a completely different ballgame. You'll need to use math in new ways on the GRE. The test-writers at ETS have an uncanny ability to take simple concepts and make very difficult questions from those concepts.

For instance, they might tell you that John is the 78th person on line and Paul is the 432nd person on line. They then ask you the following question: How many people are between John and Paul?

The first thing you (and almost everyone else) would probably do is subtract. $432 - 78 = 354$.

So you'd be looking for the answer choice with 354.

Imagine your surprise when you look at the answer choices and see the following:

(A) 352   (D) 355

(B) 353   (E) 356

(C) 354

Suddenly, you're not so sure that the correct answer is 354. What are you to do?

All of the choices are close to your answer. This is a fairly simple problem. However, the questions on the GRE will be a lot harder and it will be a lot harder to choose between similar answer choices.

The truth of the matter is that if you have not encountered a difficult type of problem before the test, you may be out of luck. It is very unlikely that you'll be able to figure out the easy way to do an unfamiliar problem during the test and you will waste precious time trying to do so.

So you need to be familiar with as many types of problems before you take the GRE. Almost any question is easy IF YOU KNOW WHAT YOU ARE DOING.

One very helpful technique for solving GRE Problem Solving questions is to take a difficult problem, simplify it, and derive a rule that can solve the simplified problem. Then take that rule and apply it to the difficult problem. The problem will now be very easy to solve.

Let's apply this technique to our example problem: You are looking for the number of numbers between 78 and 432. Those numbers are too big for you to work with. Suppose, however, you simplify the problem. How many numbers are between 3 and 8? You can easily derive in your head that the answer is four (4, 5, 6, and 7).

Important Information!

Now you know that there are four numbers between 3 and 8. But if you were to subtract 3 from 8, you'd get 5. Subtraction yields a number that is one higher than the correct answer. After you have subtracted, you must subtract 1 from the difference of the two numbers to get the correct answer.

To return to the original problem, how many numbers are between 78 and 432? First you subtract: 432 − 78 = 354. Then you subtract 1 from the difference: 354 − 1 = 353. The answer to the problem would be 353, or choice (B).

The point we wish to make is the following: IF YOU KNOW HOW TO DO THE PROBLEMS, THEY AREN'T SO DIFFICULT. GRE problems tend to involve using basic concepts in unusual ways. Which is why we've given you a review of these basic concepts! **You must take these basic concepts and apply them in the unusual ways the GRE asks you to use them.**

The good part of all this, for you, is that the people at ETS have a tendency to ask the same types of bizarre questions with a switch of the numbers. While we can't say with any certainty that the problem type illustrated above will appear on your test, we are certain that sooner or later that problem type will appear on the GRE. **After having gained a working knowledge of basic math, algebra, and geometry, you must do as many problem types as you possibly can and understand the fastest and easiest way to solve that problem type.**

But simply doing problems is not the key. **It is very important that you understand the fastest and easiest way to solve as many types of problems as you can.** One way to make sure that you understand this is to see if you can create similar problems of that type. This is why we've supplied drill questions and the practice test in this book.

Let's do a sample Problem Solving question:

If Sam lives on the 10th block of a city and Diane lives on the 181st block, how many blocks are between Sam's house and Diane's house? If you can see the similarity between this problem and our first problem, you should be able to make up and solve a similar problem of your own.

If you don't see the similarity between the two problems, then you should probably keep working with the first problem until you do. Read the problem again. Read the explanation. If you don't understand the problem, ask someone who does.

People who are good in math are often willing to help you. They may enjoy this stuff. As hard as that may be for you to believe, certain people consider GRE math problems to be fun!

So, your task between now and the exam is to, first, gain a firm grasp of the mathematical knowledge needed to complete the Problem Solving questions and, second, understand how to solve as many different GRE problem types as you can. Although there are an infinite number of variations on their themes, after a while a pattern will begin to emerge. You will develop an instinct for how to tackle each type of problem.

Now, let's look at the directions for the Problem Solving questions.

About the Directions

<u>NUMBERS:</u> All numbers used are real numbers.

<u>FIGURES:</u> Position of points, angles, regions, etc., are assumed to be in the order shown and angle measures are assumed to be positive. Figures can be assumed to lie in a plane unless otherwise indicated. Figures should not be assumed to be drawn to scale.

<u>LINES:</u> Assume that lines shown as straight are indeed straight.

That is all the directions you'll get for the Problem Solving questions on the GRE. The remainder of the directions will only apply to the Quantitative Comparison questions.

As you may have deduced, the questions in this section are quite straightforward. They are going to ask you a math question. They will give you five answer choices, and from those five answer choices, you must choose the best answer choice.

The statement that all numbers used are real numbers is something you need not worry about. There are numbers known as imaginary numbers, but you have probably completely forgotten all about them by now. They are not on the test; there is no need to worry about them.

Unless you are told otherwise, the diagrams in this section of this book are drawn to scale, and you can use them to help you answer the problems.

Attacking Arithmetic Problem Solving Questions

The arithmetic questions on the GRE fall into one of the following six question types:

1	**Fractions**
2	**Decimals**
3	**Ratios**
4	**Percentages**
5	**Averages**
6	**Exponents and Radicals**

In this section we'll introduce you to each of these six question types and teach you strategies and techniques for completing each type of question as quickly and easily as possible.

Question Type 1: FRACTIONS

There are many ways that the GRE will ask you to use fractions. The skills you need to have mastered in order to successfully attack fractions on the GRE include:

1. **Adding Fractions**

2. **Subtracting Fractions**

3. **Multiplying Fractions**

4. **Dividing Fractions**

5. **Reducing Fractions**

6. **Converting Mixed Numbers to Fractions**

Bust it!

Since the operations of fractions can be very confusing, we've given you a quick refresher on them:

A.   Parts and types of fractions:

In the fraction $\frac{a}{b}$, the *numerator* is *a* and the *denominator* is *b*. This fraction means that *a* is being divided by *b*. The denominator of a fraction can never be zero since a number divided by zero is not defined. If the numerator of a fraction is greater than the denominator, the fraction is called an *improper fraction*. A *mixed number* is the sum of a whole number and a fraction.

An example of a mixed number is:

$$4\frac{3}{8} = 4 + \frac{3}{8}$$

B. Changing a mixed number to an improper fraction:

To change a mixed number to an improper fraction, simply multiply the whole number by the denominator of the fraction and add that to the numerator. Put this sum over the denominator. For example:

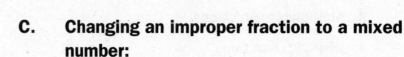

$$5\frac{2}{3} = \frac{(5 \times 3) + 2}{3} = \frac{15 + 2}{3} = \frac{17}{3}$$

Look!

Important Strategy

C. Changing an improper fraction to a mixed number:

To change an improper fraction to a mixed number, simply divide the numerator by the denominator. The remainder becomes the numerator of the fractional part of the mixed number, and the denominator remains the same. For example:

$$\frac{35}{4} = 35 \div 4 = 8\frac{3}{4}$$

D. Adding fractions that have a common denominator:

To find the sum of fractions having a common denominator, simply add together the numerators of the given fractions and put this sum over their common denominator. Do not add together the common denominators. For example:

$$\frac{11}{3} + \frac{5}{3} = \frac{11 + 5}{3} = \frac{16}{3}$$

E.   Subtracting fractions that have a common denominator:

To find the difference of fractions having a common denominator, simply subtract the numerators of the given fractions and put this difference over their common denominator. Do not subtract the common denominators. For example:

$$\frac{11}{3} - \frac{5}{3} = \frac{11-5}{3} = \frac{6}{3} = 2$$

F.   Adding fractions that have different denominators:

To find the sum of fractions having different denominators, it is necessary to find the *lowest common denominator (LCD)* of the different denominators using a process called *factoring*.

To *factor* a number means to find two numbers that when multiplied together have a product equal to the original number. These two numbers are then said to be *factors* of the original number. For example, the factors of 6 are:

          1 and 6 since $1 \times 6 = 6$
     and
          2 and 3 since $2 \times 3 = 6$

Every number is the product of itself and 1. A *prime factor* is a number that does not have any factors besides itself and 1. This is important when finding the LCD of fractions having different denominators.

To find the LCD of $\frac{11}{6}$ and $\frac{5}{16}$, we must first find the prime factors of each of the two denominators:

Important Information!

$$6 \qquad = 2 \times 3$$

$$16 \qquad = 2 \times 2 \times 2 \times 2$$

$$LCD = 2 \times 2 \times 2 \times 2 \times 3 = 48$$

Note that we do not repeat the 2 that appears in both the factors of 6 and 16.

Once we have determined the LCD of the denominators, each of the fractions must be converted into *equivalent fractions* having the LCD as the denominator.

Important Strategy

To convert the fractions $\frac{11}{6}$ and $\frac{5}{16}$ to equivalent fractions, you must rewrite them so that 48 is their denominator. To do this you must multiply the numerator and the denominator of each fraction by a number to make the denominators in both fractions 48. This can be done because the numerator and denominator of a fraction can be multiplied (or divided) by the same number without changing the value of the fraction. So, this is how to determine what number you should multiply $\frac{11}{6}$ and $\frac{5}{16}$ by so that their denominators become 48:

$$6 \times ? = 48$$
$$6 \times 8 = 48$$
$$16 \times ? = 48$$
$$16 \times 3 = 48$$

Therefore, to convert $\frac{11}{6}$ and $\frac{5}{16}$ to equivalent fractions:

$$\frac{11}{6} \times \frac{8}{8} = \frac{88}{48}$$

$$\frac{5}{16} \times \frac{3}{3} = \frac{15}{48}$$

Now add these fractions:

$$\frac{11}{6} + \frac{5}{16} = \frac{88}{48} + \frac{15}{48} = \frac{103}{48}$$

G.   Subtracting fractions that have different denominators:

To find the difference of fractions having different denominators, follow the same steps as adding fractions with different denominators, only subtract the numerators once you have made them equivalent fractions. For example:

$$\frac{11}{6} - \frac{5}{16} = \frac{88}{48} - \frac{15}{48} = \frac{73}{48}$$

H.   Multiplying fractions:

To find the product of two or more fractions, simply multiply the numerators of the given fractions to find the numerator of the product and multiply the denominators of the given fractions to find the denominator of the product. For example:

$$\frac{2}{3} \times \frac{1}{5} \times \frac{4}{7} = \frac{2 \times 1 \times 4}{3 \times 5 \times 7} = \frac{8}{105}$$

I.   Dividing fractions:

To find the quotient of two or more fractions, simply invert (or flip-over) the divisor and multiply. For example:

$$\frac{8}{9} \div \frac{1}{3} = \frac{8}{9} \times \frac{3}{1} = \frac{8 \times 3}{9 \times 1} = \frac{24}{9} = \frac{8}{3}$$

J.   Simplifying fractions:

Simplifying a fraction means reducing it to a form in which the numerator and denominator have no common factors. A common factor divides into both numbers evenly. For example:

$$\frac{12}{18} = \frac{12 \div 6}{18 \div 6} = \frac{2}{3}$$

K.   Simplifying complex fractions:

Complex fractions are fractions whose numerators and/or denominators are made up of fractions. To simplify a complex fraction, find the LCD of all the fractions. Then multiply both the numerator and denominator by this number and simplify as you would a normal fraction. For example:

$$\frac{4 + \dfrac{4}{9}}{4 - \dfrac{4}{7}}$$

Look!

Important Strategy

In order to combine terms, we must find the LCD of 9 and 7:

$$9 = 3 \times 3$$

$$7 = 7 \times 1$$

$$\text{LCD} = 3 \times 3 \times 7 = 63$$

Now multiply both the numerator and denominator by 63:

$$\frac{63\left(4 + \dfrac{4}{9}\right)}{63\left(4 - \dfrac{4}{7}\right)} = \frac{\left(\dfrac{63}{1}\right)\left(\dfrac{4}{1}\right) + \left(\dfrac{\overset{7}{\cancel{63}}}{1}\right)\left(\dfrac{4}{\cancel{9}}\right)}{\left(\dfrac{63}{1}\right)\left(\dfrac{4}{1}\right) - \left(\dfrac{63}{1}\right)\left(\dfrac{4}{\underset{1}{\cancel{7}}}\right)} = \frac{252 + 28}{252 - 36} = \frac{280}{216}$$

Finally, simplify the fraction:

$$\frac{280}{216} \div \frac{8}{8} = \frac{35}{27}$$

Testbusting Fractions Tip #1:
TURN FRACTIONS INTO DECIMALS

While it is important to know and understand the above rules for working with fractions, it often easier to solve problems on the GRE by converting fractions into decimals. The decimal value of any fraction can be found by dividing the numerator (the top number) by its denominator (the bottom number).

Converting fractions to decimals will help you on the GRE in two specific ways. First, and most importantly, by converting fractions to decimals you will have a much easier time comparing and working with values. Second, you will encounter some questions that require you to convert fractions to decimals in order to answer the question.

As we just told you, probably the best reason for converting fractions to decimals is that it makes it easier to work with values. There are questions on the GRE that are easier to solve if you can convert the fractions to decimals. Be sure to review topics involving fractions so you are comfortable working with them when you have to, but also remember that converting fractions to decimals when possible will enable you to work quicker and with more accuracy.

Comparing fractions is a common task on the GRE. You will encounter problems that ask you to compare one fraction with another. Converting fractions to decimals will make these questions a snap. The people who write the GRE like these questions because fractions are very difficult to compare. This is true because the rules that apply to fractions are confusing. A fraction may look greater than another on paper, but it is really less. For example, $\frac{3}{4}$ is greater than $\frac{2}{16}$. You may be fooled into thinking $\frac{2}{16}$ is greater than $\frac{3}{4}$ because the former's denominator is bigger. But if you convert the fractions to decimals you'll easily see that .75 $\left(\frac{3}{4}\right)$ is greater than .125 $\left(\frac{2}{16}\right)$.

Converting fractions to decimals will save you time if there is a lot of adding, subtracting, multiplying, and dividing needed to solve the question. The time it takes to convert fractions into decimals in order to add them is usually much less than the time it takes just to find the least common denominator. Working with decimals avoids having to find a least common denominator in order to add fractions and saves you the confusing and slow task of factoring a fraction in order to reduce it.

Testbusting Fractions Tip #2:
REDUCE LARGE FRACTIONS

If you encounter a fraction question that thoroughly confuses you because of the large fractions involved, and you can't convert them to decimals, try reducing the fractions.

The best way to reduce a fraction is to divide both the numerator and the denominator by the largest number that is a common factor. For example:

$$\frac{12}{48}$$

12 divides into both 12 (12 × 1) and 48 (12 × 4)

Divide both the numerator and the denominator by 12

$$\frac{12 \div 12}{48 \div 12} = \frac{1}{4}$$

By reducing fractions, you'll often find that a question that looks very hard is actually very simple.

Question Type 2: DECIMALS

You've already learned that decimals can be very helpful in dealing with fractions. But in order to work with decimals you will need to know how to perform the following operations:

1. **Adding Decimals**

2. **Subtracting Decimals**

3. **Multiplying Decimals**

4. **Dividing Decimals**

5. **Comparing Decimals**

Testbusting Decimals Tip #1:
USING THE DECIMAL POINT

Another important strategy you can learn to use with decimals on the GRE is to master the decimal point. You will be asked to compare decimals on the GRE. The placement of the decimal point is essential to determining the value of a decimal.

Here is a brief chart explaining how to determine a decimal's value:

$$2{,}330 = 2{,}000 + 300 + 30 + 0$$

$$233.0 = 233 = 200 + 30 + 3$$

$$23.30 = 23.3 = 20 + 3 + \frac{3}{10}$$

$$2.330 = 2.33 = 2 + \frac{3}{10} + \frac{3}{100}$$

$$0.2330 = 0.233 = \frac{2}{10} + \frac{3}{100} + \frac{3}{1{,}000}$$

$$0.02330 = 0.0233 = \frac{0}{10} + \frac{2}{100} + \frac{3}{1{,}000} + \frac{3}{10{,}000}$$

From this chart you can see that decimals can contain fractions. You probably knew this had to be true even before you saw this chart because you know that every fraction can be made into a decimal. So the opposite must also be possible. To find a fraction from a decimal, simply put the number over its position past the decimal point. From our example, we could take .233 and turn it into the fraction $\frac{233}{1{,}000}$ because we know the last number in .233 is in the thousandths place. Pretty simple, right?

Here are some more examples of converting decimals to fractions:

$$.40 = \frac{40}{100} = \frac{10}{25} = \frac{2}{5}$$

$$.3994 = \frac{3{,}994}{10{,}000} = \frac{1{,}997}{5{,}000}$$

$$.7 = \frac{7}{10}$$

Converting decimals to fractions is easy. But comparing decimals can be tricky. The easiest way to compare two decimals is to line up the decimal points and fill in any missing spaces with zeros. Here's an example:

Is 0.0089 greater than 0.07?

First line up the two numbers by their decimal points:

0.0089

0.07

Next, fill in the empty spaces with zeros:

0.0089

0.0700

Now compare the numbers. It's obvious that 700 is greater than 89. So now you can see that 0.07 is definitely greater than 0.0089.

You may have been confused by the number 89. Isn't 89 greater than 7, so 0.0089 has to be greater than 0.07? While understandable, your assumption is wrong and will make you lose points on the GRE. Every time you need to compare decimals, make sure that you stop and think, "Am I positive that my choice is greater than the other?" If you aren't positive, get out your scrap paper, line up the decimal points, fill in the spaces with zeros, and THEN compare the decimals.

Question Type 3: RATIOS

A ratio is simply a relationship which compares two quantities. If you have a bowl of 3 apples and 3 oranges, you can express this mixture of apples and oranges as 1:1. In this bowl there are as many apples as there are oranges. If there were 6 apples and 3 oranges, twice as many apples as oranges, you can express this as the ratio 2:1. This ratio translates as meaning there are two apples for every orange.

Since ratios can be also be written as fractions and many of the same rules that apply to fractions also apply to ratios, it is as easy to work with ratios as fractions. But remember fractions and ratios are not the same. To look at a ratio as a fraction, the ratio "two to five" would be the same as saying $\frac{2}{5}$. The traditional way of presenting this ratio is 2:5. All of this means that there are three ways of writing a ratio:

1. $\frac{2}{5}$

2. the ratio 2 to 5

3. 2:5

Bust it!

Testbusting Ratios Tip #1:
USING ESTIMATION AND LOGIC

Ratios are very easy to work with if you have a good understanding of what they are: a relationship between two quantities.

Here's an example of a ratio problem:

If a crowd has 10,000 people and the ratio of men to women is 1:3 how many women are present?

(A) 10,000   (D) 5,000

(B) 2,500   (E) 3,000

(C) 7,500

If this ratio was 1:1 there would be the same number of men and women in the crowd. If the ratio was 3:3 there would also be the same number of men and women in the crowd. This is true because a ratio is a relationship between quantities. The ratios 1:1 and 3:3 are equal in their relationship to each other, so the number of men and women that they represent must also be equal to one another. This eliminates choice (D) because if the number of men and women were equal, there must be 5,000 of each in a crowd of 10,000.

Since the ratio we are dealing with is 1:3, that means there is 1 man to every 3 women in the crowd. From this you can guess that there will be quite a few more women in the crowd than men. This would help you eliminate choices (B), 2,500, and (E), 3,000, since the question is asking you how many women there are in the crowd and there will be more women (greater than half: 5,000) than men. You can also eliminate choice (A), 10,000, because a ratio of 1:3 means there are some men in the crowd, the crowd is not all women. So, if there are 10,000 people in the crowd, choice (A) cannot be correct.

This leaves choice (C), 7,500, as the correct answer. Logically, you must agree that if there are three women for every man in a crowd of 10,000, the number 7,500 would be about right for the number of women in the crowd.

**Testbusting Ratios Tip #2:
USING THE SUM OF THE PARTS**

Unlike the example we just showed you, estimating and using logic to guess the correct answer won't work every time, so you need to learn how to *solve* ratio problems. In the previous example we used logic and the process of elimination to help answer a ratio problem. But in order to solve some GRE ratio questions you'll need to perform the mathematical steps in order arrive at the correct answer.

Let's look at our example problem again:

If a crowd has 10,000 people and the ratio of men to women is 1:3 how many women are present?

(A) 10,000　　　　**(D) 5,000**

(B) 2,500　　　　　**(E) 3,000**

(C) 7,500

To get the answer using a mathematical process, we have to use the technique of summing up the parts of a ratio.

To sum up the parts, you should add the ratio together. Using our example, that would be 1 added to 3 equals 4. That's 1 part men plus 3 parts women. Now take that sum and divide it into the total number of people in the crowd (which works out to be $\frac{10,000}{4} = 2,500$). This tells us that the crowd is made up of 4 parts of 2,500 people. We know that the ratio of men to women is 1:3, so there is 1 group of 2,500 men and 3 groups of 2,500 women. That means there are 7,500 women in the crowd (3 × 2,500). So the answer is (C), 7,500.

Let's try another one!

A moving company's fleet of trucks is made up of cargo vans and moving vans. The ratio of cargo vans to moving vans is 14:7. If there are 294 trucks in the entire fleet, how many are moving vans?

First simplify the ratio of 14:7 to 2:1 since it's the same thing and it's easier to work with smaller numbers. $\frac{14}{7}$ is equal to $\frac{2}{1}$.

Bust it!

Once again, to sum up the parts you should add the ratio together. This means 2 added to 1 equals 3. That's 2 parts cargo vans plus 1 part moving vans. Now take that sum and divide it into the total number of trucks in the fleet (which works out to be $\frac{294}{3}$ = 98). This tells us that the trucks are made up of 3 parts of 98 trucks. We know that the ratio of cargo vans to moving vans is 2:1, so there are 2 groups of 98 cargo vans and 1 group of 98 moving vans. There are 98 moving vans in the fleet.

Testbusting Ratios Tip #3:
THINK OF PROPORTIONS AS EQUAL RATIOS

Once in a while, you'll be given a question on the GRE that you think is a ratio problem, but doesn't come right out and call itself a ratio problem. Usually, this type of question reads like this:

If Mary can knit 7 sweaters with 280 feet of yarn, how many feet would it take for her to knit 25 sweaters?

You should treat this question as a ratio, even if a true ratio is never given. This is a ratio question disguised as a proportion question. You have all the information to complete the proportion except for one piece. Here is the proportion created as a ratio:

$$\frac{7 \text{ sweaters}}{280 \text{ feet of yarn}} = \frac{25 \text{ sweaters}}{x \text{ feet of yarn}}$$

Since ratios can be treated as fractions, we can cross multiply to find the value for x.

$$7x = 25 \times 280$$

$$7x = 7,000$$

$$x = 1,000$$

It would take 1,000 feet of yarn for Mary to knit 25 sweaters.

Question Type 4: PERCENTAGES

Bust it!

Percentages are simply fractions with a denominator of 100. Every percentage, when placed in decimal form, will have 100 as its denominator.

$$56\% = \frac{56}{100} = .56$$

Percentage problems are very popular with the writers of the GRE because most people don't like percentages. But, if you apply some simple techniques, you won't have the least bit of trouble answering any percentage problem you encounter.

Testbusting Percentage Tip #1:
MEMORIZE COMMON PERCENTAGE CONVERSIONS

The easiest way to answer percentage questions more quickly is to memorize common percentage conversions. This means knowing what a percentage converts to in decimals and fractions. Here is a short list of common percentages:

$$100 \text{ percent} = \frac{100}{100} = 1$$

$$75 \text{ percent} = \frac{3}{4} = 0.75$$

$$50 \text{ percent} = \frac{1}{2} = 0.50$$

$$25 \text{ percent} = \frac{1}{4} = 0.25$$

$$20 \text{ percent} = \frac{1}{5} = 0.20$$

$$10 \text{ percent} = \frac{1}{10} = 0.10$$

$$5 \text{ percent} = \frac{1}{20} = 0.05$$

$$1 \text{ percent} = \frac{1}{100} = .01$$

Testbusting Percentage Tip #2:
KNOW HOW TO CONVERT PERCENTAGES TO FRACTIONS AND DECIMALS

You will need to know how to convert percentages to fractions to decimals and back again. This skill is necessary and will prove to be an invaluable tool in attacking GRE percentage questions.

To convert a percentage to a decimal, simply move the decimal point two places to the left. This is the same as dividing the percentage by 100, but much easier and quicker! For example, 25% is equal to 0.25. And 245% is equal to 2.45.

To convert a decimal to a percentage, do the opposite: move the decimal point two places to the right! For example, 0.94 would become 94%. And 0.0043 equals 0.43%.

Unlike working with decimals, converting a percentage to a fraction takes a bit more work. To do so, place the percentage over a denominator of 100 and reduce the fraction. For example, a percentage of 28 would become $\frac{28}{100}$ and then reduce to $\frac{7}{25}$. Another example would be a percentage of 65 becoming the fraction $\frac{65}{100}$ and then reducing to $\frac{13}{20}$.

To get a percentage from a fraction, you first have to convert the fraction to a decimal. As you know, to get a decimal from a fraction, divide the numerator by the denominator. Once you get a decimal, you know to move the decimal point two places to the right. For example: $\frac{3}{4}$ would become 0.75 and then 75%. Here's another example: $\frac{14}{35}$ would become 0.4 and then 40%.

**Testbusting Percentage Tip #3:
TAKING IT ONE STEP AT A TIME**

There are percentage questions on the GRE that are specifically designed to confuse you. These types of questions usually appear as follows:

What number is 20% less than 55?

This may seem confusing at first glance, but it can be very easy to find the solution if you take it one step at a time.

First, what is 20 percent of 55? Now be careful. On the actual test you will surely see 11 as an answer choice. This is a trap. You might incorrectly pick this trap answer choice as the correct answer if you don't carefully read the question. While 11 *is* 20 percent of 55, it is *not* the correct answer to this question. You need to do some further work.

The next step is to reword the question: What number is 11 less than 55? Well, that should be easy: 44. So the correct answer is 44! Not too bad if you slow down, take a deep breath, and attack a question one step at a time.

Let's try another one, only this one will be harder:

A couple rents an apartment for $500 a year. A year later the rent is increased by 10 percent. And the year after that, another 10 percent. How much will the couple pay for the three years that they rent the apartment?

Wow! If there ever was a question that needs to be taken one step at a time, this is it! But let's take a deep breath and get started. We must first determine what we are being asked. The last sentence asks us to find out how much the couple will pay for all three years that they rent the apartment. This means we need to add the three years of rent to get the correct answer.

The next step is to find the rent for each year. You know the first year's rent is $500 because you've been told so. That means the second year's rent is $500 plus 10 percent. What's 10 percent of $500?

Bust it!

500×10 percent = $500 $\times$ .10 = $50

That's right, $50.00 So you add that to $500 to get the second year's rent: $550.00 Now find out the third year's rent: $550 (the second year's rent) plus 10 percent.

$550.00 $\times$ 10 percent = $550.00 $\times$ .10 = $55.00

So the third year's rent is $550 + $55 = $605. Now we must determine the total of all three years' rent:

$500 + $550 + $605 = $1655

So the correct answer is $1655. Again, not too bad if you sit back and take the question one step at a time!

You must be very careful with these complex percent questions. The GRE uses them (and very well, we might add) to get you to select an answer choice that seems right but is actually wrong. So take your time and be very careful to read the questions closely.

Question Type 5:
AVERAGES: MEANS, MEDIANS, AND MODES

The writers of the GRE love to use averages in questions. Why? Because they can use averages in three different ways using four different terms to confuse you. Huh? It's simple: There are three different ways you will encounter averages on the GRE and four different words to describe them. Those four words are average, mean, median, and mode.

Let's look at the first word: average. In mathematics, an average is a term used to describe a way to represent a list of numbers. But, an average can also be used to define the sum of a list of values divided by the number of values in the list. Here's an example:

Find the mean salary for four company employees who make $5.00 per hour, $8.00 per hour, $12.00 per hour, and $15.00 per hour.

$$\frac{\$5 + \$8 + \$12 + \$15}{4}_{\text{(the number of values in the list)}} = \$\frac{40}{4} = \$10$$

The mean salary is $10.00 per hour.

If you encounter the word average on the GRE, you should know that the question is asking you to find the sum of a list of values divided by the number of values in the list.

$$\text{Average} = \frac{\text{Sum of the Values}}{\text{Number of Values}}$$

The second word you need to know is mean. A mean and average are exactly the same thing when the word average is used to find the sum of a list of values divided by the number of values in the list. If you are asked to find the mean of a list of values on the GRE, you must know that you are being asked to find the average of that list.

The third word is median. A median is different than an average or mean. A median is the value that is in the exact middle of a group of values when all the numbers are arranged in order or the average of the two middle values if there is an even number of values. For example, in a list of values such as 2, 4, 9, 22, 104, 105, 229, the median would be 22 since there are three values before it in the list and three values after it.

The fourth word is mode. A mode is the value that appears most in a list of values, when all the numbers are arranged in order. For example, if you are given 3, 4, 4, 8, 8, 8, 8, 13, 14, 15, 15, 19, the mode of that list is 8 since it appears in the list four times (more than any other value in the list). There can be more than one mode in a set of values.

 Testbusting Averages Tip #1:
TO FIND THE MEAN, FIND THE NUMBER OF VALUES

Whenever you are asked to find the mean or average in a question, the first thing you need to determine is the number of values. Here's an example:

> **A teacher grades 5 papers in one night. The scores on those papers are 80, 94, 88, 72, and 79. On the second night, the teacher grades 5 more papers. The scores on the second night's papers are 99, 68, 84, 93, and 91. What is the mean of all of the scores?**

The first step, as we've told you, is to determine the number of values for which you are being asked to find the mean. In this case there are 10 papers that were graded on two nights. The next step is to add all of the papers' scores together:

$$80 + 94 + 88 + 72 + 79 + 99 + 68 + 84 + 93 + 91 = 848$$

Then divide the sum of all the scores by the number of scores:

$$848 \div 10 = 84.8$$

This means the mean of all the scores is 84.8. Pretty simple, but you had to find the number of values before you could do anything else. Remember to do this first when you are being asked to find the average or mean.

 Testbusting Averages Tip #2:
TAKE IT ONE STEP AT A TIME

Just like in percent questions, in complex average questions you need to attack the question one step at a time. Here's an example of how to attack a very hard average question:

> **A group of 20 farmers had an average truckload of 30 bales of hay. If 6 of those farmers have an average of 22 bales of hay, what is the average for the other 14 farmers?**

Okay. Slow down, take a breath, and then break the question down. You know that the first thing you have to do is find the number of farmers that you are being asked to average. There are 20 farmers total, but you are being asked to find the average for only 14.

Next, you need to determine what information you have. You know that the 20 farmers averaged 30 bales of hay. If all 20 farmers averaged 30 bales of hay, you can determine that those 20 farmers had 600 bales of hay:

30 average bales × 20 farmers = 600 bales of hay

You also know that 6 of those farmers averaged 22 bales of hay per truck.

22 average bales × 6 farmers = 132 bales of hay

You need to find out what the other 14 farmers averaged.

You should next subtract the number of bales the 6 farmers had from the total number of bales all 20 farmers had:

600 total bales – 132 bales from 6 farmers = 468 bales from 14 farmers

Now you know the number of bales the other 14 farmers had. You're almost there. You know how to find the average of a list of values, right? Divide the sum of all the values by the number of values. To answer this question simply divide the number of bales these 14 farmers had by 14:

468 bales ÷ 14 farmers = 33.43 average bales

Voila! If you take these complex questions one step at a time, they usually prove to be pretty easy!

Question Type 6: EXPONENTS AND RADICALS

The final type of arithmetic question that you'll find on the GRE involves exponents and radicals. You must be familiar with these terms in order to do well on the GRE.

Bust it!

A power of a number is the product obtained by multiplying the number by itself a given number of times. To raise a given number (let's call it a base value), multiply the base value by itself as many times as the power indicates (let's call this number an exponent). It's easier to understand if we show you an example:

$$5^3 = 5 \times 5 \times 5 = 125$$

125 can be written as 5^3

The base value is 5 and the exponent is 3. The exponent indicates how many times you should multiply the base value by itself. The exponent is always a little number (or letter) placed in the upper-right hand corner.

Here's another example:

$$4^6 = 4 \times 4 \times 4 \times 4 \times 4 \times 4 = 4,096$$

4,096 can be written as 4^6

In 4^6, 4 is the base and 6 is the exponent.

Pretty simple, right? Now let's look at radicals. This is kind of the opposite process of writing a number with an exponent. A radical indicates the square root of a value.

For example:

$$5 \times 5 = 25$$
$$\sqrt{25} = 5$$

or

$$7 \times 7 = 49$$
$$\sqrt{49} = 7$$

Sometimes, a radical can indicate the cube root of a number. For example:

$$3 \times 3 \times 3 = 27$$
$$\sqrt[3]{27} = 3$$

or

$$6 \times 6 \times 6 = 216$$
$$\sqrt[3]{216} = 6$$

Testbusting Exponents and Radicals Tip #1:
KNOW HOW TO MANIPULATE EXPONENTS

In order to succeed at exponent questions on the GRE, you'll need to know how to multiply them. It is easy to do, but the writers of the GRE love to make sure you know how to do it.

To multiply exponents that have the same base value, simply add the exponents:

$$2^4 \times 2^5 \times 2^9 = 2^{18}$$

Be extremely careful not to confuse multiplying exponents that have the same base with adding exponents that have the same base. $2^4 + 2^5 + 2^9$ does NOT equal 2^{18}. To add numbers with exponents, you need to determine their actual values and add those together:

$$2^4 + 2^5 + 2^9 = (2 \times 2 \times 2 \times 2) + (2 \times 2 \times 2 \times 2 \times 2)$$
$$+ \quad (2 \times 2 \times 2 \times 2 \times 2 \times 2 \times 2 \times 2 \times 2)$$

$$16 + 32 + 512 = 560$$

You can divide two base values that are the same; you would simply subtract the exponents.

$$4^5 \div 4^3 = 4^2$$

Again, be sure not to confuse dividing exponents with the same base with subtracting them. To subtract exponents that have the same base, you need to determine their actual values and subtract them, similar to the process of adding exponents that have the same base. Here is an example:

$$4^5 - 4^2 = (4 \times 4 \times 4 \times 4 \times 4) - (4 \times 4) = 1{,}024 - 16 = 1{,}008$$

When you multiply the exponents of two or more bases, instead of adding them, you are "raising a power to a power." This is often done when exponents appear in parentheses. Here's an example:

$$(3^4)^5 = 3^{4 \times 5} = (3^4)(3^4)(3^4)(3^4)(3^4) = 3^{20}$$

Parentheses are very important when dealing with exponents and can be confusing. For this reason, the writers of the GRE will use parentheses often. To keep yourself on track to the correct answer, be sure to employ the distributive property when working with parentheses. The distributive property, in the case of exponents, states that anything inside parentheses must be multiplied by the exponent outside the parentheses. For example:

$$(4a)^2 + 2 = 16a^2 + 2$$

not

$$(4a)^2 + 2 = 4a^2 + 2$$

 **Testbusting Exponents and Radicals Tip #2:
KNOW HOW EXPONENTS BEHAVE**

You may remember that we warned you to be careful with fractions because they sometimes don't work the way you'd expect them to. Well, exponents do the same thing. Knowing how exponents behave before you take the GRE will give you an edge and help you avoid choosing answers that look correct but are actually wrong.

Here is a quick summary of what to learn about exponents before taking the GRE:

1. A negative number raised to an even power will become positive.

    Example: $(-3)^2 = -3 \times -3 = 9$

                      or

                      $(-3)^4 = -3 \times -3 \times -3 \times -3 = 81$

2. A negative number raised to an odd power will be negative.

    Example: $-3^3 = -3 \times -3 \times -3 = -27$

3. A number raised to a negative power implies a fraction.

    Example: $(3)^{-2} = \dfrac{1}{3^2} = \dfrac{1}{3 \times 3} = \dfrac{1}{9}$

4. If you square or cube a fraction it will become less than the base value.

    Example: $\left(\dfrac{3}{4}\right)^3 = \dfrac{27}{64}$

5. If the exponent of a base is 0, the value will be 1 (unless the base is 0, then it will be 0).

    Example: $3^0 = 1$

                      $0^0 = 0$

6. If you square or cube a value greater than 1, it will become larger than the base.

Example: $3^2 = 9$

                 $4^2 = 16$

                 $5^3 = 125$

7.   If your base is 10, the exponent will equal the number of zeros in the number.

Example: $10^2 = 100$ (two zeros)

                 $10^5 = 100,000$ (five zeros)

 Testbusting Exponents and Radicals Tip #3: KNOW HOW RADICALS BEHAVE

Just like exponents, you'll have a leg up on the GRE if you know how radicals behave. This will help you avoid any traps laid by the question writers who want you to pick the answer choice that looks right but really isn't.

1.   No matter what, if you are being asked the square root of a number, the square root will be positive. The testmakers wish you only to consider the positive root. Although 3^2 and $(-3)^2$ both equal 9, the square root of 9 is only positive 3.

2.   To multiply square roots, multiply the values inside the brackets.

Example: $\sqrt{4} \times \sqrt{9} = \sqrt{36} = 6$

3.   The square root of a positive fraction is larger than the fraction you see.

Example:

$$\sqrt{\frac{1}{9}} = \frac{1}{3}$$

$$\frac{\sqrt{1}}{\sqrt{9}} < \frac{1}{3}$$

$$\frac{1}{9} < \frac{1}{3}$$

Points to Remember for Busting GRE Arithmetic Problem Solving Questions

✔   *Study the operations and behaviors of fractions. Know how to add, subtract, multiply, and divide fractions. Understand and know how to manipulate improper fractions, mixed numbers, and complex fractions.*

✔   *Whenever possible, convert fractions to decimals.*

✔   *Always reduce fractions to their lowest form. When you run into a fraction that confuses you because of the large values involved, and you can't convert it to a decimal, always reduce it. This will enable you to look at the problem more easily.*

✔   *Know how to use the placement of the decimal point to compare decimal values.*

On Target!

✔   Use estimation and logic to weed out answer choices in ratio problems.

✔   Know how to mathematically solve ratio problems by summing up the parts because guessing and using logic will not always get you to the correct answer.

✔   Understand that ratio questions can appear as proportion problems even if they don't include the word "ratio." Know how to identify and solve such questions.

✔   Memorize the most common percentages and their fractional and decimal equivalents.

✔   Know how to convert percentages to fractions and decimals.

On Target!

✔   When presented with a complex percentage question, slow down; take a deep breath; and attack it one step at a time. Usually, a complex question that looks intimidating turns out to be several simple problems put together.

✔   To find the mean of a set of values, your first step is to determine the number of values in the set. Only then can you begin to find the mean.

On Target!

✔   Just like with complex percentage problems, if you run into a complex mean, median, or mode question, slow down; take a deep breath; and attack it one step at a time. Don't be intimidated by a question that is really simple if you just look at it in parts.

✔   Know how to manipulate exponents through addition, subtraction, multiplication, and division.

✔   Understand how exponents and radicals behave to avoid making mistakes because the correct answer "looks wrong" or an incorrect answer "looks right."

Attacking Algebra Problem Solving Questions

The algebra questions on the GRE use letters, or variables, to represent numbers. In these questions, you will be required to solve existing algebraic expressions or translate word problems into algebraic expressions.

Sound difficult? If it does, you're not alone. Most students find algebra difficult, but in this section we'll teach you some strategies and help you review the algebraic principles that will enable you to successfully attack the algebra questions on the GRE.

All the algebra questions on the GRE fall into one of the following two question types:

1. Algebraic Expressions and Equations

2. Word Problems

There are just these two types of questions! Of course each of these question types can require you to use a wide variety of algebraic skills. But we'll tell you what skills you'll need and teach you some strategies to make working out algebra questions quicker and easier.

Let's learn more about these strategies before we go into a discussion about the types of questions. The strategies you'll learn will help you solve algebra problems faster than if you use the techniques you learned in school. "What's wrong with the way I learned in school?" you may ask. Well, to put it bluntly: it takes too long! The

Bust it!

Look!

Important Strategy

clock is one of your worst enemies on the GRE and the way you learned algebra in school eats up too much time.

The strategies that will help you save the most time on algebra questions are "Starting from the Choices" and "Testing Choices." As you can see from their names, both strategies involve the use of the answer choices. This is because the GRE is a multiple-choice test and you should use that to your best advantage. When you took an algebra class in school, more often than not your teacher didn't give you multiple-choice tests. This forced you to work through each problem using the algebraic functions you learned in class. But the GRE is a multiple-choice test and you can use the answer choices as a way to get the correct answer easier and quicker. Let's begin with Starting from the Choices.

Important Strategy

Testbusting Algebra Tip #1:
STARTING FROM THE CHOICES

As you probably know, algebra is a form of math that uses letters, or variables, to represent numbers. This is why so many students are afraid of algebra questions. The variables are strange and unfamiliar. Most other math problems have regular numbers that are easy to understand and work with. But the variables in algebra questions are numbers too, it's just a little harder to see them.

This is the first step to doing well in algebra: think of the variables as numbers. Most algebra problems ask you to take an equation and find the numbers that are represented by the variables. For example:

$$2x + 5 = 15$$

The *x* is the variable in this problem. You should read this as "what number (*x*) times 2 added to 5 equals 15?" You would multiply *x* and 2 because, in algebra, two numbers that are placed right next to one another implies that they are to be multiplied. Now, on a basic question like this it's pretty simple to figure out the right answer.

And on the GRE it would be even easier. Why? Because the test would give you the correct answer! Let's look at this example as it would appear on the GRE:

$$2x + 5 = 15$$

(A) 1   (D) 2

(B) –3   (E) 0

(C) 5

Remember that this question is asking you to find the value (or number) for *x*. Since one of the answer choices is correct, that means one of the answer choices is *x*! All you have to do is look at the answer choices, pick one that looks correct, plug it into the equation, and see if it works! That's what we mean by Starting from the Choices!

Look!

Important Strategy

Here's how to use the Starting from the Choices strategy:

First, you need to make some decisions. For our example you are being asked what number multiplied by 2 and added to 5 equals 15. From this, you need to decide which answer choice to pick and place in the equation first.

It is best to pick a number that is in the middle of all the possible choices. This is because, if the choice you pick is wrong, you'll be able to tell whether the correct answer is greater or lesser than your first choice and then your second choice is guaranteed to be closer to the correct answer. Picking the middle number first saves you time, lots of time.

Look at the answer choices again:

(A) 1   (D) 2

(B) –3   (E) 0

(C) 5

The middle number would be 1 or 2 since a negative number is given and 5 is the highest positive number. Let's use choice (D) 2:

2 times 2 plus 5 = 15

4 plus 5 = 15

9 ≠ 15

Too low. Since 2 gives you a number that is lower than 15, the next number you plug in the equation should be higher than 2. Let's look at what choices remain:

(A̶) 1   (D̶) 2

(B̶) –3   (E̶) 0

(C) 5

The only number that is higher than 2 is choice (C), 5. You could simply select (C) at this time, but it is wise to check that your assumption is correct by working the equation out using 5:

2 times 5 plus 5 = 15

10 plus 5 = 15

15 = 15

So choice (C) is correct. You only had to pick two choices and you didn't need to perform any algebra to find the right answer choice!

Using the strategy of Starting from the Choices will help you get the correct answer easier (because you won't have to do the algebra) and quicker (because you'll probably be able to eliminate wrong answer choices and plug in the remaining choices faster than it would take you to actually do the question)!

Let's do another problem, only this time a bit harder:

Eliminating Answer Choices

Important Strategy

Bust it!

Gregg wants to buy a new car but doesn't have enough money to buy one. He has $300 in savings and makes $150 a week as a gas station attendant. The car he wants is $1,200. How many weeks must he work before he can afford the car?

(A) 3   (D) 8

(B) 1   (E) 6

(C) 22

"But that's not an algebra question!" Yes, it is. You just have to write the equation. So writing the equation is your first step. You know Gregg needs $1,200 to buy the car, so let's place this on one side of the equal sign:

$$= \$1,200$$

You know that he already has $300 in savings, so let's place this on the other side of the equal sign:

$$\$300 = \$1,200$$

Next, you know that he makes $150 per week as a gas station attendant. The question you need to answer is how many weeks he needs to work in order to afford the car. The number of weeks is what you need to find and, thus, is the variable. So, let's finish the equation by writing how many weeks (x) of $150, plus the $300 he already has, would give Gregg the $1,200 he needs to buy the car. We would write this equation as:

$$\$150x + \$300 = \$1,200$$

You are now ready to Start from the Choices. Let's look at the answer choices:

(A) 3   (D) 8

(B) 1   (E) 6

(C) 22

As we stated earlier, it is a good idea to use the middle number first. The closest number to middle would be choice (D), 8. Plugging 8 into our equation we would get:

$150(8) + $300 = $1,200

$1,200 + $300 = $1,200

$1,500 ≠ $1,200

You know $1,500 doesn't equal $1,200, so choice (D) is not correct. You can tell from the answer using 8 as *x* that the correct answer is going to be lower than 8. So, looking at our choices again, you should try choice (E), 6, the next number lower than 8:

$150(6) + $300 = $1,200

$900 + $300 = $1,200

$1,200 = $1,200

Found it! So choice (E), 6, is the correct answer. See how easy Starting from the Choices can be!

Before moving onto the Testing Choices strategy, we have a few words of advice about Starting from the Choices:

On Target!

1.   *It should be pretty obvious that the algebra questions you will want to use this strategy on must have answer choices that are numbers.*

2.   *Make sure you plug in the answer choice everywhere the variable appears. Algebra questions can use a variable in more than one place. For instance:*

$$3x + 8 - \frac{3}{4}x + x = 200$$

In this example, you must find a number that will be used in three different places in the equation and still come up with the answer of 200. When plugging in the choices, make sure that you plug the choices in all three places. If you don't, you won't find the correct answer.

3.   Don't worry if you can't tell which answer choice is exactly the middle number. Just pick one that's close and work from there. You may have to work through all the answer choices to find the correct answer, but by picking one that's close to the middle first, you should find the answer quicker than by just randomly picking a number.

On Target!

 Testbusting Algebra Tip #2:
TESTING CHOICES

This strategy will help you attack algebra questions that don't have numbers in their answer choices (where you should use the Starting from the Choices strategy). Testing Choices is very similar to Starting from the Choices, but you use clues in the question to determine what numbers you plug into the equation instead of looking at the answer choices (as you would when using Starting from the Choices).

Questions with phrases like "solving for *y*" or "in terms of *x*" are tip-offs that you should use the Testing Choices strategy. Trying to solve questions like these using traditional algebra methods is extremely slow and the chances that you will make errors is very high. So whenever you see phrases like "solving for *y*" or "in terms of *x*", be sure to employ the Testing Choices strategy.

Look!

Important Strategy

To use the Testing Choices strategy, you must first pick numbers to represent the variables in the question. Second, you have to use the numbers you've picked to find the answer to the question. Finally, you have to use the numbers you've picked and plug them into the answer choices to determine which choice will give you the answer to the question (which you found in Step 2).

Confused? Don't be. Here's an example to clarify the steps:

Nancy scored an average of x number of points per game during the entire basketball season. If Nancy's team played 20 games in the season, how many points, in terms of x, did Nancy score?

(A) $\dfrac{2}{x}$ (D) $20 + x$

(B) $20x$ (E) x^2

(C) $\dfrac{x}{2}$

Okay, the first step is to pick numbers to represent the variables in the question. The only variable is x, the average number of points Nancy scored per game during the entire season. You have to pick a number for x, something easy to work with, like 10.

Next, work out the question using 10:

Nancy scored an average of 10 points per game during the entire basketball season. If Nancy's team played 20 games in the season, how many points did Nancy score?

The answer would be 200 since Nancy's team played 20 games and she averaged 10 points per game (20 games × 10 points per game = 200 points).

The final step would be to use 10 in the answer choices to see which one will give you the correct answer 200. Unlike Starting from the Choices questions, it doesn't really matter which answer choice you start with. If one choice looks to you to be more likely to be correct than the others, choose this one first. Here are the answer choices for our example:

Bust it!

(A) $\dfrac{2}{x}$ (D) $20 + x$

(B) $20x$ (E) x^2

(C) $\dfrac{x}{1}$

Let's try choice (A), $\dfrac{2}{x}$, first. Remember we're substituting 10 for x:

$$\frac{2}{x} = \frac{2}{10} = \frac{1}{5}$$

Definitely not the correct answer since $\dfrac{1}{5}$ does not equal 200. Let's try choice (B) next:

$$20x = 20(10) = 200$$

Got it! Choice (B) is the correct answer because it represents the correct relationship between the average number of points Nancy scored per game and the total number of points she scored in the season.

Let's try another one! This time the question will not be as easy to recognize using the Testing Choices strategy:

Bust it!

If 500 people each paid the same amount of money for 500 concert tickets, and the people spent a total of x dollars, 25 of these tickets cost how much?

(A) $\dfrac{5}{x}$

(B) $\dfrac{x}{40}$

(C) $10x$

(D) $\dfrac{x}{20}$

(E) $\dfrac{80}{x}$

There are lots of numbers here to confuse you, but the question is really not that hard if you know the correct strategy. The first step is to pick a number to use in the question. Let's pick 2. If each ticket cost $2, then 500 people spent $1,000 on 500 tickets. That means $1,000 is the value for x. Also, if each ticket costs $2, then 25 tickets would cost $50.

In order to answer this question, you need to plug–in $1,000 for x in the answer choices to find the choice that gives you $50 (what 25 tickets would cost).

Let's start with (A):

$$\frac{5}{x} = \frac{5}{1,000} = \frac{1}{200}$$

Now let's try (B):

$$\frac{x}{40} = \frac{1,000}{40} = \frac{500}{20} = \frac{250}{10} = \frac{25}{1} = 25$$

Still not it. How about choice (C)?

$$10x = 10(1,000) = 10,000$$

Nope. Let's try choice (D):

$$\frac{x}{20} = \frac{1,000}{20} = \frac{500}{10} = \frac{50}{1} = 50$$

So the correct answer is choice (D). See how easy that was!

There are many ways that the GRE will present algebra questions that can be solved using the Testing Choices strategy. Just remember, the same steps apply to every question that you can answer using this strategy. The trick is to recognize the types of problems for which you can use this strategy to solve the question. Here are some types of problems and how to solve them using the Testing Choices strategy:

INEQUALITIES:

An inequality is an expression that doesn't have an equal sign (=) but, in its place, another sign. These types of signs include lesser than (<); greater than (>); lesser-than-or-equal ($\leq$); or greater-than-or-equal ($\geq$).

You can use the Testing Choices strategy to answer inequalities, but you have to follow some special rules: Sometimes you'll need to pick a few numbers to solve an inequality problem, and you might have to pick specific numbers to help yourself out. Picking numbers like 0 or 1, or negative numbers and fractions, will enable you to work with inequalities because those numbers behave in strange ways when they are multiplied or squared.

Sometimes you don't even have to use the Testing Choices strategy on an inequality problem if you can simplify the question. Here's an example:

$-4y + 13 \geq 21$, **so which of the following is true?**

(A) $y \leq -4$ (D) $y \geq 6$

(B) $y \leq 6$ (E) $y = 1$

(C) $y \leq -2$

Simplify the problem as much as possible:

$$-4y + 13 \geq 21$$

$$-4y \geq 8$$

$$-y \geq \frac{8}{4}$$

$$-y \geq 2$$

$$y \leq -2$$

It is extremely important that you multiply the variable $-y$ by -1 so you get a positive variable. Remember to switch the inequality sign in direction when you multiply the other side by a negative.

The correct answer choice is (C), $y \leq -2$, and you didn't have to do anything but simplify the problem!

IT CANNOT BE DETERMINED:

Once in a while, you'll see a question on the GRE regular multiple-choice math that has "It Cannot Be Determined" as answer choice (E). This doesn't pose any problem to you except that if you plan to use the Testing Choices strategy, you'll need to test every answer choice just to be sure that choice (E) "It Cannot Be Determined" is not the correct choice.

EVEN AND ODD:

Many of the questions that you encounter involving even and odd numbers will contain the word "could." If this is the case, all you have to do is pick a number, use it in the problem and find just one instance where the conditions of the problem are met. Once you've done this, you've solved the problem. Here's an example:

If a is an odd number and b is even, which of the following could be an even number?

(A) $a - b$ (D) $\dfrac{a}{2} - b$

(B) $a + b$ (E) $\dfrac{a}{b} - \dfrac{a}{2}$

(C) $a + \dfrac{b}{2}$

When dealing with questions containing even and odd numbers, it is best to pick 1 and 2 for the numbers you'll plug into the question. Using 1 for *a* and 2 for *b*, let's look at the answer choices again:

(A) $a - b = 1 - 2 = -1$

(B) $a + b = 1 + 2 = 3$

(C) $a + \dfrac{b}{2} = 1 + \dfrac{2}{2} = 1 + 1 = 2$

Having found that (C) is an even number, you can stop trying out the answer choices. Choice (C) is correct because, by using 1 and 2 for *a* and *b*, this choice could be an even number. No further searching is necessary.

Now that you know two extremely effective strategies for approaching GRE algebra questions, let's review the types of algebra questions you'll see on the Problem Solving section of the GRE.

Question Type 1: ALGEBRAIC EXPRESSIONS

Problems involving algebraic expressions will often ask you to compare two expressions, or rearrange and simplify them. To successfully complete questions on algebraic expressions, you'll need to know the following skills:

1. Combining like terms

2. Factoring an expression

1. Combining like terms: To combine like terms you need to look at values in an expression that differ only in their numerical coefficients. Here's a quick review of terminology: You've learned that a *variable* is a letter that represents a number. However, a

Look!

Important Strategy

variable can take on several values at a given time. A *constant*, on the other hand, is a symbol which takes on only one value at a given time. A *term* is a constant, a variable, or a combination of constants and variables. For example: 7.76, 3x, xyz, $\dfrac{5z}{x}$, (0.99)x^2 are terms. If a term is a combination of constants and variables, the constant part of the term is referred to as the *coefficient* of the variable (such as the "2" in 2x or the "4" in 4x^2). If a variable is written without a coefficient, the coefficient is assumed to be 1.

So, to combine like terms, you need to combine terms which differ only in their numerical coefficients. For example:

$$P(x) = (x^2 - 3x + 5) + (4x^2 + 6x - 3)$$

By using the commutative and associative laws, you can rewrite this expression as:

$$P(x) = (x^2 + 4x^2) + (6x - 3x) + (5 - 3)$$

Then, using the distributive law, we can rewrite the expression as:

$$P(x) = (1 + 4)x^2 + (6 - 3)x + (5 - 3)$$
$$P(x) = 5x^2 + 3x + 2$$

This is combining like terms. Here's another example:

$$= (5x^2 + 4y^2 + 3z^2) - (4xy + 7y^2 - 3z^2 + 1)$$
$$= 5x^2 + 4y^2 + 3z^2 - 4xy - 7y^2 + 3z^2 - 1$$
$$= 5x^2 + (4y^2 - 7y^2) + (3z^2 + 3z^2) - 4xy - 1$$
$$= 5x^2 + (-3y^2) + 6z^2 - 4xy - 1$$

2.   Factoring an expression: To factor a polynomial completely is to find the prime factors of the polynomial with respect to a specified set of numbers.

The following concepts are important while factoring or simplifying expressions:

a.   The factors of an algebraic expression consist of two or more algebraic expressions which, when multiplied together, produce the given algebraic expression.

b.   A prime factor is a polynomial with no factors other than itself and 1. The *Least Common Multiple (LCM)* for a set of numbers is the smallest quantity divisible by every number of the set. For algebraic expressions the least common numerical coefficients for each of the given expressions will be a factor.

c.   The *Greatest Common Factor (GCF)* for a set of numbers is the largest factor that is common to all members of the set.

d.   For algebraic expressions, the greatest common factor is the polynomial of highest degree and the largest numerical coefficient which is a factor of all the terms in a given expression.

The procedure for factoring an algebraic expression completely is as follows:

STEP 1   First, find the greatest common factor, if there is any. Then examine each factor remaining for greatest common factors.

STEP 2 | Continue factoring the factors obtained in Step 1 until all factors other than monomial (consisting only of one term) factors are prime.

For example:

Factor $4 - 16x^2$:

$$4 - 16x^2 = 4(1 - 4x^2) = 4(1+2x)(1 - 2x)$$

Here's another example:

Express each of the following as a single term:

$$3x^2 + 2x^2 - 4x^2 \text{ and } 5axy^2 - 7axy^2 - 3xy^2$$

Step 1: Factor x^2 in the expression.

$$3x^2 + 2x^2 - 4x^2 = (3 + 2 - 4)x^2 = 1x^2 = x^2$$

Step 2: Factor xy^2 in the expression and the factor a.

$$5axy^2 - 7axy^2 - 3xy^2 = (5a - 7a - 3)\, xy^2$$

$$= [(5 - 7)a - 3]xy^2$$

$$= (-2a - 3)xy^2$$

Question Type 2: Word Problems

Bust it!

The vast majority of word problems found on the GRE can be easily and quickly solved using the Starting with the Choices and Testing Choices strategies. There will, however, be some problems that cannot be solved using either of these strategies. For these types of questions, you'll need to rewrite the word problem as an equation and solve it using traditional algebra.

In order to rewrite word problems as equations, you'll need to pay attention to key words in the problems. Here is a quick list of key words and what they should mean to you:

KEYWORD	EQUIVALENT
is	equals
sum	add
plus	add
more than, older than	add
difference	subtract
less than, younger than	subtract
twice, double	multiply by 2
half as many	divide by 2
increase by 3	add 3
decrease by 3	subtract 3

Important Information!

Here's an example of a word problem as you might see one on the GRE:

Adam has 50 more than twice the number of frequent flier miles that Erica has. If Adam has 200 frequent flier miles, how many does Erica have?

(A) 25

(B) 60

(C) 75

(D) 100

(E) 250

The keywords in this problem are "more" and "twice." If you let:

A = the number of frequent flier miles that Adam has

and

E = the number of frequent flier miles that Erica has

If Adam has twice the number of miles that Erica has plus 50 more you can write:

A (Adam) $= 50 + 2E$

Since $A = 200$, the solution becomes:

$200 = 50 + 2E$

Bust it!

Therefore,

$$200 = 50 + 2E$$

$$200 - 50 = 2E$$

$$150 = 2E$$

$$75 = E$$

So choice (C), 75, would be the correct answer.

Points to Remember for Busting GRE Algebra Problem Solving Questions

✔   *Using the Starting from the Choices strategy to answer algebra questions will be faster and easier than using traditional algebra. To use this strategy,*

1)   *think of variables as numbers,*

2)   *pick an answer choice and use it to answer the question,*

3)   *if it works, that's the correct choice, and*

4)   *if it doesn't work, keep trying different answer choices until you find the right one.*

✔   *When a question doesn't have numbers in its answer choices, use the Testing Choices strategy to solve it. The first step for using the Testing Choices strategy is to pick a number. Second, use the number you've picked to solve the problem. Third, use the number you picked and plug it into the answer choices to determine which answer choice will give you the answer to the question. The answer choice that gives you the answer to the question is the correct answer.*

✔   *If you are being asked a question about an inequality, you can use the same Testing Choices strategy to solve the problem. But, you may be*

On Target!

able to simplify the inequality and solve it without even having to test choices.

✔   If the question you are working has "It Cannot Be Determined" as its answer choice (E), be sure to test every answer choice before selecting your answer. This is the only way to be absolutely sure that (E) is not the correct answer.

✔   If the word "could" appears in the question you are working on, you only have to find one instance where the numbers you pick satisfy the conditions of the question. Once you find numbers that meet these conditions, you've found the correct answer. This applies mostly to questions that involve even and odd numbers.

✔   Know the fundamental rules and terminology of algebraic expressions. Know how to combine like terms and how to factor an expression.

✔   Understand that most word problems can be solved using the Starting with the Choices or Testing Choices strategies, but that there will be instances where you'll need to rewrite a word problem as an equation. Know how to recognize the keywords in a word problem and be able to translate those key words into equations.

On Target!

Attacking the Geometry Problem Solving Questions

The final type of basic math skill you'll need for the GRE is geometry. Like arithmetic and algebra, you will not need to know complex formulas, theorems, or proofs to solve GRE geometry. In fact, whatever formulas you need (such as the area of a circle or the number of degrees in a straight line), will be given to you at the beginning of the GRE math section. In this section we'll teach:

Bust it!

1. **Geometry rules and principles that are frequently tested on the GRE**

2. **How to use the strategy of Starting from the Choices to answer geometry questions**

The Fundamental Rules of GRE Geometry

Most geometry problems on the GRE can be solved with basic knowledge of lines, angles, triangles, rectangles, parallelograms, and circles. Some problems will require knowledge of solids and coordinate geometry. You will not have to work with proofs on this test.

Important Information!

While you do not need to know a great deal of geometry, what you need to know is essential. Because the same formulas tend to be used over and over again, failure to memorize a basic principle can cost you not just one question, but several.

Common Symbols

SYMBOL	DEFINITION
$\parallel$	is parallel to
$\perp$	is perpendicular to
$\angle$	angle
$\overline{AB}$	line segment AB (any letters can be used)
$\llcorner$	right angle

Point: A *point* is a particular and definite position. Although we represent points on paper with small dots, a point has no size, thickness, or width.

Plane: A *plane* is a collection of points lying on a flat surface that extends indefinitely in all directions.

Lines

A line in geometry is defined as a straight line. A line can be named by a single letter or by two points on the line. Example:

line *l*; line segment $\overline{MN}$

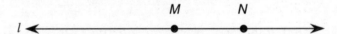

A line segment is all the points on a line between and including two points; for example, $\overline{MN}$.

The bisector of a line segment divides the line segment into two equal parts. Example:

$\overline{LM}$ bisects $\overline{AB}$; $\overline{AM} = \overline{MB}$

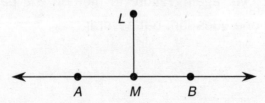

Degrees and Angles

At the extreme basic level, geometry is all about degrees and angles. A *degree* is a unit that is used to measure angles. There are 360° in a circle (the little symbol after "360" denotes "degrees"). It doesn't matter how big or how small the circle is—it will always contain 360°.

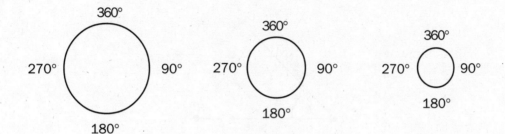

An angle is formed when two lines extend from one point. It is easier to understand angles if you think of a circle. If the point from which the two lines extend is at the center of the circle, the measure of the angle is determined by the number of degrees enclosed by the lines as they cross the edge of the circle:

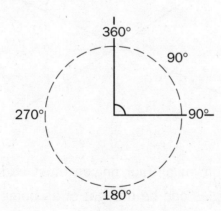

Angles can be referred to in any of the three following ways:

1. By a capital letter which names its *vertex* (the point where the two lines converge), for example: ∠A

2.   By a lowercase letter or number placed inside the angle, for example: ∠x

3.   By three capital letters, where the middle letter is the vertex and the other two letters are not on the same line, for example: ∠CAB or ∠BAC, both of which represent the angle that follows:

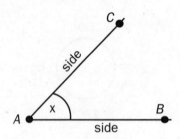

Vertical angles are formed when two lines intersect. The angles opposite to each other are equal: ∠a = ∠c and ∠b = ∠d.

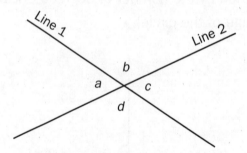

The sum of all four angles must add up to 360°. This is true because all angles can be thought of as being part of a circle (see figure below).

Important Information!

If two lines form an angle that measures 90°, it is said to be a *right angle*. Also, the two lines making a right angle are said to be *perpendicular*. In the case of a right angle formed by the intersection of two perpendicular lines, all four angles will be 90°:

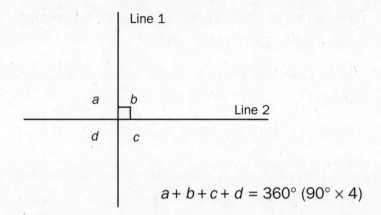

$$a+b+c+d = 360° \ (90° \times 4)$$

Two lines are called parallel lines if, and only if, they are in the same plane and DO NOT intersect. This means the two lines will run alongside one another in both directions and will never intersect. If two or more lines are perpendicular (form right angles) to the same line, then these lines are parallel to each other:

Important Information!

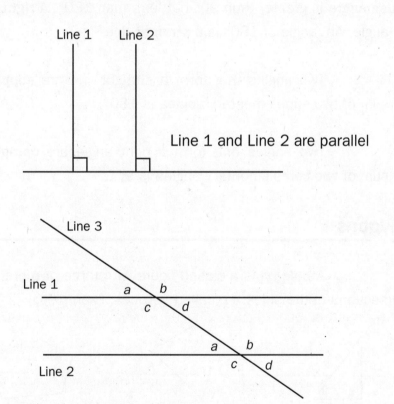

Look at the figure above. If two parallel lines (Lines 1 and 2) are cut by a transversal line (Line 3) then the following is always true:

1.   The sum of the adjacent angles is equal to 180° (e.g. $a + b = 180°$, $b + d = 180°$, etc.)

2. $\angle a$ on Line 1 is equal to angle $\angle a$ on Line 2, $\angle b = \angle b$ and so forth

3.   Opposite angles are equal (e.g. $\angle a = \angle d$, $\angle b = \angle c$)

Bust it!

> Properties of parallel lines are among the most frequently used concepts in GRE test questions. Whenever you see two parallel lines cut by a transversal, you should immediately look for pairs of angles that are equal or supplementary.

Special Angles

An **acute angle** is greater than 0° but less than 90°. An **obtuse angle** is greater than 90° but less than 180°. A **right angle** is a 90° angle. An angle of 180° is a **straight line**.

Two angles that form a straight line are **supplementary.** The sum of two supplementary angles is 180°.

Two angles that form a right angle are **complementary.** The sum of two complementary angles is 90°.

Polygons

A *polygon* is a closed figure with three or more sides. The intersections of the sides are called *vertices*. Examples:

      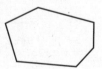

Triangle (3 sides)   Quadrilateral (4 sides)   Hexagon (6 sides)

The sum of the measures of the interior angles of an *n*-sided polygon is $(n-2)(180°)$. For example,

The sum for a triangle ($n = 3$) is $(3 - 2)(180°) = 180°$

The sum for a hexagon ($n = 6$) is $(6 - 2)(180°) = 720°$

A polygon whose sides are all the same length and whose interior angles are all equal in measure is called a *regular polygon*. Examples:

Regular Triangle

Regular Rectangle

Regular Hexagon

The *perimeter* of a polygon is the sum of the lengths of its sides. For example, the total length of a fence which encloses a field would be the field's perimeter.

The *area* of a polygon is the measure of the space enclosed by the polygon. For example, the total amount of carpeting needed to cover the floor of a room would be the area of that room.

Important Information!

Triangles

A closed three-sided geometric figure is called a triangle. The sides of a triangle are straight lines. The points of intersection of the sides of a triangle are called the vertices of the triangle. For example, in the triangle that follows, the vertices are *ABC*. The perimeter of a triangle is the sum of its sides:

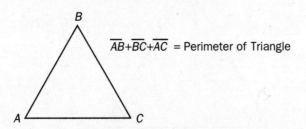

$\overline{AB} + \overline{BC} + \overline{AC}$ = Perimeter of Triangle

The sum of the lengths of any two sides of a triangle must be greater than the length of the third side.

The **area of a triangle** is its height multiplied by its base divided by 2.

Important Information!

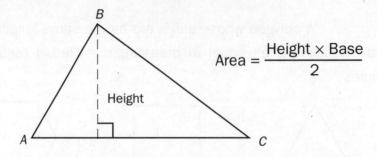

$$\text{Area} = \frac{\text{Height} \times \text{Base}}{2}$$

Every triangle is made up of three interior angles that equal 180°. Since many GRE geometry questions cover this rule, it is important to remember it.

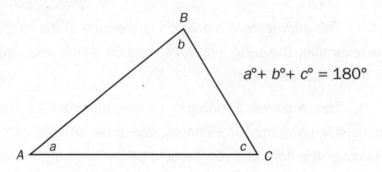

$$a° + b° + c° = 180°$$

There are three main types of triangles: equilateral, isosceles, and right. **An equilateral triangle is a triangle having three equal sides.** Because the sides of an equilateral triangle are the same, so are the angles. This is true because angles opposite equal sides are also equal. **The angles of an equilateral triangle are always 60°.**

Important Information!

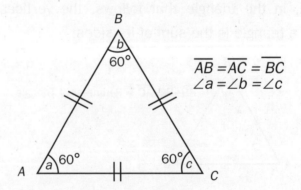

$$\overline{AB} = \overline{AC} = \overline{BC}$$
$$\angle a = \angle b = \angle c$$

An isosceles triangle is a triangle in which two of the sides are equal. And since angles opposite equal sides are equal, two of the angles in an isosceles triangle are equal:

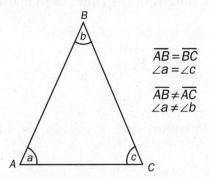

$$\overline{AB} = \overline{BC}$$
$$\angle a = \angle c$$

$$\overline{AB} \neq \overline{AC}$$
$$\angle a \neq \angle b$$

Important Information!

A triangle with a right angle (90°) is called a right triangle. The side opposite the right angle is called the hypotenuse of the right triangle. The other two sides are called the arms or legs of the right triangle.

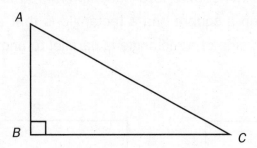

Pythagorean theorem: For a right triangle, the square of the length of the hypotenuse is equal to the sum of the squares of the other two sides. Example:

$$a^2 + b^2 = c^2$$

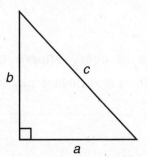

Important Information!

This formula can be used to find the length of one side of a right triangle if the lengths of the other two sides are known. For example, if one leg of a right triangle is 4 and the hypotenuse is 5, then you can figure out the length of the other side like this:

$$5^2 = 4^2 + x^2$$

$$25 = 16 + x^2$$

$$9 = x^2$$

So the unknown side, x, equals $\sqrt{9}$, which is 3.

Quadrilaterals

A *quadrilateral* is a polygon with four sides. Every quadrilateral has four sides and four interior angles, the sum of whose measures is 360°. A *square* is a *quadrilateral*, so is a *rectangle*. The difference between a square and a rectangle is that a square has four equal sides. Each side of a rectangle is parallel to another side of equal length.

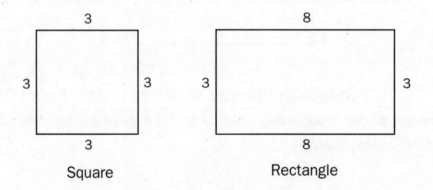

Square   Rectangle

All angles in every square or rectangle must be 90°. Opposite sides are parallel and have equal length.

To determine the perimeter of a quadrilateral, simply add the lengths of its sides:

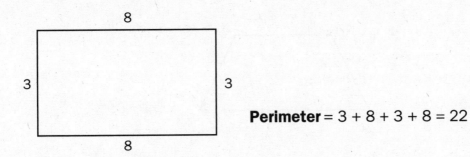

Perimeter = 3 + 8 + 3 + 8 = 22

To determine the area of a rectangle or square, multiply its base by its height:

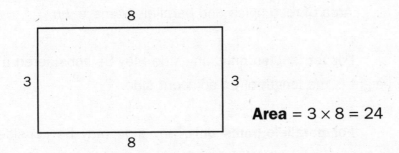

Area = 3 × 8 = 24

A **parallelogram** is a four-sided figure in which opposite sides are parallel. In a parallelogram, opposite sides are equal and opposite angles are equal. Example:

$AB = CD$ and $AC = BD$;

$\angle A = \angle D$ and $\angle B = \angle C$

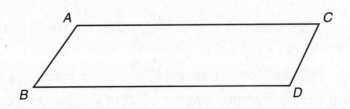

Important Information!

When you have a quadrilateral and only one pair of opposite sides is parallel, it is called a *trapezoid*. Example:

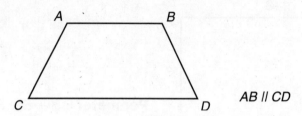

$AB \parallel CD$

To determine the area of rectangles and parallelograms, multiply the base (*b*) by the height (*h*):

Area of rectangles and parallelograms = *bh*

Important Information!

For rectangles only, any side may be considered a base, and the height is the length of an adjacent side.

For parallelograms only, any side may be considered a base, and the height is the length of a perpendicular line drawn from the base to the opposite side. Example:

Rectangle

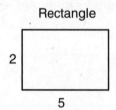

Parallelogram

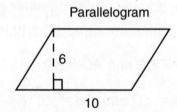

Area = (5)(2) = 10   Area = (10)(6) = 60

The area of a **trapezoid** is a little harder to figure out. First find half the sum of the lengths of the two parallel sides (b_1 and b_2). Then multiply the result by the height (*h*), which you would find the same way as you would find the height for a parallelogram: by drawing a perpendicular line from b_1 to b_2.

Area of a trapezoid = ½ (b_1 + b_2)(*h*)

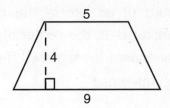

Area = ½ (5 + 9)(4) = 28.

Circles

A **circle** is a set of points equidistant from one point, called the center. A circle is named by the letter of its center. Example:

circle *O*

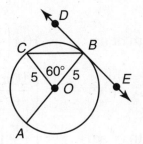

A line passing through the center of a circle connecting two points on the circle is called a **diameter** ($\overline{AB}$).

A line from the center of the circle to any point on the circle is called a **radius** ($\overline{CO}$). The radius is ½ the diameter.

A line segment that has its end points on a circle is called a **chord** ($\overline{CB}$).

A **tangent** is a line that intersects a circle at one point ($\overleftrightarrow{DE}$).

The **circumference** is the distance around a circle. In any circle, the ratio of the circumference *c* to the diameter *d* is a fixed constant, denoted by the Greek letter π.

$$\frac{c}{d} = \pi$$

An **arc** is a portion of the circumference. The GRE will refer to an arc by naming three points which lie on that arc. In the figure below, arc *XYZ* is the short arc which runs clockwise from *X* to *Z*, but arc *XWZ* is the long arc which runs counterclockwise from *X* to *Z*.

The measure of an arc is the measure of its **central angle** (an angle whose vertex is at the center of the circle—∠*COB*). The measure of an arc is measured in degrees. The length of an arc is a portion of the circle's circumference.

There is an equation that will help you find the *length* of an arc. The ratio of arc length to the circumference of the entire circle is equal to the ratio of arc measure (in degrees) to 360.

$$\frac{\text{length of arc}}{10\pi} = \frac{60}{360}$$

$$\text{length of arc} = 10\pi\left(\frac{60}{360}\right)$$

$$\text{length of arc} = 10\pi\left(\frac{1}{6}\right)$$

$$\text{length of arc} = \left(\frac{10\pi}{6}\right)$$

$$\text{length of arc} = \left(\frac{5\pi}{3}\right)$$

The formula for the *area* of a circle with radius *r* is

$$\text{Area of a circle} = \pi r^2$$

For example, the area of the circle above is $\pi(5)^2 = 25\pi$.

In this circle, the wedge-shaped region formed by arc *ABC* and the two radii is called a *sector* of the circle. Here, its central angle is 60°. The ratio of the area of the sector to the area of the whole circle is equal to the ratio of the arc measure to 360. So, if *S* represents the area of the sector with a central angle of 60°, then

$$\frac{S}{25\pi} = \frac{60}{360}$$

$$S = 25\pi\left(\frac{60}{360}\right)$$

$$S = 25\pi\left(\frac{1}{6}\right)$$

$$S = \left(\frac{25\pi}{6}\right)$$

A radius whose endpoint lies on the point of tangency is perpendicular to the tangent line. Example:

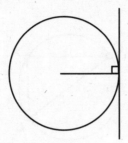

Formulas for Circles:

The degree measure of a circle is 360°.

Area: $A = \pi r^2$; where r = radius

Circumference: $C = \pi d$ or $2\pi r$, where d = diameter, r = radius

Length of an Arc: $Arc\ AB = (x/360) \times 2\pi r$, where x = the measure of arc AB, r = radius

It is essential that you know the approximate value of π, which is 3.14 or $^{22}/_{7}$.

Bust it!

Inscribed Figures

An angle drawn inside a circle with its vertex lying on the circle is called an **inscribed angle**. The measure of an inscribed angle is half the measure of its intercepted arc.

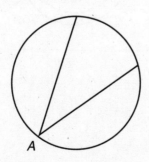

*Important
Information!*

A figure drawn inside a circle with all of its vertices lying on the circle is inscribed in the circle. The circle is said to be circumscribed about the polygon.

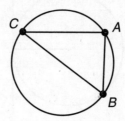

A circle drawn inside a figure with each side of the figure tangent to the circle is inscribed in the figure. The polygon is said to be circumscribed about the circle.

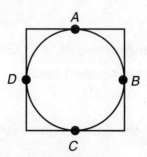

Two or more circles that have the same center are called *concentric* circles. Example:

Three-Dimensional Figures

The following are some examples of three-dimensional figures: rectangular solids, cubes, cylinders, spheres, pyramids, and cones.

A *rectangular solid* has six rectangular surfaces which are called *faces*. They are like the six sides of a cardboard box. Each line segment is called an *edge* (there are 12 edges, like the edges of a box). Each point at which the edges meet is called a *vertex* (there are 8 vertices, like the corners of a box). The three dimensions of a rectangular solid are length (*l*), width (*w*), and height (*h*).

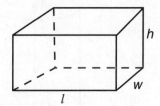

A **cube** is a rectangular solid in which all edges are equal because all faces are squares. The surface area of a cube of edge length *a* is $S = 6a^2$. Example:

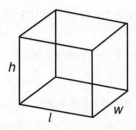

Formulas for Solids:

Volume: $V = l \times w \times h$; where l = length, w = width, and h = height.

Surface area: The sum of the areas of all the faces.

Surface area of rectangular solid = $2(wl + lh + wh)$

Bust it!

For example, if a rectangular solid has length 4, width 3, and height 5, then its volume is:

Volume of rectangular solid = (4)(3)(5) = 60,

and its surface area is:

Surface area of a rectangular solid = 2[(3)(4)+(4)(5)+(3)(5)] = 94.

The following is a *right circular cylinder*. Its bases are circles with equal areas and equal radii. Think of the top and bottom of a soup can. The centers of the bases are points *A* and *B*, and the cylinder's height, *AB*, is perpendicular to both bases.

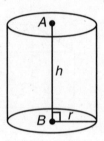

The *volume* of a right circular cylinder is the area of the base (the bottom of the soup can) multiplied by the height. Remember that the formula for the area of a circle is πr^2. This is the base of the cylinder. Therefore, multiply it by the height to find the volume:

$$\text{Volume of a cylinder} = \pi r^2 h$$

Important Information!

The *surface area* of a right circular cylinder is the sum of the two base areas (the top and bottom of the soup can) and the area of the curved surface (think of the soup can label). You know how to find the area of the circular bases. Now imagine unrolling the curved surface of the cylinder. Think of taking the soup can label, cutting it straight down the long end, and then flattening it. You would see a rectangle. The side of the label is equal to the height of the cylinder (*h*). The top of the label is equal to the diameter of the circle ($2\pi r$). Therefore,

$$\text{Surface area of a cylinder} = 2(\pi r^2) + 2\pi r h$$

For example, if a cylinder has a base radius of 3 and a height of 7, then its volume is:

$$V = \pi (3)^2 (7)$$
$$= \pi (9) (7)$$
$$= 63\pi,$$

and its surface area is:

$$A = (2)(\pi)(3)^2 + (2)(\pi)(3)(7)$$
$$= (2)(\pi)(9) + (2)(\pi)(21)$$
$$= (18)(\pi) + (42)(\pi)$$
$$= 6\pi.$$

 Testbusting Geometry Tip:
STARTING FROM THE CHOICES

As you learned to do for algebra questions, Starting from the Choices can help you find the correct answer to a question faster and easier than if you used traditional methods. This is also true of geometry questions!

Bust it!

You should remember that there are three steps to using the Starting from the Choices strategy. Here's a summary of those steps amended to fit geometry questions:

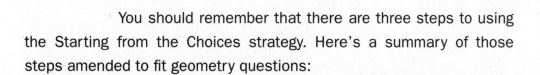

STEP 1 | Read the question and look at the answer choices. Pick one of the answer choices that you think would most likely be the correct answer. If this doesn't help you, pick the most likely answer quickly, just pick the number that is in the middle of all the values.

STEP 2
Use the answer choice you've picked to see if it works in the question.

STEP 3
If the answer choice you picked doesn't work, choose another answer choice. Keep trying choices until you find one that works. This is your correct answer.

This strategy will help you answer any geometry questions that ask you to find measurements or determine missing information.

Let's do an example:

What is the value of x in the triangle below?

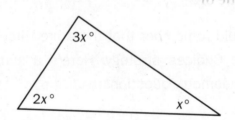

(A) 25   (D) 55

(B) 30   (E) 90

(C) 40

Looking at the choices, you should pick the number in the middle. In this case, the middle number is choice (C) 40. Your next step is to plug in that answer into the problem to see if it works.

You know that the sum of a triangle's interior angles must equal 180°. So, using 40 for x, see if choice (C) is the correct answer:

$$2(40)° + 3(40)° + 40° = 180°$$

$$80° + 120° + 40° = 180°$$

$$240° \neq 180°$$

Wrong! That's okay. Choice (C) gave you a number that was too big. Your next step is to go back to the answer choices and pick a choice that is less than 40. The next choice that is less than 40 would be choice (B), 30. Plug 30 into the question and see if it works:

$$2(30)° + 3(30)° + 30° = 180°$$

$$60° + 90° + 30° = 180°$$

$$180° = 180°$$

Bust it!

That's it! Choice (B), 30, is the correct answer. Just to be sure, let's solve the question in the traditional manner:

What is the value of x in the triangle below?

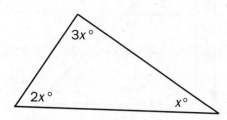

(A) 25

(D) 55

(B) 30

(E) 90

(C) 40

As you knew before, the sum of the interior angles of a triangle must equal 180°. So, let's create an equation to find x:

$$2x° + 3x° + x° = 180°$$

Now, combine like terms:

$$6x° = 180°$$

Finally, isolate the variable:

$$x° = 30°$$

So you chose the correct answer! Using the strategy of Starting from the Choices will help you get the correct answer easier (because you won't have to work out the question from scratch) and quicker (because you'll probably be able to eliminate wrong answer choices and plug in the remaining few choices faster than it would take you to actually do the question)! Let's do another problem, only this time a little harder:

Bust it!

If the perimeter of the larger triangle is 48, what could be the value of *x* in the triangles below?

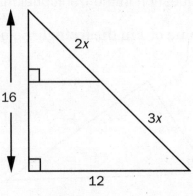

(A) 1   (D) 4

(B) 6   (E) –1

(C) 7

For this example, the answer choice you should pick first is probably (D), 4, since this is the middle number. Now plug 4 into the question:

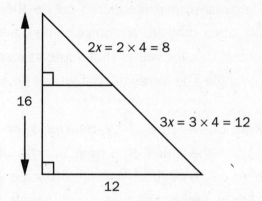

You should know that the perimeter of a triangle is the sum of its sides. So, if *x* equals 4, the hypotenuse is 20 (8 + 12). From this you can determine that the large triangle's perimeter would be 48 (12 + 16 + 20 = 48). Choice (D) is correct!

There is another strategy you can use to get the answer to this question, one that is even easier than Starting from the Choices. This alternate method can be used for any problem that contains a right triangle—and you will see a lot of right triangles on the GRE.

The reason right triangles are so special is because there is a rule that applies to them—a rule called the **PYTHAGOREAN THEOREM**. This theorem can be used to find the measure of the hypotenuse, or any leg, of a right triangle. The theorem states that the square of the length of a right triangle's hypotenuse equals the sum of the squares of the lengths of the two other sides. This equation reads as $a^2 + b^2 = c^2$:

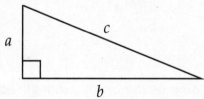

GRE geometry problems often involve right triangles with sides measuring 3, 4, and 5—or multiples of these numbers. The GRE writers do this because these measures create the smallest possible right triangle with sides that are all integers (no decimals or fractions). The great part about this for you is that you can learn the multiples of the 3–4–5 right triangle and save yourself lots of time on the GRE!

What do we mean by **multiples of the 3–4–5 right triangle**? Well, since the sides of a right triangle are related by their squares ($a^2 + b^2 = c^2$), a larger 3–4–5 right triangle will be proportional in its measure. For instance, the next larger triangle based on a 3–4–5 triangle would be 6–8–10; then 12–16–20; and then 24–32–40, etc....

Look!

Important Strategy

Keep these relationships in mind when you are faced with a right triangle question on the GRE. If a question asks you to find the length of one of the sides of a right triangle, look at the other measures. If you recognize the triangle as a 3–4–5 triangle (or one of its multiples) you will be able to find the missing measure from memory. For example:

Find the length of c:

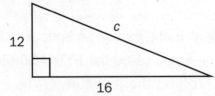

(A) 20   (D) 28

(B) 22   (E) 41

(C) 26

You should recognize this triangle as a 3–4–5 triangle and from this know that measure of the side c (the hypotenuse) must be a multiple of 5. The only answer choice that is a multiple of 5 is choice (A), 20. So this is the correct answer.

Try and answer this question using the 3–4–5 triangle strategy:

If the perimeter of the larger triangle is 24, what could be the value of *x* in the triangles below?

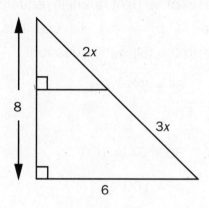

Bust it!

(A) 1 (D) 2

(B) 6 (E) –1

(C) 7

First, you should recognize this triangle as a 3–4–5 triangle. To answer the question through that method, you must find a value for *x* that gives us 10. You know this because, according to the 3–4–5 triangle theory, a triangle with one side that equals 6 (3 × 2) and one side that equals 8 (4 × 2), the third side must equal 10 (5 × 2). Thus, to find the value of *x*, you must use the following equation:

$$2x + 3x = 10$$

Combine like terms:

$$5x = 10$$

Isolate the variable:

$$\frac{5x}{5} = \frac{10}{5}$$

$$x = 2$$

So the answer to this question is choice (D), 2. Pretty simple, right?

Now let's answer the question using the Pythagorean Theorem. You remember that the Pythagorean Theorem states that the square of the hypotenuse of a right triangle equals the sum of the squares of its sides ($a^2 + b^2 = c^2$). To use this theorem in this problem, we need to set up the following equation:

$$6^2 + 8^2 = c^2$$

Simplify:

$$36 + 64 = 100$$

$$c^2 = 100$$

$$c = \sqrt{100} = 10$$

Now you know that the hypotenuse of the triangle equals 10, but you don't know the value of x (which is what the question is asking you). To find the value of x, you must use the following equation:

$$2x + 3x = 10$$

Combine like terms:

$$5x = 10$$

Isolate the variable:

$$\frac{5x}{5} = \frac{10}{5}$$

$$x = 2$$

So, once again you've found that the correct answer to this problem is choice (D), 2. And along the way you've learned three different ways to solve the problem. Some are easier than others, some are faster than the others. It really doesn't matter which technique you use ("Eyeballing," 3–4–5 Triangle, or the Pythagorean Theorem), as long as you feel comfortable and arrive at the correct answer. It is important that you feel comfortable with all of these techniques, because you will take too much time to answer a question and will make careless mistakes while answering the question. So practice these techniques, figure out how to use them in different situations and how to use them when you encounter a right triangle on the GRE.

Back to the Starting with the Choices strategy we were discussing before we introduced the Pythagorean Theorem and 3–4–5 Triangles. As with the algebra questions, there are some things you should look out for when using the Starting with the Choices strategy on geometry questions:

Look!

Important Strategy

1.   You will want to use this strategy only for questions that have answer choices that are numbers.

2.   Don't worry if you can't tell which answer choice is exactly the middle number. Just pick one that's close and work from there. You may have to work through all the answer choices to find the correct answer, but by picking one that's close to the middle first, you should find the answer quicker than by just randomly picking a number.

Points to Remember for Busting GRE Geometry Problem Solving Questions

On Target!

✔   *Know the basic terminology of geometry: point, line, plane, and line segment.*

✔   *Understand degrees and angles. Know the different ways to write an angle. Become knowledgeable about the different types of angles and the relationship between angles.*

✔   *Know what a triangle is and the different types of triangles. Understand that the three interior angles of a triangle must add up to 180°. Be able to determine the perimeter (the sum of the measure of its sides) and area $\left(\dfrac{base \times height}{2} \right)$ of a triangle.*

✔   *Understand what a circle is and what its parts are called and how they are measured. Be able to determine a circle's circumference ($2\pi r$ or πD) and its area (πr^2).*

✔   *Know what a quadrilateral is and the difference between a square and a rectangle. Understand that the sum of all angles for any quadrilateral must equal 360°. Be able to determine a quadrilateral's perimeter (the sum of the measure of its sides) and the area of a rectangle or parallelogram (base $\times$ height).*

✔   *Know how to estimate the value of π and common square roots.*

✔   *Using the Starting from the Choices strategy to answer geometry questions will be faster and easier than using traditional geometry. To use this strategy, 1) pick an answer choice and use it to answer the question; 2) if it works, that's the correct choice; 3) if it doesn't work, keep trying answer choices until you find the right one.*

✔   *Know how to use the 3–4–5 Triangle strategy and the Pythagorean Theorem ($a^2+b^2=c^2$) when attacking questions that involve right triangles.*

✔   *Understanding these principles and using them to answer right triangle questions will save you a lot of time and headaches on GRE geometry questions. Expect to see a lot of right triangles on the GRE, and become comfortable with both of these techniques to find the measure of their sides.*

On Target!

Attacking Chart Problem Solving Questions

One of the unique question types that you will encounter on the GRE Quantitative Ability section is the Chart question. Technically part of the Problem Solving questions, charts can be seen as a separate question-type and should be studied separately from the normal Problem Solving questions.

Chart questions consist of a group of questions based on a chart or graph (or sometimes more than one chart or graph).

The concepts that are tested in Chart questions are basic arithmetic skills; the same basic arithmetic skills you'll need to know in order to successfully answer the Problem Solving and Quantitative Comparison questions. The only difference is how you attack Chart questions.

The trick to answering Chart questions correctly is to understand the chart or graph BEFORE even looking at it. The writers of the GRE love to create charts and graphs that are extremely difficult to decipher.

 Chart Questions Testbusting Tip #1:
LOOK FOR PERTINENT AND IMPORTANT INFORMATION IN THE CHART OR GRAPH

One of the first places to look when trying to understand a chart or graph is the title. If there is more than one chart, note the differences between the charts' titles. Be especially careful when there are terms like "in thousands" or "in millions" in a chart title. When a title contains wording such as this, the units of measurement have been abbreviated. Usually you can ignore the units when performing calculations, but you must take them into consideration when selecting your answer.

Finally, pay attention to any asterisks, footnotes, items in parentheses, and any small print.

Chart Questions Testbusting Tip #2:
KNOW WHEN TO ESTIMATE

Look!

Important Strategy

Using estimations when working with charts will save you time and headaches. You don't need to make exact calculations whenever a chart or graph contains the words "approximately" or "roughly." Also, you can always estimate if the values in the answer choices are spread very far apart.

Let's do an example:

QUESTIONS 1 – 3 are based on the following graph:

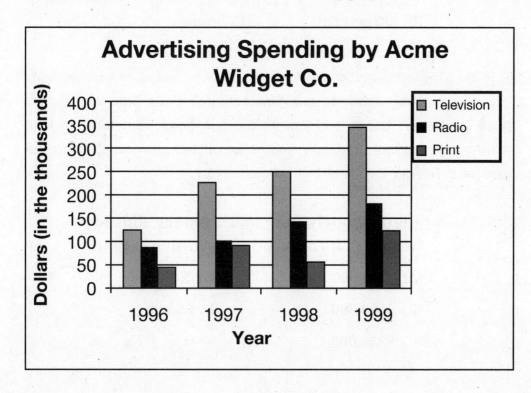

Advertising Spending by Acme Widget Co.

1. Approximately how much money did Acme Widget Co. spend on print advertising in 1997?

   (A) $300,000   (D) $100,000

   (B) $400,000   (E) $5,000

   (C) $250,000

2. How much did Acme Widget Co. spend on television advertising in 1999?

   (A) $200,000   (D) $100,000

   (B) $348,000   (E) $50,000

   (C) $188,000

Bust it!

3. Roughly how much of an increase in spending on radio advertising did Acme Widget Co. see from 1997 to 1999?

   (A) 25 percent   (D) 10 percent

   (B) 50 percent   (E) none

   (C) 100 percent

Okay, ready to see how estimating can help you answer these questions? Before you look at the questions, remember to look at the chart or graph and fully understand it before moving on to the questions. Ready? Let's start with Question 1:

1. Approximately how much money did Acme Widget Co. spend on print advertising in 1997?

   (A) $300,000   (D) $100,000

   (B) $400,000   (E) $5,000

   (C) $250,000

In order to answer this question, you must first find information that represents print advertising spending in 1997. To do this you should see that the x-axis (horizontal) represents the years and that the y-axis (vertical) represents dollars in the thousands. Remember to be careful whenever a chart presents units in a special way. In this case, you should understand that the numbers on the y-axis are abbreviated and when you look at the answers, you must multiply the numbers on the y-axis by 1,000.

Next, you must locate the bar that represents print advertising. From the legend you can determine that the lightest-color bars represent spending on print advertising. By looking at this chart, you should see that Acme Widget Co. spent just under $100,000 on print advertising in 1997.

It is important to note that the question asked you "Approximately how much money... ." Since the question is worded as such, you can estimate your answer. You've already determined that the chart shows just under $100,000 was spent on print advertising in 1997. This may be all you need to know. To find out, look at the answer choices.

Choices (A) through (C) are clearly too high to be the correct answer. Choice (D), $100,000, looks correct. Finally, choice (E), $5,000 is obviously too low. Thus, choice (D), $100,000, is your correct answer.

See how easy that was? You should have recognized that you could estimate and that estimation led you to the correct answer.

Now let's look at Question 2:

2. **How much did Acme Widget Co. spend on television advertising in 1999?**

   (A) $200,000   (D) $100,000

   (B) $348,000   (E) $50,000

   (C) $188,000

This question is very similar to Question 1. Your first step is to find the information the question is looking for: You must first find information that represents television advertising spending in 1999.

As before, the *x*-axis (horizontal) represents the years and the *y*-axis (vertical) represents dollars in the thousands. From the legend you can determine that the gray-color bars represent spending on television advertising.

By looking at this chart, you should see that Acme Widget Co. spent just under $350,000 on television advertising in 1999.

The question did not have any estimation clues in it such as "approximately" or "roughly" so you should quickly look at the answer choices to see how far apart they place their values. In this case, you should recognize that your estimate of just under $350,000 should be close enough to reach the correct answer.

Choice (A), $200,000, is quite a bit smaller than $350,000 and can be eliminated. Choice (B), $348,000 is very close to your estimate of $350,000 and should be kept. Choices (C), $188,000; (D), $100,000; and (E), $50,000 are less than your estimate by quite a large amount so they can be eliminated. This leaves you with choice (B), $348,000, as your correct answer.

On to Question 3:

3. **Roughly how much of an increase in spending on radio advertising did Acme Widget Co. see from 1997 to 1999?**

    (A) 25 percent   (D) 10 percent

    (B) 50 percent   (E) none

    (C) 100 percent

You should recognize the possibility to estimate from the key phrase in this question: "Roughly how much... ." With this in mind, your next step is to determine what information you need to find in order to answer the question.

Since we are dealing with the same chart as in Questions 1 and 2, the *x*-axis (horizontal) represents the years and that the *y*-axis (vertical) represents dollars in the thousands. From the legend you can determine that the black-color bars represent spending on radio advertising.

The question is asking you to determine the percentage increase in radio advertising spending from 1997 to 1999. You should be able to see that the company spent about $100,000 in 1997 and about $200,000 in 1999 on radio advertising. From this information you can estimate that the spending on radio advertising doubled in that time span.

But you need to come up with a percentage. Well, think about how much of a percent increase you have when a value is doubled. Don't worry about working this question out exactly and using the percentage skills you've learned. Using your estimation, it is simple to determine that you have a 100 percent increase when you double something. You should memorize this as one of the common percentage figures.

Too easy? Okay, we'll answer the question the hard way: by doing the math.

We have approximately $100,000 in radio advertising spending in 1997. We have approximately $200,000 in 1999. The question is asking you how much the spending increased from 1997 to 1999, so you must determine how much more was spent on radio advertising in 1999 than in 1997:

$200,000 in 1999 – $100,000 in 1997 = $100,000 more spending

From this you need to find out how this increase compares to the original amount. Since we have $100,000 in spending in 1997 and a $100,000 increase in 1999, you must use the percent increase formula:

Percent Increase = $x/100 \times$ original figure

In this formula, x equals the percent increase.

Plugging in our figures, you would get:

$$100,000 = \frac{x}{100} \times 100,000$$

$$100,000 = \frac{100,000x}{100}$$

$$100,000 = 1,000x$$

$$\frac{100,000}{1,000} = \frac{1,000x}{1,000}$$

$$100 = x$$

Bust it!

Thus, there was an approximate 100 percent increase in radio advertising spending from 1997 to 1999.

Now look at the answer choices: choice (C), 100 percent, is the only choice that even comes close to your estimated answer. Thus, choice (C) is the correct answer.

Take a moment and think about how much easier it was to determine that there was a 100 percent increase based on your memory of common percentages when compared to actually working the problem out mathematically. This question should be a motivator for both estimation when working on Chart questions and memorizing common percentages!

Points to Remember for Busting GRE Chart Problem Solving Questions

✔ _Learn how to understand charts and graphs._

✔ _Carefully read the title of a chart or graph. If there is more than one chart, note the differences between the charts' titles._

✔ _Be especially careful with terms like "in thousands" or "in millions" in a chart title._

On Target!

✔   Pay attention to any asterisks, footnotes, items in parentheses, and any small print.

✔   Use estimations when working with charts and graphs.

✔   Look for key words like "approximately" or "roughly" in the questions to indicate when to estimate. Also, you can always estimate if the values in the answer choices are spread very far apart.

Drill: Problem Solving

1. If a measurement of 2.25 inches on a map represents 50 miles, what distance does a measurement of 18 inches on the map represent?

(A) 350 miles   (D) 425 miles
(B) 375 miles   (E) 450 miles
(C) 400 miles

3. If $\dfrac{3}{x-1}=\dfrac{2}{x+2}$, then x =

(A) -8.   (D) 1.
(B) -1.   (E) 5.
(C) 0.

2. A teacher earns $25,000 a year and receives a 4% cost of living increase in salary, and a $275 merit increase. His salary increased by

(A) 4.5%.   (D) 5.1%.
(B) 4.9%.   (E) 5.2%.
(C) 5.0%.

4. Ballpoint pens cost $1.50 a dozen for the first 200 dozen a store buys from a wholesaler and $1.25 a dozen for those bought in addition to the first 200 dozen. If the store buys 250 dozen pens from the wholesaler, then its average cost of ballpoint pens per dozen is

(A) $1.50.   (D) $1.30.
(B) $1.45.   (E) $1.25.
(C) $1.38.

Question 5 pertains to the following table.

ANNUAL INCOME BY SEX OF HEAD OF THE HOUSEHOLD

Sex	Less than $15,000	$15,000–$34,999	$35,000–$49,999	$50,000 and above
Male	12	25	35	8
Female	22	10	6	2

5. What percent of the males earn less than $35,000?

(A) 31
(B) $46^1/_4$
(C) $57^1/_2$
(D) 60
(E) 90

6. If p and q are prime numbers, each greater than 2, which of the following must be true?

I. pq is an even integer.
II. $p + q$ is an even integer.
III. pq is an odd integer.

(A) I only
(B) II only
(C) III only
(D) I and II only
(E) II and III only

7. Rachel has 30 pounds of a mixture of candy that sells for $1.00/lb. Candy A sells for $.95/lb and Candy B sells for $1.10/lb. How many pounds of Candy A is in the mixture?

(A) 5
(B) 10
(C) 15
(D) 20
(E) 35

8. If the product of two numbers is 14 and one of the numbers is $3^1/_2$ times the other, then the sum of the two numbers is

(A) 2.
(B) 5.
(C) 7.
(D) 9.
(E) 14.

9. If $AB = 10$ in the given figure, the area of the triangle ABC is

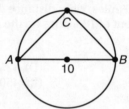

(A) 65.
(B) 40.
(C) 28.
(D) 16.
(E) 25.

10. The sum of three consecutive even integers is 270. What is the largest integer?

(A) 86
(B) 88
(C) 90
(D) 92
(E) 94

11. A 2,000-foot-long fence will be used to enclose a rectangular field that is three times as long as it is wide. The length of the field is

(A) 250 feet.   (D) 600 feet.
(B) 400 feet.   (E) 750 feet.
(C) 500 feet.

12. The mean distance from Mars to the sun is 1.41×10^8 miles and the mean distance from Earth to the sun is 9.3×10^7 miles. How much closer to the sun is Earth than Mars?

(A) 4.8×10^7 (D) 4.8×10^8
(B) 7.89×10^7 (E) 7.89×10^8
(C) 7.89×10^{10}

13. In a chess match, a win counts 1 point, a draw counts $^1/_2$ point, and a loss counts 0 points. After 15 games, the winner was 4 points ahead of the loser. How many points did the loser have?

(A) $4^1/_2$ (D) 7
(B) $5^1/_2$ (E) 9
(C) 6

14. What is the measure of the angle made by the minute and hour hands of a clock at 3:00?

(A) 60°   (D) 115°
(B) 75°   (E) 120°
(C) 90°

15. A box of 61 pieces of candy was passed around a classroom and each student took one piece of candy. The box was passed around again in the same way, and again each student took one piece. This process was continued until there was no candy left. A particular child got the first and last piece. Which of the following is a FALSE sentence?

(A) There could have been 15 students in class.
(B) There could have been 12 students in class.
(C) There could have been 10 students in class.
(D) There could have been 7 students in class.
(E) There could have been 6 students in class.

16. During the one-hour period between 5:00 and 6:00, how many minutes is exactly one "2" displayed on an electronic digital clock?

(A) 12   (D) 15
(B) 13   (E) 16
(C) 14

17. For the triangle pictured below, the degree measure of the three angles are x, $3x$, and $3x + 5$. Find x.

(A) 25   (D) 28.3
(B) 27   (E) 29
(C) 28

18. A rectangular parking lot is 400 feet by 300 feet. How many feet can be saved by walking across the diagonal from A to C rather than going along the outer edge from A to C?

(A) 200   (D) 500
(B) 300   (E) 700
(C) 400

In Question 24, the formulas V(cylinder) $= \pi r^2 h$ and V(cone) $= {}^1/_3 \pi r^2 h$ may be helpful.

19. A cone of radius 3 inches and a cylinder of radius 4 inches have equal volumes. Find the ratio of the height of the cone to that of the cylinder.

(A) $\dfrac{16}{9}$ (D) $\dfrac{3}{4}$

(B) $\dfrac{16}{3}$ (E) $\dfrac{3}{16}$

(C) $\dfrac{9}{16}$

20. The solution of the equation $x^{-2} + x^{-1} - 6 = 0$ is

(A) $x = {}^{-1}/_3$ and $x = {}^1/_2$.
(B) $x = -6$.
(C) $x = 3$ and $x = -2$.
(D) $x = {}^{-1}/_6$.
(E) $x = {}^1/_3$ and $x = {}^{-1}/_2$.

21. The fraction

$$\frac{7x-11}{x^2-2x-15}$$

was obtained by adding the two factors

$$\frac{A}{x-5} + \frac{B}{x+3}.$$

The values of A and B are

(A) $A = 7x$, $B = 11$.   (D) $A = 5$, $B = -3$.
(B) $A = -11$, $B = 7x$.   (E) $A = -5$, $B = 3$.
(C) $A = 3$, $B = 4$.

22. A large cube has a surface of 216 square inches. What is the total surface area of two smaller cubes whose edges are half as long as those of the large cube?

(A) 108   (D) 30
(B) 216   (E) 72
(C) 54

23. If the hypotenuse of a right triangle is $x + 1$ and one of the legs is x, then the other leg is

(A) $\sqrt{2x+1}$.   (D) 1.

(B) $\sqrt{2x}+1$.   (E) $2x + 1$.

(C) $\sqrt{x^2+(x+1)^2}$.

24. The expression $(x + y)^2 + (x - y)^2$ is equivalent to

(A) $2x^2$.   (D) $2x^2 + y^2$.
(B) $4x^2$.   (E) $x^2 + 2y^2$.
(C) $2(x^2 + y^2)$.

25. If $1 - x^{-1}$ is divided by $1 - x$, the quotient is

(A) 1.   (D) $\dfrac{1}{x}$.

(B) $-\dfrac{1}{x}$.   (E) $\dfrac{1}{1-x}$.

(C) $-\dfrac{1}{x^2}$.

26. When x is decreased by 129 and then that number is multiplied by 129, the result is 129. What is the value of x?

(A) 130   (D) 3
(B) 129   (E) 16,770
(C) 2

27. A 6 meter rope is cut into four pieces with each piece twice as long as the previous one. How long is the longest piece?
(A) .4 m   (D) 3.2 m
(B) 1 m   (E) 4 m
(C) 3 m

28. A book that is 7.5 inches by 9.5 inches has a 1 inch top margin, .75 inch bottom margin and right side margin, and 2 inch left side margin. What is the area of the printed part of the page?

(A) 35.625   (D) 38.8125
(B) 36   (E) 39
(C) 36.8125

29. If $3a + 4a = 14$, and $b + 6b = 21$, then $7(a + b) =$

(A) 21.   (D) 40.
(B) 28.   (E) 42.
(C) 35.

30. If $m < n < 0$, which expression must be < 0?

(A) The product of m and n
(B) The square of the product of m and n
(C) The sum of m and n
(D) The result of subtracting m from n
(E) The quotient of dividing n by m

31.

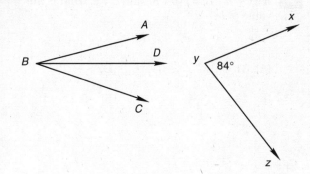

In the figure shown, if $\overline{BD}$ is the bisector of angle ABC, and angle ABD is one-fourth the size of angle XYZ, what is the size of angle ABC?

(A) 21°   (D) 63°
(B) 28°   (E) 168°
(C) 42°

32. A cube of volume 8 cubic centimeters is placed directly next to a cube of volume 125 cubic centimeters. What is the perpendicular distance in centimeters from the top of the larger cube to the top of the smaller cube?

(A) 7   (D) 2
(B) 5   (E) 0
(C) 3

33. The length of a rectangle is four more than twice the width. The perimeter of the rectangle is 44 meters. Find the length.

(A) 6 m   (D) 16 m
(B) 8 m   (E) 22 m
(C) 11 m

34. If $21 - (a - b) = 2(b + 9)$, and $a = 8$, what is the value of b?

(A) 31   (D) $-\dfrac{5}{3}$

(B) 13   (E) -5

(C) 4

35. Five years ago, Tim's mom was three times Tim's age today. Now their combined ages are 45. How old is Tim's mom today?

(A) 40   (D) 50
(B) 35   (E) 30
(C) 45

Questions 36 – 40 refer to the following information.

In the Growing Strong Hospital, a survey was taken of the marital status of each of the 2,000 employees. The results are shown below. No two employees are married to each other.

GROWING STRONG HOSPITAL EMPLOYEES

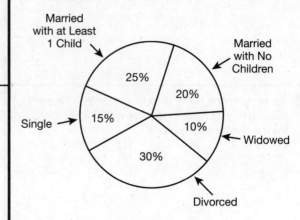

36. How many employees are neither married nor widowed?

(A) 300   (D) 900
(B) 500   (E) 1100
(C) 700

37. How many employees are not widowed?

(A) 1,800   (D) 600
(B) 1,500   (E) 200
(C) 1,000

38. Sixty percent of the employees are women. How many male employees are there?

(A) 600
(B) 800
(C) 1,000

(D) 1,200
(E) 1,400

39. There are 150 male employees who are married with at least one child. How many female employees are in this category?

(A) 150
(B) 250
(C) 350

(D) 450
(E) 550

40. Fifty percent of all the widowed employees are men. In the category of "Married with No Children," only ten percent of these employees are men. The total number of male employees in these two categories is what percent of the total number of employees?

(A) 60
(B) 30
(C) 15

(D) 10
(E) 7

Problem Solving Drill
ANSWER KEY

1. (C)	21. (C)
2. (D)	22. (A)
3. (A)	23. (A)
4. (B)	24. (C)
5. (B)	25. (B)
6. (E)	26. (A)
7. (D)	27. (D)
8. (D)	28. (C)
9. (E)	29. (C)
10. (D)	30. (C)
11. (E)	31. (C)
12. (A)	32. (C)
13. (B)	33. (D)
14. (C)	34. (E)
15. (D)	35. (B)
16. (C)	36. (D)
17. (A)	37. (A)
18. (A)	38. (B)
19. (B)	39. (C)
20. (A)	40. (E)

Attacking Quantitative Comparison Questions

In the Quantitative Ability section of the GRE you will also encounter a series of Quantitative Comparison questions. In Quantitative Comparison questions, you are asked to compare two quantities. Since you only have to compare quantities, the questions in this section usually take less time to solve than regular multiple-choice questions.

The two quantities are always presented in two columns, Column A and Column B.

<u>Column A</u>	<u>Column B</u>
2^3	2^2

Bust it!

Your job is to determine which quantity, if either, is greater. The directions tell you that there are four possible choices. Having only four answer choices makes the Quantitative comparison questions even more different than the other sections of the GRE. But in this case that's good: less answer choices means less work to find the correct answer!

Let's take a look at the Quantitative Comparison answer choices. These choices will be the same for EVERY Quantitative Comparison question you encounter:

Bust it!

- If the quantity in Column A is greater than the quantity in Column B, the correct choice is (A).

- If the quantity in Column B is greater than the quantity in Column A, the correct choice is (B).

- If the two quantities are equal, the correct choice is (C).

- If the relationship cannot be determined, the correct choice is (D).

What would the correct choice be for the problem on the previous page? Since the quantity in Column A is equal to 8 and the quantity in Column B is equal to 4, and 8 > 4, the correct choice is (A).

About the Directions

Now that you have seen some of the directions, let's go over the rest of them. It's important to become familiar with the directions before the test so you don't waste time reading them during the test. You will also see the same reference information that appeared before the regular multiple-choice problems. Become familiar with this material before you take the GRE. If you have to refer to any part of this page during the test, you are taking away valuable time needed to solve the problems.

DIRECTIONS: Each of the following questions consist of two quantities, one in Column A and one in Column B. You are to compare the two quantities and choose
 	
  (A) if the quantity in Column A is greater;
  (B) if the quantity in Column B is greater;
  (C) if the two quantities are equal;
  (D) if the relationship cannot be determined from the information given.
 	
NOTES:
 	
1. In certain questions, information concerning one or both of the quantities to be compared is centered above the two columns.
2. In a given question, a symbol that appears in both columns represents the same thing in Column A as it does in Column B.
3. Since there are only four choices, never mark (E).
	EXAMPLES:
	
	Column A Column B
	
	E1 $3 + 4$ 3×4
	
	$x°$ $30°$
	
	E2 x 150
		Answer
		
		Ⓐ ● Ⓒ Ⓓ Ⓔ
		
		Ⓐ Ⓑ ● Ⓓ Ⓔ

About the Questions

Important Information!

The following section will take you through the different types of Quantitative Comparison questions that you will encounter on the GRE. Five main types exist and will be described here.

Question Type 1: CALCULATIONS

This type of question will ask you to perform addition, subtraction, multiplication, or division. The question may ask you to perform one or more of these operations in order to compare the quantities in columns A and B.

Important Strategy

? PROBLEM

Column A	Column B
$(13 + 44)(37 - 40)$	$(13 - 44)(37 - 40)$

! SOLUTION

You could do the addition and subtraction in each column, but if you use your number knowledge, you can get the right answer in a matter of seconds! Try working with just signs. Remember that a smaller number minus a larger number yields a negative result so the answers to all the subtractions are negative. You'll get:

$$(+)(-) \quad \text{and} \quad (-)(-)$$

which becomes

$$(-) \quad \text{and} \quad (+)$$

The correct choice is (B).

Question Type 2: CONVERSIONS

This type of question may require you to convert the quantities given by asking you to find a percentage of a number, find a fraction of a number, or find the area if given length and width, etc., in order to compare the quantities in columns A and B.

 PROBLEM

Look !

Important Strategy

Column A	Column B
60% of $\frac{3}{4}$	75% of $\frac{3}{5}$

 SOLUTION

Change the way the quantities look; change the percents to fractions. You'll get:

$$60\% = \frac{60}{100} = \frac{3}{5} \qquad\qquad 75\% = \frac{3}{4}$$

$$\left(\frac{3}{5}\right)\left(\frac{3}{4}\right) = \left(\frac{9}{20}\right) \qquad \left(\frac{3}{4}\right)\left(\frac{3}{5}\right) = \left(\frac{9}{20}\right)$$

You can now *compare parts*. The correct choice is (C).

Question Type 3: EXPONENTS AND ROOTS

This type of question will ask you to determine a number's value, and then may ask you to use the value to perform an indicated operation in order to compare the quantities in columns A and B.

Important
Strategy

? PROBLEM

Column A	Column B
$\sqrt{.81}$	$\sqrt[3]{.81}$

! SOLUTION:

In this problem, $\sqrt{.81}$ is not hard to compute—it's 0.9. The problem is finding $\sqrt[3]{.81}$. There is no procedure to find $\sqrt[3]{.81}$ except estimating and multiplying. Since you are really concerned with seeing how $\sqrt[3]{.81}$ compares to 0.9 and not finding out exactly what it is, try 0.9 as an estimate. That means you have to cube 0.9. 0.9^3 is .729. Since .729 is less than .81, then $\sqrt[3]{.81}$ must be greater than 0.9. The correct choice is (B).

Question Type 4: VARIABLES

This type of question will present you with variables of unknown quantities. You will be provided with additional information which must be applied in order to compare the quantities in columns A and B.

? PROBLEM

Column A	Column B

$y^* = y(y + 1)$ if y is even

$y^* = y(y - 1)$ if y is odd

Column A	Column B
7^*	6^*

SOLUTION

Change the way the quantities look by applying the rules that appear between the two columns:

$$7* = (7)(7-1) \qquad\qquad 6* = 6(6+1)$$
$$7* = (7)(6) \qquad\qquad\quad 6* = (6)(7)$$
$$= 42 \qquad\qquad\qquad\quad = 42$$

Look!

Important Strategy

The factors are identical in the two columns. The correct choice is (C).

Question Type 5: FIGURES

This type of question will include a figure. You will be asked to use the figure provided to compare the quantities in columns A and B. The figures may or may not be drawn to scale.

PROBLEM

Column A	Column B

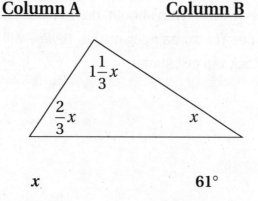

x	$61°$

SOLUTION

The sum of the three angles of a triangle equals 180°. Therefore, we can add together the angles in the triangle above and set them equal to 180° to solve for x.

$$1\frac{1}{3}x + \frac{2}{3}x + x = 180$$

If we multiply this equation by three, we can eliminate the fractions.

Look!

Important Strategy

$$3\left(\frac{4}{3}x + \frac{2}{3}x + x = 180\right)$$

$$4x + 2x + 3x = 540$$

Simplifying the equation, we obtain

$$9x = 540$$
$$x = 60$$

Therefore, the correct choice is (B), since 60° is less than 61°.

As you attempt to answer Quantitative Comparison questions, it is not completely necessary that you be able to classify each question. However, you should be familiar with how to handle each question type. The remainder of this review will teach you how to approach and attack the questions.

Points to Remember

✔ *Always examine **both columns and** the information in the **center**, if there is any, before you begin to work. By doing this, you won't overlook any information and you will be able to decide upon the appropriate strategy to use.*

✔ *If a problem seems to involve a lot of calculations, there is probably a faster way to do it. The numbers that are used in the problems are not selected to make you do a lot of calculations; they are selected so that, if you are aware of certain mathematical relationships or properties, you can do the problems relatively quickly.*

✔ *Since you only have to compare quantities, don't work out the problems completely once you have enough information to make the comparison.*

✔ *Keep your work neat and in the appropriate columns so it will be easier to make comparisons.*

✔ *Be suspicious of problems with obvious answers if they occur toward the end of the section. The problems at the end of the section are always the more difficult ones. If the answer seems obvious, you have probably overlooked something important.*

✔ *If you have to guess, remember if a problem contains only numbers in both columns, the answer cannot be (D). If a problem contains only numbers, you can get an exact value for the quantities in each column and a comparison can be made.*

On Target!

Answering Quantitative Comparison Questions

As you go through Quantitative Comparison questions, some seem to require a lot of calculations. On the other hand, there are some questions for which the answer seems immediately obvious. Often neither is the case. Excessive calculations can often be avoided and questions for which the answer seems obvious are often tricky.

The following steps will help guide you through answering Quantitative Comparison questions. These steps will cover strategies for every situation that you may encounter. Therefore, you may not need to go through every step for every question.

Important Strategy

STEP 1   **When you are presented with an addition or multiplication problem, you can often avoid these calculations just by comparing individual quantities.**

Bust it!

?   **PROBLEM**

Column A	Column B
$\dfrac{1}{3}+\dfrac{1}{6}+\dfrac{1}{12}$	$\dfrac{1}{4}+\dfrac{1}{8}+\dfrac{1}{16}$

SOLUTION

Both columns contain an addition problem. Don't bother to add! Compare the fractions in each column:

Column A		Column B
$\frac{1}{3}$	>	$\frac{1}{4}$
$\frac{1}{6}$	>	$\frac{1}{8}$
and $\frac{1}{12}$	>	$\frac{1}{16}$

Bust it!

For each fraction in Column B, there is a greater fraction in Column A. Therefore, the sum in Column A must be greater than the sum in Column B. The correct choice is (A).

PROBLEM

Column A	Column B
The area of a rectangle with a base of 3 and a height of 4	The area of a circle with a radius of 2

SOLUTION

You have to compare the area of a rectangle to the area of a circle. Your two columns will look like:

Area of rectangle	Area of circle
(3)(4)	$\pi 2^2 = 4\pi$

Bust it!

Both columns contain a multiplication problem with positive numbers. Don't multiply! Compare the factors in each column:

3	<	π
and 4	=	4

The factors in Column B are greater than or equal to the factors in Column A so the product in Column B (the area of the circle) must be greater than the product in Column A (the area of the rectangle). The correct choice is (B).

Important Strategy

STEP 2 | Sometimes you are faced with problems in which comparing parts seems to apply but you can't compare the quantities the way they are presented in the problem. If you change the way the quantities look, you may be able to compare parts.

? PROBLEM

Column A	Column B
20% of 368	$\frac{1}{4}$ of 368

Bust it!

! SOLUTION

Both columns contain multiplication of positive quantities:

$$(20\%)(368) \qquad \left(\frac{1}{4}\right)(368)$$

This means that you can compare individual quantities to avoid multiplication. Both columns contain 368 but Column A contains a percent and Column B contains a fraction. You can either change the percent to a fraction or the fraction to a percent.

If you change 20% to a fraction, the columns will look like:

$$\left(\frac{1}{5}\right)(368) \qquad \left(\frac{1}{4}\right)(368).$$

Now you can compare quantities:

$$\frac{1}{5} \quad < \quad \frac{1}{4}$$

$$368 \quad = \quad 368$$

or

If you change $\frac{1}{4}$ to a percent, the columns will look like:

$$(20\%)(368) \qquad (25\%)(368)$$

Now you can compare quantities in the two columns:

$$20\% \quad < \quad 25\%$$
$$368 \quad = \quad 368$$

Using either approach, the product in Column B is greater than the product in Column A. The correct choice is (B).

 PROBLEM

Column A	Column B
The area of a rectangle with length of 2.5 feet and width of 2 feet	The area of a rectangle with length of 27 inches and width of 23 inches

Bust it!

 SOLUTION

Since you multiply length by width to find the area of a rectangle, both columns contain multiplication of positive quantities:

$$(2.5)(2) \qquad (27)(23)$$

If you write the problem this way and forget about the units, you have:

$$2.5 < 27$$
$$2 < 23$$

The product in Column B seems to be greater than the product in Column A. But this is **wrong!** Column A contains feet and Column B contains inches. Make sure you change feet to inches or inches to feet before you make the comparisons!

Let's change the feet to inches and see what happens. 2.5 feet equals 30 inches and 2 feet equals 24 inches. Now all the quantities are in inches so you can make the comparisons. Your two columns look like:

Column A	Column B
(30) (24)	(27) (23)

The factors in Column A are greater than the factors in Column B. The correct choice is (A).

 PROBLEM

Column A	Column B
The number of ounces in 2 pints	The number of pints in 2 gallons

 SOLUTION

In this problem you must make sure to convert to the units specified in each column.

1 pint = 16 ounces	1 gallon = 8 pints
2 pints = 32 ounces	2 gallons = 16 pints

There are more *ounces* in 2 pints (Column A) than there are *pints* in 2 gallons (Column B). The correct choice is (A).

Bust it!

 PROBLEM

Column A	Column B
(4.37) (125)	(437) (1.25)

Bust it!

SOLUTION

Each column contains a multiplication problem with positive numbers but comparing parts doesn't work since:

Column A		Column B
4.37	<	437
but 125	>	1.25

Even if you switch the numbers around, it still won't help:

	Column A		Column B
	125	<	437
but	4.37	>	1.25

You may think that you are forced to multiply, but you don't have to if you notice that all the digits are the same. The only differences between the quantities in the two columns are where the decimal points are. You can move the decimal points to try to get some or all of the numbers to look the same and then make the comparisons. When you move the decimal points, you are really multiplying or dividing by powers of 10 and what you do in one column must be done in the other column.

You can move the decimal point in 4.37 to the right 2 places in Column A (you're really multiplying by 100). You must then move the decimal point in Column B two places to the right.

Column A	Column B
(4.37) (125)	(437) (1.25)

becomes

$$(437)(125) \qquad\qquad (437)(125)$$

Now you have identical factors in both columns. The correct choice is (C).

 PROBLEM

Column A	Column B
$\dfrac{(14)(15)}{(35)(8)}$	1

Bust it!

! **SOLUTION**

Sometimes changing the way quantities look won't help you compare parts, but it will make the arithmetic a lot easier!

Column A contains multiplication and division of positive numbers. Factor and reduce and you will make the problem a lot easier to solve.

When you factor,

Column A	Column B
$\dfrac{(14)(15)}{(35)(8)}$	1

becomes

$\dfrac{(2)(7)(3)(5)}{(2)(7)(4)(5)}$	1

When you reduce, you get:

$$\frac{3}{4} \qquad\qquad 1$$

The quantity in Column B is greater than the quantity in Column A so the correct choice is (B).

> **STEP 3** | Make sure to look at the numbers presented. Numbers have important properties that can be used to save time. There are many properties that will be useful to know for the GRE. We'll highlight a few here.

Look!

Important Strategy

 PROBLEM

Column A	Column B
(17) (15) (13)	(18) (16) (14) (0)

 SOLUTION

You may be tempted to compare factors in this problem, but you don't have to if you remember to look at both columns before you do any work. Notice that 0 is a factor in Column B. The quantity in Column B is equal to 0 since 0 times any number is 0. The quantity in Column A is greater than 0 since all the factors are positive. The correct choice is (A).

Bust it!

 PROBLEM

Column A	Column B
$(2)^5 + (-2)^5$	$(3)^5 + (-3)^5$

Bust it!

! **SOLUTION**

When you first look at this problem, you probably want to compare parts. To do that, you might think that you have to find the values of each part, but you don't! Getting the values involves a lot of multiplication. There is a faster way. Analyze the numbers in each column:

$(2)^5$ = some positive number $(3)^5$ = some positive number
$(-2)^5$ = the same as $(2)^5$ but $(-3)^5$ = the same as $(3)^5$ but
with a negative sign   with a negative sign

The two numbers in each column are the same but opposite in sign. What does that mean when you add the two numbers in each column? The sum in each column is 0. The quantities in the two columns are equal. The correct choice is (C).

? **PROBLEM**

Column A	Column B
$\dfrac{(-1)^7+(-1)^9}{(-1)^4+(-1)^6}$	1

! **SOLUTION**

When -1 is raised to an odd power, the result is -1. When -1 is raised to an even power, the result is $+1$. Using that information, you get the following:

$\dfrac{(-1)+(-1)}{(+1)+(+1)}$	1
$\dfrac{-2}{+2}$	1
-1	1

The correct choice is (B).

> ## STEP 4
> Try substituting values for the variables, in particular 0, 1, − 1, and fractions between 0 and − 1. Sometimes you can use values that appear in the problem. To get a better understanding of how this will help you solve problems, let's look at a few.

Look!

Important Strategy

 ? PROBLEM

Column A	Column B
x is positive	
2^X	2^3

Bust it!

! SOLUTION

In order to compare the two quantities, you have to know the value of *x*. According to the information centered above the two columns, *x* can be any positive number. You could try different values for *x*, but where do you begin? Column B gives you a starting point. What happens if *x* = 3? The quantities in the two columns would be equal. Now that you have tried one value for *x* and established that the two quantities can be equal, try another value to see if you can make one quantity greater than the other. What if *x* > 3? Then the quantity in Column A would be greater than the quantity in Column B (you shouldn't have to do the arithmetic!). By making these two comparisons, you have determined that:

the quantity in Column A = the quantity in Column B

or

the quantity in Column A > the quantity in Column B

The correct choice is (D).

(It's unnecessary to check values for $x < 3$ since you have already determined that (D) is the correct choice.)

Bust it!

? PROBLEM

Column A	Column B

The average of a, b, and c is 10.
$$a > b > c$$

$a - b$	$b - c$

! SOLUTION

Try some values for a, b, and c. The choice of numbers is up to you, but keep it simple. If you have 3 numbers with an average of 10, then their sum is 30. This may help you choose numbers.

You could start with $a = 11$, $b = 10$, and $c = 9$. Then you would have:

$$a - b = 11 - 10 = 1 \quad \text{and} \quad b - c = 10 - 9 = 1$$

The quantities in the two columns can be equal. But can there be some other relationship? Try some more numbers.

What if $a = 12$, $b = 11$, and $c = 7$? Then you would have:

$$a - b = 12 - 11 = 1 \quad \text{and} \quad b - c = 11 - 7 = 4$$

In this case, the quantity in Column B is greater than the quantity in Column A.

You have determined that:

the quantity is Column A = the quantity in Column B

or

the quantity in Column A < the quantity in Column B

The correct choice is (D).

PROBLEM

Bust it!

Column A	Column B

x is positive
$x \neq 1$

x	x^2

SOLUTION

Once again you have to try different values for x. Keep the arithmetic as simple as possible.

If $x = 2$, then you get:

2	4

If $x = 3$, then you get:

3	9

The answer seems obvious, doesn't it! Column B > Column A.

But if you try $x = \dfrac{1}{2}$, you get:

$\dfrac{1}{2}$	$\dfrac{1}{4}$

Column A > Column B!

Depending upon the value selected for x, the quantity in Column A can be greater or less than the quantity in Column B. The correct choice is (D).

PROBLEM

Bust it!

Column A	Column B

A pound of apples costs 89 cents.
A pound of pears costs 99 cents.

The number of apples in a pound	The number of pears in a pound

Bust it!

! SOLUTION

Although a pound of pears costs more than a pound of apples, that does not mean that there are more pears than apples in a pound. There is no way to know how many pears or apples make up a pound. The correct choice is (D).

? PROBLEM

Column A	Column B

A rectangle has an area of 8.

The perimeter of the rectangle	12

! SOLUTION

The centered information tells you the area of the rectangle. Since the area is 8, the length could be 4, and if the length is 4, the width would be 2. If these are the measurements, then the perimeter would equal 12. But could the length and width have other values? What if the length is 8 and the width is 1? The area would still be 8 but the perimeter would be 18. We have found one set of values which make the quantities in Column A and Column B equal (4 and 2) and another set which make the quantities not equal (8 and 1). The correct choice is (D).

Look!

Important Strategy

STEP 5 | Estimation is useful when the numbers in the problem are close to any number that is easy to work with like $\frac{1}{2}$ or 1, or when an approximation will do.

PROBLEM

Column A	Column B
$\dfrac{3}{8} + \dfrac{3}{7}$	1

Bust it!

SOLUTION

In this problem, you have to compare the sum of two fractions, with different denominators, to 1. One way to do this is to change both fractions so that they have a common denominator and then do the arithmetic. A faster way is to estimate values. In Column A, $\dfrac{3}{8}$ is close to $\dfrac{1}{2}$, but a little less. $\dfrac{3}{7}$ is also close to $\dfrac{1}{2}$, but a little less. Since both numbers are each a little less than $\dfrac{1}{2}$, their sum must be less than 1, the quantity in Column B. The correct choice is (B).

PROBLEM

Column A	Column B
(16.8) (.51)	(8.4) (.99)

Bust it!

SOLUTION

Each column contains a multiplication problem with positive numbers but comparing parts doesn't work since:

Column A		Column B
16.8	>	8.4

but

.51	<	.99

Even if you switch the numbers around, it still won't help:

	16.8	>	.99
but	.51	<	8.4

You may think that you are forced to multiply, but you don't have to if you notice that .51 is a little more than .5 and .99 is a little less than 1. Using these estimates will help you work out the problem without doing all the multiplication in the original problem! (You may find it faster to use $\frac{1}{2}$ instead of .5 to multiply 16.8 by.)

Using these estimated values in the columns, you get:

Column A	**Column B**
$(16.8)\left(\dfrac{1}{2}\right)$	$(8.4)(1)$

which becomes

8.4	8.4

But remember that you are using estimated values! The real value in Column A is a little more than 8.4 since you really had to multiply 16.8 by .51. The real value in Column B is a little less than 8.4 since you really had to multiply 8.4 by .99. The correct choice is (A).

Look!

Important Strategy

STEP 6 If figures are not drawn to scale or do not look accurate, do not use them to help you solve the problem. These types of figures can throw you off and cause you to select the wrong answer.

? **PROBLEM**

Column A	**Column B**

Line ℓ 1 is parallel to line ℓ 2.
Line ℓ 2 is parallel to line ℓ 3.

The distance between ℓ 1 and ℓ 2	The distance between ℓ 2 and ℓ 3

SOLUTION

This problem involves parallel lines but there is no figure. Draw a figure that fits the description in the problem, and then try to draw another figure that also fits the description but shows a different relationship. Two acceptable figures for this problem follow. Note that if you draw only one figure, you will get an incorrect answer.

In this first figure, the lines are evenly spaced so the distance between lines $\ell 1$ and $\ell 2$ is the same as the distance between lines $\ell 2$ and $\ell 3$. If this is the only figure you draw, you would choose (C) as your answer.

_____ $\ell 1$ _____

_____ $\ell 2$ _____

_____ $\ell 3$ _____

In this second figure, the distance between lines $\ell 1$ and $\ell 2$ is greater than the distance between lines $\ell 2$ and $\ell 3$ If this is the only figure you draw, you would choose (B) as your answer.

_____ $\ell 1$ _____

_____ $\ell 2$ _____

_____ $\ell 3$ _____

But if you draw both figures, you will choose the correct answer. The correct choice is (D).

The following questions should be completed to further reinforce what you have just learned. After you have completed all of the questions, check your answers against the answer key. Make sure to refer back to the review for help.

Drill: Quantitative Comparisons

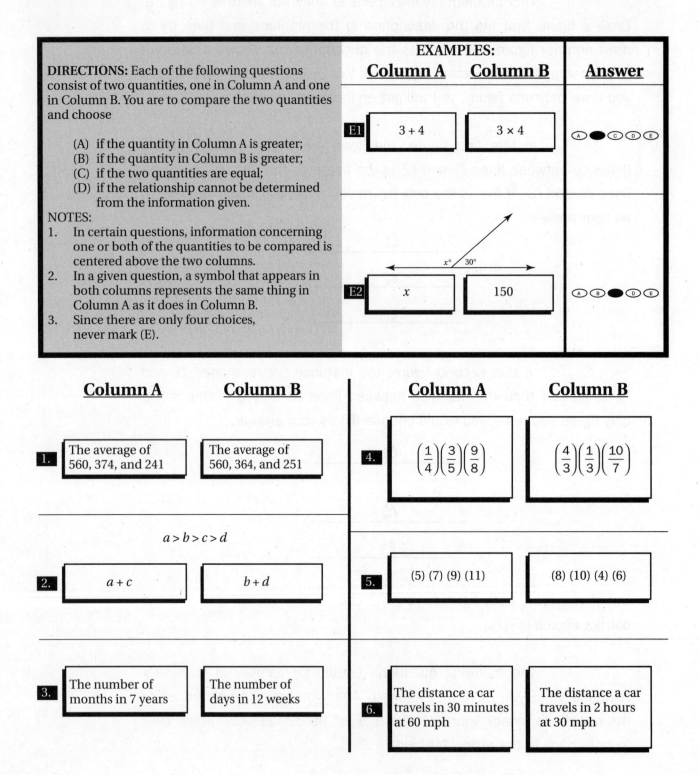

DIRECTIONS: Each of the following questions consist of two quantities, one in Column A and one in Column B. You are to compare the two quantities and choose

(A) if the quantity in Column A is greater;
(B) if the quantity in Column B is greater;
(C) if the two quantities are equal;
(D) if the relationship cannot be determined from the information given.

NOTES:
1. In certain questions, information concerning one or both of the quantities to be compared is centered above the two columns.
2. In a given question, a symbol that appears in both columns represents the same thing in Column A as it does in Column B.
3. Since there are only four choices, never mark (E).

EXAMPLES:

	Column A	Column B	Answer
E1	$3 + 4$	3×4	Ⓐ ● Ⓒ Ⓓ Ⓔ
E2	x	150	Ⓐ Ⓑ ● Ⓓ Ⓔ

Column A	Column B
1. The average of 560, 374, and 241	The average of 560, 364, and 251

$$a > b > c > d$$

Column A	Column B
2. $a + c$	$b + d$
3. The number of months in 7 years	The number of days in 12 weeks

Column A	Column B
4. $\left(\dfrac{1}{4}\right)\left(\dfrac{3}{5}\right)\left(\dfrac{9}{8}\right)$	$\left(\dfrac{4}{3}\right)\left(\dfrac{1}{3}\right)\left(\dfrac{10}{7}\right)$
5. (5) (7) (9) (11)	(8) (10) (4) (6)
6. The distance a car travels in 30 minutes at 60 mph	The distance a car travels in 2 hours at 30 mph

Column A	Column B

7. $(1.75)(24)$ | $(175)(2.4)$

8. $\dfrac{(14)(21)}{(49)(6)}$ | 1

9. $(3)^2(4)^3$ | $(\pi)^2(2)^6$

10. $(2.17)(682)$ | $(196)(6.7)$

11. 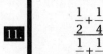 $\dfrac{\frac{1}{2}+\frac{1}{4}}{\frac{1}{3}+\frac{1}{5}}$ | 1

12. $\dfrac{(78-94)}{(35-41)}$ | $\dfrac{(175-123)}{(134-167)}$

Column A	Column B

13. $\dfrac{(5)(0)}{(19)(3)(21)}$ | $(-3)^7+(9)(3)^5$

14. $\dfrac{(-2)^4(-5)^3}{(-3)^2}$ | $\dfrac{(174-356)}{(97-132)}$

15. $-\dfrac{7}{8}$ | $-\dfrac{8}{7}$

$$\frac{x}{y}=7$$

16. x | y

There are 40 students in Class A.
There are 30 students in Class B.
There are more boys in each class than girls.

17. The number of boys in Class A | The number of boys in Class B

Column A	Column B

$$a > b, c > d, c \neq 0, d \neq 0$$

18. $\dfrac{a}{c}$ $\dfrac{b}{d}$

$$|X| > 1$$

19. X^3 X^2

$$XY = 1, X > 0$$

20. X Y

21. $\dfrac{9}{10} \times \dfrac{12}{13}$ $\dfrac{5}{9} \times \dfrac{6}{11}$

22. $\sqrt{37} + \sqrt{27}$ $\sqrt{37 + 27}$

23. $\sqrt{\dfrac{7}{3} \times \dfrac{1}{5} \times \dfrac{11}{5}}$ $\sqrt{\dfrac{5 \times 2}{6}}$

Column A	Column B

24.

$\dfrac{1}{\sqrt{2}} + \dfrac{1}{\sqrt{3}}$ $\dfrac{1}{\sqrt{6}}$

25. $(6.9)(8.9)$ $\sqrt{(50)(82)}$

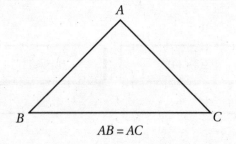

$$AB = AC$$

26. $\angle A$ $\angle B$

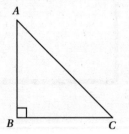 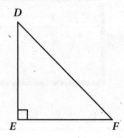

$$S_1 = S_2$$

Note: S_1 and S_2 are the areas of the two triangles.

27. AC DF

Column A	**Column B**

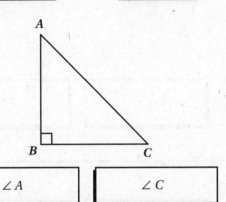

28. $\angle A$ | $\angle C$

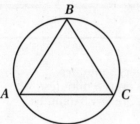

29. AB | AC

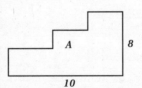

$AB = BC$

30. AD | DC

Column A	**Column B**

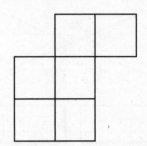

6 congruent squares. The area of the figure is 150.

31. The perimeter of the figure | 65

$A + B = 18$

32. The maximum value of AB | 70

$$x = \left(.03 \div \frac{3}{5}\right)$$

33. x | .0025

All lines are perpendicular or parallel.

34. The perimeter of A | The perimeter of B

Column A	**Column B**	**Column A**	**Column B**

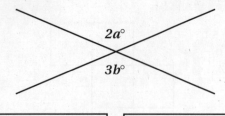

35.

a	b

$$N = \frac{7}{12}$$

38. The value of $\dfrac{N^{12}}{N^{10}}$ | $\dfrac{1}{2}$

$$N > 0$$

36.

N^{10}	N^{12}

39. The average of all numbers ending in 8 between 200 and 310 | 250

It takes a motorist 1 minute and 40 seconds to go 1 mile.

A bell rings every 5 minutes.
A light flashes every 6 minutes.
A buzzer buzzes every 8 minutes.

37. The motorist's speed in m.p.h. | 35 m.p.h.

40. If the 3 of them start together, the number of minutes the 3 happen again together | 110 minutes

Quantitative Comparisons Drill
ANSWER KEY

1.	(C)	21.	(A)
2.	(A)	22.	(A)
3.	(C)	23.	(B)
4.	(B)	24.	(A)
5.	(A)	25.	(B)
6.	(B)	26.	(D)
7.	(B)	27.	(D)
8.	(C)	28.	(D)
9.	(B)	29.	(D)
10.	(A)	30.	(C)
11.	(A)	31.	(B)
12.	(A)	32.	(A)
13.	(C)	33.	(A)
14.	(B)	34.	(C)
15.	(A)	35.	(A)
16.	(D)	36.	(D)
17.	(D)	37.	(A)
18.	(D)	38.	(B)
19.	(D)	39.	(A)
20.	(D)	40.	(A)

GRE Practice Test Answer Sheet

SECTION 3

1. Ⓐ Ⓑ Ⓒ Ⓓ Ⓔ
2. Ⓐ Ⓑ Ⓒ Ⓓ Ⓔ
3. Ⓐ Ⓑ Ⓒ Ⓓ Ⓔ
4. Ⓐ Ⓑ Ⓒ Ⓓ Ⓔ
5. Ⓐ Ⓑ Ⓒ Ⓓ Ⓔ
6. Ⓐ Ⓑ Ⓒ Ⓓ Ⓔ
7. Ⓐ Ⓑ Ⓒ Ⓓ Ⓔ
8. Ⓐ Ⓑ Ⓒ Ⓓ Ⓔ
9. Ⓐ Ⓑ Ⓒ Ⓓ Ⓔ
10. Ⓐ Ⓑ Ⓒ Ⓓ Ⓔ
11. Ⓐ Ⓑ Ⓒ Ⓓ Ⓔ
12. Ⓐ Ⓑ Ⓒ Ⓓ Ⓔ
13. Ⓐ Ⓑ Ⓒ Ⓓ Ⓔ
14. Ⓐ Ⓑ Ⓒ Ⓓ Ⓔ
15. Ⓐ Ⓑ Ⓒ Ⓓ Ⓔ
16. Ⓐ Ⓑ Ⓒ Ⓓ Ⓔ
17. Ⓐ Ⓑ Ⓒ Ⓓ Ⓔ
18. Ⓐ Ⓑ Ⓒ Ⓓ Ⓔ
19. Ⓐ Ⓑ Ⓒ Ⓓ Ⓔ
20. Ⓐ Ⓑ Ⓒ Ⓓ Ⓔ
21. Ⓐ Ⓑ Ⓒ Ⓓ Ⓔ
22. Ⓐ Ⓑ Ⓒ Ⓓ Ⓔ
23. Ⓐ Ⓑ Ⓒ Ⓓ Ⓔ
24. Ⓐ Ⓑ Ⓒ Ⓓ Ⓔ
25. Ⓐ Ⓑ Ⓒ Ⓓ Ⓔ
26. Ⓐ Ⓑ Ⓒ Ⓓ Ⓔ
27. Ⓐ Ⓑ Ⓒ Ⓓ Ⓔ
28. Ⓐ Ⓑ Ⓒ Ⓓ Ⓔ
29. Ⓐ Ⓑ Ⓒ Ⓓ Ⓔ
30. Ⓐ Ⓑ Ⓒ Ⓓ Ⓔ

SECTION 4

1. Ⓐ Ⓑ Ⓒ Ⓓ Ⓔ
2. Ⓐ Ⓑ Ⓒ Ⓓ Ⓔ
3. Ⓐ Ⓑ Ⓒ Ⓓ Ⓔ
4. Ⓐ Ⓑ Ⓒ Ⓓ Ⓔ
5. Ⓐ Ⓑ Ⓒ Ⓓ Ⓔ
6. Ⓐ Ⓑ Ⓒ Ⓓ Ⓔ
7. Ⓐ Ⓑ Ⓒ Ⓓ Ⓔ
8. Ⓐ Ⓑ Ⓒ Ⓓ Ⓔ
9. Ⓐ Ⓑ Ⓒ Ⓓ Ⓔ
10. Ⓐ Ⓑ Ⓒ Ⓓ Ⓔ
11. Ⓐ Ⓑ Ⓒ Ⓓ Ⓔ
12. Ⓐ Ⓑ Ⓒ Ⓓ Ⓔ
13. Ⓐ Ⓑ Ⓒ Ⓓ Ⓔ
14. Ⓐ Ⓑ Ⓒ Ⓓ Ⓔ
15. Ⓐ Ⓑ Ⓒ Ⓓ Ⓔ
16. Ⓐ Ⓑ Ⓒ Ⓓ Ⓔ
17. Ⓐ Ⓑ Ⓒ Ⓓ Ⓔ
18. Ⓐ Ⓑ Ⓒ Ⓓ Ⓔ
19. Ⓐ Ⓑ Ⓒ Ⓓ Ⓔ
20. Ⓐ Ⓑ Ⓒ Ⓓ Ⓔ
21. Ⓐ Ⓑ Ⓒ Ⓓ Ⓔ
22. Ⓐ Ⓑ Ⓒ Ⓓ Ⓔ
23. Ⓐ Ⓑ Ⓒ Ⓓ Ⓔ
24. Ⓐ Ⓑ Ⓒ Ⓓ Ⓔ
25. Ⓐ Ⓑ Ⓒ Ⓓ Ⓔ
26. Ⓐ Ⓑ Ⓒ Ⓓ Ⓔ
27. Ⓐ Ⓑ Ⓒ Ⓓ Ⓔ
28. Ⓐ Ⓑ Ⓒ Ⓓ Ⓔ
29. Ⓐ Ⓑ Ⓒ Ⓓ Ⓔ
30. Ⓐ Ⓑ Ⓒ Ⓓ Ⓔ
31. Ⓐ Ⓑ Ⓒ Ⓓ Ⓔ
32. Ⓐ Ⓑ Ⓒ Ⓓ Ⓔ
33. Ⓐ Ⓑ Ⓒ Ⓓ Ⓔ
34. Ⓐ Ⓑ Ⓒ Ⓓ Ⓔ
35. Ⓐ Ⓑ Ⓒ Ⓓ Ⓔ
36. Ⓐ Ⓑ Ⓒ Ⓓ Ⓔ
37. Ⓐ Ⓑ Ⓒ Ⓓ Ⓔ
38. Ⓐ Ⓑ Ⓒ Ⓓ Ⓔ

SECTION 5

1. Ⓐ Ⓑ Ⓒ Ⓓ Ⓔ
2. Ⓐ Ⓑ Ⓒ Ⓓ Ⓔ
3. Ⓐ Ⓑ Ⓒ Ⓓ Ⓔ
4. Ⓐ Ⓑ Ⓒ Ⓓ Ⓔ
5. Ⓐ Ⓑ Ⓒ Ⓓ Ⓔ
6. Ⓐ Ⓑ Ⓒ Ⓓ Ⓔ
7. Ⓐ Ⓑ Ⓒ Ⓓ Ⓔ
8. Ⓐ Ⓑ Ⓒ Ⓓ Ⓔ
9. Ⓐ Ⓑ Ⓒ Ⓓ Ⓔ
10. Ⓐ Ⓑ Ⓒ Ⓓ Ⓔ
11. Ⓐ Ⓑ Ⓒ Ⓓ Ⓔ
12. Ⓐ Ⓑ Ⓒ Ⓓ Ⓔ
13. Ⓐ Ⓑ Ⓒ Ⓓ Ⓔ
14. Ⓐ Ⓑ Ⓒ Ⓓ Ⓔ
15. Ⓐ Ⓑ Ⓒ Ⓓ Ⓔ
16. Ⓐ Ⓑ Ⓒ Ⓓ Ⓔ
17. Ⓐ Ⓑ Ⓒ Ⓓ Ⓔ
18. Ⓐ Ⓑ Ⓒ Ⓓ Ⓔ
19. Ⓐ Ⓑ Ⓒ Ⓓ Ⓔ
20. Ⓐ Ⓑ Ⓒ Ⓓ Ⓔ
21. Ⓐ Ⓑ Ⓒ Ⓓ Ⓔ
22. Ⓐ Ⓑ Ⓒ Ⓓ Ⓔ
23. Ⓐ Ⓑ Ⓒ Ⓓ Ⓔ
24. Ⓐ Ⓑ Ⓒ Ⓓ Ⓔ
25. Ⓐ Ⓑ Ⓒ Ⓓ Ⓔ
26. Ⓐ Ⓑ Ⓒ Ⓓ Ⓔ
27. Ⓐ Ⓑ Ⓒ Ⓓ Ⓔ
28. Ⓐ Ⓑ Ⓒ Ⓓ Ⓔ
29. Ⓐ Ⓑ Ⓒ Ⓓ Ⓔ
30. Ⓐ Ⓑ Ⓒ Ⓓ Ⓔ

SECTION 6

1. Ⓐ Ⓑ Ⓒ Ⓓ Ⓔ
2. Ⓐ Ⓑ Ⓒ Ⓓ Ⓔ
3. Ⓐ Ⓑ Ⓒ Ⓓ Ⓔ
4. Ⓐ Ⓑ Ⓒ Ⓓ Ⓔ
5. Ⓐ Ⓑ Ⓒ Ⓓ Ⓔ
6. Ⓐ Ⓑ Ⓒ Ⓓ Ⓔ
7. Ⓐ Ⓑ Ⓒ Ⓓ Ⓔ
8. Ⓐ Ⓑ Ⓒ Ⓓ Ⓔ
9. Ⓐ Ⓑ Ⓒ Ⓓ Ⓔ
10. Ⓐ Ⓑ Ⓒ Ⓓ Ⓔ
11. Ⓐ Ⓑ Ⓒ Ⓓ Ⓔ
12. Ⓐ Ⓑ Ⓒ Ⓓ Ⓔ
13. Ⓐ Ⓑ Ⓒ Ⓓ Ⓔ
14. Ⓐ Ⓑ Ⓒ Ⓓ Ⓔ
15. Ⓐ Ⓑ Ⓒ Ⓓ Ⓔ
16. Ⓐ Ⓑ Ⓒ Ⓓ Ⓔ
17. Ⓐ Ⓑ Ⓒ Ⓓ Ⓔ
18. Ⓐ Ⓑ Ⓒ Ⓓ Ⓔ
19. Ⓐ Ⓑ Ⓒ Ⓓ Ⓔ
20. Ⓐ Ⓑ Ⓒ Ⓓ Ⓔ
21. Ⓐ Ⓑ Ⓒ Ⓓ Ⓔ
22. Ⓐ Ⓑ Ⓒ Ⓓ Ⓔ
23. Ⓐ Ⓑ Ⓒ Ⓓ Ⓔ
24. Ⓐ Ⓑ Ⓒ Ⓓ Ⓔ
25. Ⓐ Ⓑ Ⓒ Ⓓ Ⓔ
26. Ⓐ Ⓑ Ⓒ Ⓓ Ⓔ
27. Ⓐ Ⓑ Ⓒ Ⓓ Ⓔ
28. Ⓐ Ⓑ Ⓒ Ⓓ Ⓔ
29. Ⓐ Ⓑ Ⓒ Ⓓ Ⓔ
30. Ⓐ Ⓑ Ⓒ Ⓓ Ⓔ
31. Ⓐ Ⓑ Ⓒ Ⓓ Ⓔ
32. Ⓐ Ⓑ Ⓒ Ⓓ Ⓔ
33. Ⓐ Ⓑ Ⓒ Ⓓ Ⓔ
34. Ⓐ Ⓑ Ⓒ Ⓓ Ⓔ
35. Ⓐ Ⓑ Ⓒ Ⓓ Ⓔ
36. Ⓐ Ⓑ Ⓒ Ⓓ Ⓔ
37. Ⓐ Ⓑ Ⓒ Ⓓ Ⓔ
38. Ⓐ Ⓑ Ⓒ Ⓓ Ⓔ

GRE Practice Test
Answer Sheet

SECTION 3

1. Ⓐ Ⓑ Ⓒ Ⓓ Ⓔ
2. Ⓐ Ⓑ Ⓒ Ⓓ Ⓔ
3. Ⓐ Ⓑ Ⓒ Ⓓ Ⓔ
4. Ⓐ Ⓑ Ⓒ Ⓓ Ⓔ
5. Ⓐ Ⓑ Ⓒ Ⓓ Ⓔ
6. Ⓐ Ⓑ Ⓒ Ⓓ Ⓔ
7. Ⓐ Ⓑ Ⓒ Ⓓ Ⓔ
8. Ⓐ Ⓑ Ⓒ Ⓓ Ⓔ
9. Ⓐ Ⓑ Ⓒ Ⓓ Ⓔ
10. Ⓐ Ⓑ Ⓒ Ⓓ Ⓔ
11. Ⓐ Ⓑ Ⓒ Ⓓ Ⓔ
12. Ⓐ Ⓑ Ⓒ Ⓓ Ⓔ
13. Ⓐ Ⓑ Ⓒ Ⓓ Ⓔ
14. Ⓐ Ⓑ Ⓒ Ⓓ Ⓔ
15. Ⓐ Ⓑ Ⓒ Ⓓ Ⓔ
16. Ⓐ Ⓑ Ⓒ Ⓓ Ⓔ
17. Ⓐ Ⓑ Ⓒ Ⓓ Ⓔ
18. Ⓐ Ⓑ Ⓒ Ⓓ Ⓔ
19. Ⓐ Ⓑ Ⓒ Ⓓ Ⓔ
20. Ⓐ Ⓑ Ⓒ Ⓓ Ⓔ
21. Ⓐ Ⓑ Ⓒ Ⓓ Ⓔ
22. Ⓐ Ⓑ Ⓒ Ⓓ Ⓔ
23. Ⓐ Ⓑ Ⓒ Ⓓ Ⓔ
24. Ⓐ Ⓑ Ⓒ Ⓓ Ⓔ
25. Ⓐ Ⓑ Ⓒ Ⓓ Ⓔ
26. Ⓐ Ⓑ Ⓒ Ⓓ Ⓔ
27. Ⓐ Ⓑ Ⓒ Ⓓ Ⓔ
28. Ⓐ Ⓑ Ⓒ Ⓓ Ⓔ
29. Ⓐ Ⓑ Ⓒ Ⓓ Ⓔ
30. Ⓐ Ⓑ Ⓒ Ⓓ Ⓔ

SECTION 4

1. Ⓐ Ⓑ Ⓒ Ⓓ Ⓔ
2. Ⓐ Ⓑ Ⓒ Ⓓ Ⓔ
3. Ⓐ Ⓑ Ⓒ Ⓓ Ⓔ
4. Ⓐ Ⓑ Ⓒ Ⓓ Ⓔ
5. Ⓐ Ⓑ Ⓒ Ⓓ Ⓔ
6. Ⓐ Ⓑ Ⓒ Ⓓ Ⓔ
7. Ⓐ Ⓑ Ⓒ Ⓓ Ⓔ
8. Ⓐ Ⓑ Ⓒ Ⓓ Ⓔ
9. Ⓐ Ⓑ Ⓒ Ⓓ Ⓔ
10. Ⓐ Ⓑ Ⓒ Ⓓ Ⓔ
11. Ⓐ Ⓑ Ⓒ Ⓓ Ⓔ
12. Ⓐ Ⓑ Ⓒ Ⓓ Ⓔ
13. Ⓐ Ⓑ Ⓒ Ⓓ Ⓔ
14. Ⓐ Ⓑ Ⓒ Ⓓ Ⓔ
15. Ⓐ Ⓑ Ⓒ Ⓓ Ⓔ
16. Ⓐ Ⓑ Ⓒ Ⓓ Ⓔ
17. Ⓐ Ⓑ Ⓒ Ⓓ Ⓔ
18. Ⓐ Ⓑ Ⓒ Ⓓ Ⓔ
19. Ⓐ Ⓑ Ⓒ Ⓓ Ⓔ
20. Ⓐ Ⓑ Ⓒ Ⓓ Ⓔ
21. Ⓐ Ⓑ Ⓒ Ⓓ Ⓔ
22. Ⓐ Ⓑ Ⓒ Ⓓ Ⓔ
23. Ⓐ Ⓑ Ⓒ Ⓓ Ⓔ
24. Ⓐ Ⓑ Ⓒ Ⓓ Ⓔ
25. Ⓐ Ⓑ Ⓒ Ⓓ Ⓔ
26. Ⓐ Ⓑ Ⓒ Ⓓ Ⓔ
27. Ⓐ Ⓑ Ⓒ Ⓓ Ⓔ
28. Ⓐ Ⓑ Ⓒ Ⓓ Ⓔ
29. Ⓐ Ⓑ Ⓒ Ⓓ Ⓔ
30. Ⓐ Ⓑ Ⓒ Ⓓ Ⓔ
31. Ⓐ Ⓑ Ⓒ Ⓓ Ⓔ
32. Ⓐ Ⓑ Ⓒ Ⓓ Ⓔ
33. Ⓐ Ⓑ Ⓒ Ⓓ Ⓔ
34. Ⓐ Ⓑ Ⓒ Ⓓ Ⓔ
35. Ⓐ Ⓑ Ⓒ Ⓓ Ⓔ
36. Ⓐ Ⓑ Ⓒ Ⓓ Ⓔ
37. Ⓐ Ⓑ Ⓒ Ⓓ Ⓔ
38. Ⓐ Ⓑ Ⓒ Ⓓ Ⓔ

SECTION 5

1. Ⓐ Ⓑ Ⓒ Ⓓ Ⓔ
2. Ⓐ Ⓑ Ⓒ Ⓓ Ⓔ
3. Ⓐ Ⓑ Ⓒ Ⓓ Ⓔ
4. Ⓐ Ⓑ Ⓒ Ⓓ Ⓔ
5. Ⓐ Ⓑ Ⓒ Ⓓ Ⓔ
6. Ⓐ Ⓑ Ⓒ Ⓓ Ⓔ
7. Ⓐ Ⓑ Ⓒ Ⓓ Ⓔ
8. Ⓐ Ⓑ Ⓒ Ⓓ Ⓔ
9. Ⓐ Ⓑ Ⓒ Ⓓ Ⓔ
10. Ⓐ Ⓑ Ⓒ Ⓓ Ⓔ
11. Ⓐ Ⓑ Ⓒ Ⓓ Ⓔ
12. Ⓐ Ⓑ Ⓒ Ⓓ Ⓔ
13. Ⓐ Ⓑ Ⓒ Ⓓ Ⓔ
14. Ⓐ Ⓑ Ⓒ Ⓓ Ⓔ
15. Ⓐ Ⓑ Ⓒ Ⓓ Ⓔ
16. Ⓐ Ⓑ Ⓒ Ⓓ Ⓔ
17. Ⓐ Ⓑ Ⓒ Ⓓ Ⓔ
18. Ⓐ Ⓑ Ⓒ Ⓓ Ⓔ
19. Ⓐ Ⓑ Ⓒ Ⓓ Ⓔ
20. Ⓐ Ⓑ Ⓒ Ⓓ Ⓔ
21. Ⓐ Ⓑ Ⓒ Ⓓ Ⓔ
22. Ⓐ Ⓑ Ⓒ Ⓓ Ⓔ
23. Ⓐ Ⓑ Ⓒ Ⓓ Ⓔ
24. Ⓐ Ⓑ Ⓒ Ⓓ Ⓔ
25. Ⓐ Ⓑ Ⓒ Ⓓ Ⓔ
26. Ⓐ Ⓑ Ⓒ Ⓓ Ⓔ
27. Ⓐ Ⓑ Ⓒ Ⓓ Ⓔ
28. Ⓐ Ⓑ Ⓒ Ⓓ Ⓔ
29. Ⓐ Ⓑ Ⓒ Ⓓ Ⓔ
30. Ⓐ Ⓑ Ⓒ Ⓓ Ⓔ

SECTION 6

1. Ⓐ Ⓑ Ⓒ Ⓓ Ⓔ
2. Ⓐ Ⓑ Ⓒ Ⓓ Ⓔ
3. Ⓐ Ⓑ Ⓒ Ⓓ Ⓔ
4. Ⓐ Ⓑ Ⓒ Ⓓ Ⓔ
5. Ⓐ Ⓑ Ⓒ Ⓓ Ⓔ
6. Ⓐ Ⓑ Ⓒ Ⓓ Ⓔ
7. Ⓐ Ⓑ Ⓒ Ⓓ Ⓔ
8. Ⓐ Ⓑ Ⓒ Ⓓ Ⓔ
9. Ⓐ Ⓑ Ⓒ Ⓓ Ⓔ
10. Ⓐ Ⓑ Ⓒ Ⓓ Ⓔ
11. Ⓐ Ⓑ Ⓒ Ⓓ Ⓔ
12. Ⓐ Ⓑ Ⓒ Ⓓ Ⓔ
13. Ⓐ Ⓑ Ⓒ Ⓓ Ⓔ
14. Ⓐ Ⓑ Ⓒ Ⓓ Ⓔ
15. Ⓐ Ⓑ Ⓒ Ⓓ Ⓔ
16. Ⓐ Ⓑ Ⓒ Ⓓ Ⓔ
17. Ⓐ Ⓑ Ⓒ Ⓓ Ⓔ
18. Ⓐ Ⓑ Ⓒ Ⓓ Ⓔ
19. Ⓐ Ⓑ Ⓒ Ⓓ Ⓔ
20. Ⓐ Ⓑ Ⓒ Ⓓ Ⓔ
21. Ⓐ Ⓑ Ⓒ Ⓓ Ⓔ
22. Ⓐ Ⓑ Ⓒ Ⓓ Ⓔ
23. Ⓐ Ⓑ Ⓒ Ⓓ Ⓔ
24. Ⓐ Ⓑ Ⓒ Ⓓ Ⓔ
25. Ⓐ Ⓑ Ⓒ Ⓓ Ⓔ
26. Ⓐ Ⓑ Ⓒ Ⓓ Ⓔ
27. Ⓐ Ⓑ Ⓒ Ⓓ Ⓔ
28. Ⓐ Ⓑ Ⓒ Ⓓ Ⓔ
29. Ⓐ Ⓑ Ⓒ Ⓓ Ⓔ
30. Ⓐ Ⓑ Ⓒ Ⓓ Ⓔ
31. Ⓐ Ⓑ Ⓒ Ⓓ Ⓔ
32. Ⓐ Ⓑ Ⓒ Ⓓ Ⓔ
33. Ⓐ Ⓑ Ⓒ Ⓓ Ⓔ
34. Ⓐ Ⓑ Ⓒ Ⓓ Ⓔ
35. Ⓐ Ⓑ Ⓒ Ⓓ Ⓔ
36. Ⓐ Ⓑ Ⓒ Ⓓ Ⓔ
37. Ⓐ Ⓑ Ⓒ Ⓓ Ⓔ
38. Ⓐ Ⓑ Ⓒ Ⓓ Ⓔ

Analytical Writing
Answer Sheets

_____

_____

_____

_____

_____

_____

_____

_____

_____

_____

_____

_____

_____

_____

_____

_____

_____

_____

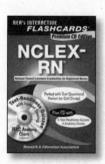

REA's Test Preps

The Best in Test Preparation

- *REA "Test Preps" are **far more** comprehensive than any other test preparation series*
- *Each book contains full-length practice tests based on the most recent exams*
- ***Every** type of question likely to be given on the exams is included*
- *Answers are accompanied by **full** and **detailed** explanations*

REA publishes hundreds of test prep books. Some of our titles include:

Advanced Placement Exams (APs)
Art History
Biology
Calculus AB & BC
Chemistry
Economics
English Language & Composition
English Literature & Composition
European History
French Language
Government & Politics
Latin
Physics B & C
Psychology
Spanish Language
Statistics
United States History
World History

College-Level Examination Program (CLEP)
Analyzing and Interpreting Literature
College Algebra
Freshman College Composition
General Examinations
History of the United States I
History of the United States II
Introduction to Educational Psychology
Human Growth and Development
Introductory Psychology
Introductory Sociology
Principles of Management
Principles of Marketing
Spanish
Western Civilization I
Western Civilization II

SAT Subject Tests
Biology E/M
Chemistry
French
German
Literature
Mathematics Level 1, 2
Physics
Spanish
United States History

Graduate Record Exams (GREs)
Biology
Chemistry
Computer Science
General
Literature in English
Mathematics
Physics
Psychology

ACT - ACT Assessment

ASVAB - Armed Services Vocational Aptitude Battery

CBEST - California Basic Educational Skills Test

CDL - Commercial Driver License Exam

CLAST - College Level Academic Skills Test

COOP, HSPT & TACHS - Catholic High School Admission Tests

FE (EIT) - Fundamentals of Engineering Exams

FTCE - Florida Teacher Certification Examinations

GED

GMAT - Graduate Management Admission Test

LSAT - Law School Admission Test

MAT - Miller Analogies Test

MCAT - Medical College Admission Test

MTEL - Massachusetts Tests for Educator Licensure

NJ HSPA - New Jersey High School Proficiency Assessment

NYSTCE - New York State Teacher Certification Examinations

PRAXIS PLT - Principles of Learning & Teaching Tests

PRAXIS PPST - Pre-Professional Skills Tests

PSAT/NMSQT

SAT

TExES - Texas Examinations of Educator Standards

THEA - Texas Higher Education Assessment

TOEFL - Test of English as a Foreign Language

USMLE Steps 1,2,3 - U.S. Medical Licensing Exams

For information about any of REA's books, visit www.rea.com

Research & Education Association
61 Ethel Road W., Piscataway, NJ 08854
Phone: (732) 819-8880